Learning to Practise Social Work

of related interest

Social Work in the British Isles
Edited by Malcolm Payne and Steven M. Shardlow
ISBN 1 85302 833 9

Innovative Education and Training for Care Professionals
A Providers' Guide
Edited by Rachel Pierce and Jenny Weinstein
ISBN 1 85302 613 1

The Changing Role of Social Care
Edited by Bob Hudson
ISBN 1 85302 752 9
Research Higlights in Social Work 37

The Working of Social Work
Edited by Juliet Cheetham and Mansoor A. F. Kazi
ISBN 1 85302 498 8

Competence in Social Work Practice
A Practical Guide for Professionals
Edited by Kieran O'Hagan
ISBN 1 85302 332 9

Research in Social Care and Social Welfare
Issues and Debates for Practice
Edited by Beth Humphries
ISBN 1 85302 900 9

Handbook of Theory for Practice Teachers in Social Work
Edited by Joyce Lishman
ISBN 1 85302 098 2

Cultural Competence in the Caring Professions
Kieran O'Hagan
ISBN 1 85302 759 6

Practice Teaching Changing Social Work
Edited by Hilary Lawson
ISBN 1 85302 478 3

User Involvement and Participation in Social Care
Research Informing Practice
Edited by Hazel Kemshall and Rosemary Littlechild
ISBN 1 85302 777 4

Learning to Practise Social Work

International Approaches

Edited by
Steven M. Shardlow and Mark Doel

Jessica Kingsley Publishers
London and Philadelphia

Acknowledgement

We would like to thank Arena for permission to adapt the glossary from: Doel, M. and Shardlow, S. M. (eds) (1996) *Social Work in a Changing World: An International Perspective on Practice Learning.* Aldershot: Arena.

First published in the United Kingdom in 2002 by
Jessica Kingsley Publishers Ltd,
116 Pentonville Road, London
N1 9JB, England
and
325 Chestnut Street,
Philadelphia PA 19106, USA.

www.jkp.com

Library of Congress Cataloging in Publication Data
A CIP catalog record for this book is available from the Library of Congress

British Library Cataloguing in Publication Data
A CIP catalogue record for this book is available from the British Library

ISBN 1 85302 763 4

Printed and Bound in Great Britain by
Athenaeum Press, Gateshead, Tyne and Wear

Contents

LIST OF FIGURES AND TABLES   7

ACRONYMS   9

Introduction: International Themes in Educating Social Workers for Practice   *11*
Mark Doel, *School of Social Work and RNIB Rehabilitation Studies, University of Central England, Birmingham, England,*
and Steven M. Shardlow, *School of Community, Health Sciences and Social Care, University of Salford, England*

Part I   SOCIAL WORK STUDENTS: A FORCE FOR CHANGE

1   *University–Community Partnerships: Practicum Learning for Community Revitalization*   *25*
Therese J. Dent and Alice Tourville, *School of Social Work, Washington University, St. Louis, Missouri, USA*

2   *Social Work Placements in Police Stations: a Force for Change*   *43*
Kalindi S. Muzumdar, *Mumbai, India,* and Rashida A. Atthar, *Tata Institute of Social Sciences, Mumbai, India*

3   *Integrating People and Services: A Practice and Learning Experience through Field Instruction*   *59*
Anna Y. L. Leung, Heidi S. K. Hui and Frances Y. S. Ip, *Department of Social Work, University of Hong Kong, China*

4   *Learning Opportunities and Placements with Asylum Seekers*   *77*
Dee Underhill with Claire Betteridge, Ben Harvey and Karen Patient, *Cambridgeshire Social Services, England*

Part II   SOCIAL WORK LEARNING: MODELS AND METHODS

5   *Student Supervision in Context: A Model for External
    Supervisors*   *93*
    Jane Maidment, *School of Social Inquiry, Deakin University,
    Australia* and Pauline Woodward, *University of Canterbury, New Zealand*

6   *Student Practice Placements as Gatekeepers
    to the Profession*   *110*
    Sigrún Júliusdóttir, Steinnun Hrafnsdóttir and Bjarney Kristjánsdóttir,
    Department of Social Work, University of Iceland, Iceland

7   *Becoming a Social Worker: Using Student Job Descriptions
    in Child Care and Family Support Placements*   *130*
    Nicoleta Neamtu, *Babes-Bolyai University, Cluj-Napoca, Romania*
    with Silvia Cioaza, *Romanian Foundation for Child Family
    and Community, Cluj-Napoca, Romania*

8   *Practice Teaching Using the Case Record*   *147*
    Lesley Cooper, *School of Social Administration and Social Work, Flinders
    University, Australia* and Paul Searston, *Department of Human Services,
    Mt Gambier, Australia*

Part III   SOCIAL WORK LEARNING IN DIFFERENT SETTINGS

9   *Practice Learning in Hospital-based Settings*   *167*
    Nigel Hall, *School of Social Work, Kopje, Zimbabwe* and Revai Senzere,
    Department of Social Welfare, Chegutu, Zimbabwe

10 *Practice Learning in the Voluntary Sector*   *179*
    Elaine King, Rob Mackay and Joyce Lishman, *Robert Gordon
    University, Aberdeen, and the Voluntary Service, Aberdeen, Scotland*

11 *Culturally Competent Mental Health Services for Latinos:
    An Examination of Three Practice Settings*   *200*
    Kurt C. Organista, Peter G. Manoleas and Rafael Herrera, *School
    of Social Welfare, University of California, Berkeley, USA*

12 *Field Instruction in University Teaching Hospitals* *222*
Marion Bogo and Judith Globerman, *Faculty of Social Work, University of Toronto, Canada,* and Lorie Shekter-Wolfson, *Ministry of Health, Ontario, Canada*

KEYWORDS *237*

ABOUT THE AUTHORS 242

BIBLIOGRAPHY 250

SUBJECT INDEX *261*

AUTHOR INDEX 269

Figures and Tables

Table 1.1 Residents' characteristics according to 1990 US Census Data 27

Table 2.1 Improvement of communication skills and interpersonal relationships *51*

Table 2.2 Problem-solving with police as different systems 52

Figure 3.1 Levels of project development 64

Table 3.1 Summary of the project development 74

Figure 5.1 Understanding external supervision from an ecological perspective 100

Table 5.1 A bicultural continuum 102

Figure 5.2 Map for scenario 1 104

Figure 5.3 Map for scenario 2 105

Table 5.2 Utilizing an ecological perspective for external supervision 107

Table 7.1 Dimensions for analysing a social service organization or institution 133

Table 7.2 Organizational assessment tool 140

In memory of George Simpson
and Joan Francis

Acronyms

AASW	Australian Association of Social Workers (this body accredits Australian schools of social work)
ANZASW	Aotearoa New Zealand Association of Social Workers
BSW	Bachelor of Social Work (basic qualifying degree in social work at baccalaureate level)
CASSW	Canadian Association of Schools of Social Work (this body accredits Canadian social work programmes)
CCETSW	Central Council for Education and Training in Social Work (this body accredited UK social work training programmes until 2001)
CSWE	Council on Social Work Education (this body accredits social work programmes in the USA)
DipSW	Diploma in Social Work (social work qualifying award in the UK)
IFSW	International Federation of Social Workers
MSW	Master of Social Work
NASW	National Association of Social Workers (USA)
NGO	Non-governmental organization

Introduction

International Themes in Educating Social Workers for Practice

Mark Doel and Steven M. Shardlow

What is social work? Globalization and localization

Social work takes many different forms around the globe. The nature of professional practice in any particular state is grounded in the historical and cultural context as mediated through political, economic and social systems (Lorenz 1994). This makes social work difficult to define at the global level, and attempts to identify a universal essence of social work are problematic. Despite this apparent difficulty, the International Federation of Social Workers (IFSW) has developed and adopted a new definition of social work:

> The social work profession promotes social change, problem solving in human relationships and the empowerment and liberation of people to enhance well-being. Utilizing theories of human behaviour and social systems, social work intervenes at the points where people interact with their environments. Principles of human rights and social justice are fundamental to social work. (IFSW Montréal, Canada, July 2000)

Definitions of this kind provoke many questions. Is it possible to develop a universal definition of social work? If so, how well does this definition describe social work throughout the world? Indeed, does this definition apply to social work where I live? It may be relatively easy to judge the 'fit' of the IFSW definition of social work in one's own country, but much harder to make a judgement about other countries or at a global level. Behind these questions lie some of the reasons for exploring social work comparatively, across national borders. Midgley (2001) suggests there is a need to develop a broad international approach to the study of social work to generate 'a global awareness that enhances the ability of social workers to transcend their preoccupation with the local and contextualize their role within a global setting' (p25).

Opinion is divided about the impact and desirability of global forces upon social work practice. For example, Dominelli (1999) highlights the detrimental effects of the 'marketization' of social work. Júliusdóttir, Hrafnsdóttir and Kristjánsdóttir point to the market competition which social work faces from other professions (Chapter 6). Markets, we are told, are becoming increasingly globalized, a fashionable term intended to capture a central element of life in the late twentieth and early twenty-first centuries. Despite a lack of clarity about the precise nature of globalization, there is an intuitive sense in which social work seems to be located at the interface between the local and the global. Thus, when a steel works closes in South Yorkshire, Pennsylvania or Silesia, the consequent unemployment generates a range of social problems that attract the attention of social work organizations and practitioners. In such circumstances, social work must react to the localized impact of global forces. Undoubtedly, there is a need to understand social work within a frame of reference that is international and global.

We make no claim that this book provides definitive answers to questions about the nature of social work across different countries. However, the book does concern itself with an exploration of the varying forms of professional practice in different nation-states, and specifically the types of learning opportunities they promote for students of social work. Raskin, Skolnik and Wayne's (1991, p.259) observation that international comparative studies in field instruction (practice teaching) are sparse remains true. This book is not a comparative study as such, but it does build on our experiences as editors of *Social Work in a Changing World: An International Perspective on Practice Learning* (Doel and Shardlow 1996), which encouraged us to believe that we have much to learn from discovering how others organize and conceptualize the way students learn social work in practice settings.

The culture of student learning on placement is inseparable from the culture of social work practice;[1] not least in how high pressure workloads actively discourage learning – or in some cases undermine the willingness of practice teachers to provide student placements altogether (see Cooper and Searston, Chapter 8 in this book). What we see reflected in the learning experience of students is the local or national view of what social work is. This varies from nation to nation, from an individual, competent clinician to a collective, community development strategist.

Dent and Tourville (Chapter 1) state that their 'School of Social Work's office of field education was specifically charged with improving the quality of life for lower income residents', thus imposing a duty on students to engage with local communities to promote a higher quality of life; a form of political action. In contrast, a different engagement of social work and politics is evident in India, where the freedom fighters who participated in the struggle for independence were also known as 'social workers' (Muzumdar and Atthar, Chapter 2). From these two examples we might ask, is social work about fighting injustice with and on behalf of the poor, the weak and the exploited? Or, should social work more properly concern itself with developing skills such as 'care management' to assess the need for packages of help for individuals?

It is important to ask who is to define the nature and function of social work. Consider for example the case of the Latino trainees described by Organista, Manoleas and Herrera (Chapter 11). They experience relatively experimental social services, but they are not the authors of the experimentation and have limited influence on the development of these services. Likewise, Leung, Hui and Ip (Chapter 3) describe the success of the Shek Wai Kok project, which relied on an unstructured working and learning environment, with attendant uncertainties and 'learning pains'. Underhill *et al.* (Chapter 4) recount the evolution of a project to work with asylum seekers in a highly politicized atmosphere and the part played by students on placement in the development of the project itself. These different forms of practice have profound implications for the recipients of services and for the experience of students.

Social work is different again in the context of a country emerging from a long period of dictatorship and no strong tradition of social work. Neamtu and Cioaza (Chapter 7) describe a relatively prescriptive approach to student training, with a tight job description of what a social worker should do as the guideline for student learning. Perhaps it is surprising that a similar level of prescription can be found in Scotland, where social work and democratic traditions are well established, yet the kind of experimentation noted by a number of our authors is very difficult. This makes Underhill *et al.*'s (Chapter 4) account of the asylum seekers' project in eastern England all the more impressive, with its need to marry prescribed learning outcomes with a highly experimental placement setting. In Iceland, Júliusdóttir, Hrafnsdóttir and Kristjánsdóttir describe the social work placement as functioning as a gatekeeper to the profession, with a focus on the assessment of the student's competence to do a prescribed job (Chapter 6).

The experience of reading this book will, we are sure, happily confound most generalizations, either about the nature of social work or about the locus for learning professional practice!

Organization of the book

The book is a partnership between the academy and practice. Most of the chapters are written as the result of a collaboration between academy-based social work theoreticians and community, practice-based social workers. One is a collaboration between a practitioner and students (Chapter 4). These partnerships symbolically bridge the often-presumed divide between the worlds of social work theory and social work practice. For some of our authors, this has provided the opportunity to build on longstanding partnerships, while for others the book has provided the opportunity for establishing a new partnership. In either case, the act of writing about social work practice and learning from two different perspectives has been stimulating and enriching. We hope that this leads to a more inclusive book, which incorporates a range of very diverse views and perspectives about social work education.

The book explores a large number of different themes in respect of social work education and practice learning. These themes interweave across the various chapters, inevitably some in more detail in one chapter than another. Each chapter could stand as a separate contribution to the discussion about the nature of professional social work education in practice settings. However, it seems more helpful to group the contributions according to the major themes addressed. Hence, the book is divided into three parts, each reflecting a key and dominant theme of professional learning.

The themes are social work students as a force for change; social work learning: models and methods; and social work learning in different settings. The content of each chapter does not confine itself to the key sectional theme, but each grouping reflects a number of common concerns. Taken together, we have evidence of the richness of approaches to practice learning around the world.

Social work students: bringing about change through contributing to the community

Recent writings about learning how to do social work have emphasized the importance of the nature and quality of students' educational experiences. Learning about social work has been located within an educational rather than a practice paradigm. In part, the construction of this paradigm results from a reaction to earlier constructions, reflecting dissatisfaction with the student-as-client paradigm drawn from professional practice. Educational paradigms place the student at the centre of the placement experience, with student and practice teacher seeking to maximize the learning potential during the available time.

However, there are also dangers in the educational model. Clients, families or communities can be seen as the raw material for student learning. This minimizes the possibility of seeing the contribution of the student to the work of the agency or the development of services for and with the community. Moreover, clients' and service users' needs can become of secondary importance when compared to the learning needs of the student. For example, if the practice curriculum determines that the student requires an opportunity for working with a client experiencing a certain kind of problem, this may be provided without sufficient thought to the best interests of the client.

Clearly, a student's labour on placement should not be exploited, but it can be harnessed. It is now time to reflect once more on the contribution that those students can make to the work of the social work agency in developing the community, and there are several examples in this book of such contributions. We should not forget that the ability of students to make an effective contribution to the community depends upon a sense of mutuality. 'To work and learn effectively, students need both university and community support behind them' (Dent and Tourville, Chapter 1). It is time to evaluate more carefully and extensively the extent of the contribution made by students to the work of the agency and the development of communities. Most student placements are not the burden on the agency and hard-pressed practitioner as they are sometimes presented. They can provide a considerable force for change and revitalization; the valuable partnerships that students help to construct is a theme running throughout this book.

'Partnership', in its many guises, has assumed a central importance in social work practice in recent years. The idea of sharing power, information and decision-making between the person using social work and the provider of social work has been incorporated into legislation, policy guidance and, most importantly, practice itself. Despite some of the fogginess that surrounds the notion of partnership, it nevertheless signifies a central element of good practice. The notion of partnership pervades the *content* as well as the *form* of the book. Hence, in several of the chapters, there is considerable emphasis upon the partnership between student and community. It is a role that presents the student as a catalyst for change. The student is seen as a person who can be more free than employees who are constrained by job role, status and hierarchy. Students can take what King, Mackay and Lishman suggest is a 'fresh perspective' (Chapter 10).

As editors of the book, we have been pleasantly surprised at the emergence of the theme of the impact of student placements on practice itself. As Muzumdar and Atthar comment, 'the field practicum ... can be used as a vehicle for social change' (Chapter 2), especially in those situations where there is an active partnership between the educational institution (usually a university) and the community. Moreover, the students in Muzumdar and Atthar's study have developed new settings in which social work can be practised (Rapp, Chamberlain and Freeman 1989: 182). Dent and Tourville remind us that university–community relations have often been experienced by the latter as the former using them for research projects and data collection, with no reciprocity. For, Leung, Hui and Ip (Chapter 3), students have become a resource to develop a partnership with the community through a housing project in Hong Kong. For Underhill *et al.* (Chapter 4), students have been instrumental in developing a new service, while for Hall and Senzere (Chapter 9) students are a force to challenge the persistence of superstition.

Partnership and the force for change extend into other aspects of professional practice and learning. The boundaries that define and limit the spheres of competence of professional groups have been shifting over time, and there is the potential for developing interprofessional partnerships, especially with healthcare professions. Here also, students can be a force for change. Some tasks and work are shared across the health–social care divide, while others remain the preserve of one or other professional group. A feature of the developing role of the social care professions in general and social work in particular has been a willingness to develop interdisciplinary approaches to professional practice.

There are many examples in the book of social work students engaging with other professionals during placement. The project which Underhill *et al.* describe in Chapter 4 was led by a former police officer. King, Mackay and Lishman (Chapter 10) recount the way in which a student social worker empowered a service user in her relationship with a psychiatrist. Organista, Manoleas and Herrera (Chapter 11) explore the significance of mediation with a psychiatrist in learning about work with Latino clients. Bogo, Globerman and Shekter-Wolfson (Chapter 12) analyse the opportunities for students to learn interprofessional work and teamwork in hospital settings. Dent and Tourville (Chapter 1) remind us that interprofessional work is not solely about collaboration with health professionals, as witnessed by the joint work between students of social work and architecture to promote good housing and urban development.

There are also issues of power in relation to other professions, such as the difficulty which individual field instructors might experience in making a case for student placements when social work as a discipline and training as an activity are both devalued (Bogo, Globerman and Shekter-Wolfson, Chapter 12). Relationships with other professional groups are complex and unequal, as students discover.

So, Part I emphasizes the fact that practice learning can maximize the opportunities for students to make a difference to communities; for students to become a force for change.

Social work learning: models and methods – students, practice teachers and university tutors

As a learner undergoing a period of assessed education, it is inevitable that the student is at the centre of various unequal power relationships linking the educational establishment, the practice agency, the community and the student. This book recognizes the importance of acknowledging rather than denying these complex interrelationships and of mitigating the extreme effects of such power structures.

It may not only be students who feel themselves to be disadvantaged by virtue of an unequal distribution of power; experiences of power differentials are influenced by the way in which practice learning is organized. Throughout the book, there are many examples of the variety of different ways in which practice learning can be organized: field instructors employed directly by the university as described by Leung, Hui and Ip (Chapter 3); practising social workers in agencies, sometimes with the agency receiving payment for the student as recounted by King, Mackay and Lishman (Chapter 10), 'long-arm' or off-site supervisors as described by Maidment and Woodward (Chapter 5).

Whatever the organizational framework, it is essential that the value of each participant is recognized. King, Mackay and Lishman (Chapter 10) point to the importance of recognizing that the practice teacher (field instructor) is an equal partner in the educational process. Relations between practice teachers and college tutors have not always been easy, and we should not lose sight of the student as an active learner rather than a passive trainee, someone who can have an impact on the placement agency or community. This can be at the level of agency policy or perhaps in joint working with supervisors and practice teachers, as in the case of 'Consuela' described by Organista, Manoleas and Herrera

(Chapter 11), where the student works with the client while the supervisor plays with the children in another room – a model of good practice.

The 'template' model of practice learning is a social work student taught by one practice teacher based in an agency. However, there is evidence of a growing interest in group-based approaches to practice learning. The power of groups of students, placed together and working towards a common goal is evidenced in a number of chapters. Dent and Tourville (Chapter 1) describe the significance of weekly student group meetings; Muzumdar and Atthar (Chapter 2) emphasize the impact which students working together had on the police service in Mumbai. The success of the projects described by Leung, Hui and Ip (Chapter 3) and Underhill et al. (Chapter 4) similarly relied on students working together – all models of good practice.

One of the most important features of practice learning in agencies is that students should feel inspired by the possibilities of future professional practice. For example, Cooper and Searston (Chapter 8) analyse how to inspire students with the potentiality of practice using the case record – at first glance not perhaps the most likely of inspirational vehicles. The quality of the relationship between student, practice teacher and tutor is vital in helping students to experience that potential. We can perhaps speculate that students who are able to develop initiatives on placement will feel creative about the possibilities for future practice. To what extent are students able to do so? Much depends on the extent to which they are constrained or liberated by the curriculum. Although competence-based curricula detail the outcomes of learning, they do not necessarily prescribe the content, especially if they are written at generalist and generic levels. However, the move towards a national curriculum (such as in the countries of the UK) is likely to reduce rather than broaden opportunities for innovation. Models to assess students' practice competence beg the question, competent to do what (see for example, Júliusdóttir, Hrafnsdóttir and Kristjánsdóttir, Chapter 6)?

It is ironic that where the role of the social worker is tightly defined, it becomes difficult to develop the kinds of innovation in student placements as recounted by Dent and Tourville (Chapter 1). Leung, Hui and Ip (Chapter 3) describe placements as a 'venue for experimentation' and a process of learning by doing when the goals of a project are clear but the pathway to reach those goals is not so obvious:

> The student workers ... had the advantage of not having to work within predefined areas of responsibilities ... As a neutral, third party in the neighbourhood, they were in an excellent position to play a mediator role (Leung, Hui and Ip, Chapter 3).

As Leung, Hui and Ip note, time spent developing new services is time not spent learning about 'conventional modes of working in and negotiating through social service bureaucracies'. Underhill *et al.* (Chapter 4) express concern that certain competencies such as assessment and care management skills may not be tested by experimental placements. With an eye on future employment, students may be less willing to stride out, even when the opportunity is available. Nonetheless, students contribute to the rediscovery of basic principles for individual practice teachers and the revitalization of the life of the team by posing questions which practitioners have sometimes forgotten how to ask.

Social work learning in different settings: contexts for learning about social work practice

The practice placement provides a specific context for learning about how to do social work. The conceptualization about the nature of learning that occurs on placement varies greatly. For example, the placement may be viewed as the opportunity to *apply* learning already acquired in a class setting. Alternatively, the placement may be viewed as a site for new and novel learning; a place for the development of reflective practice derived from the practice experience itself (Schön 1987, 1995).

Irrespective of the way the connection between agency-based learning and class-based learning setting is viewed, the impact of the *context* for learning is evident throughout the book. Hence, a major theme is the extraordinary diversity of the settings in which social workers learn their trade (police stations, hospitals, and so on). This diversity enriches the profession by stretching our understanding of what social work practice is and what it is capable of becoming. Some of these settings present extreme challenges, not only in the form of learning that confronts students but even in respect of personal safety. Students may have to face difficult and sometimes dangerous situations, such as the communal riots described by Muzumdar and Atthar (Chapter 2) or the vitriol of the media in the face of social work with asylum seekers (Underhill *et al.* Chapter 4).

Less dramatically, social work students need to understand the complexity and dynamics of different systems; the ecological model espoused by Maidment and Woodward provides a good example (Chapter 5). The differing settings that host social work learning enable many diverse opportunities for learning. King, Mackay and Lishman (Chapter 10) outline the learning opportunities that the voluntary sector can offer students,[2] involving arrangements where agencies are paid for offering placements. In addition to the specific setting, there are other contexts that are significant but not concrete, such as the legal context of practice learning (Neamtu and Cioaza, Chapter 7).

A feature of many placements will be differing expectations of specific cultural or ethnic groups in society. The potential for conflict and discrimination in minority–majority relations is high. Social work practice is at the intersection between such potential conflicts. Some of these issues are explored by Organista, Manoleas and Herrera in the context of the experience of Latinos in the USA (Chapter 11). They note that 'trainees working with Latino clients are usually Spanish speaking Latinos themselves', while non-Latino students who can speak Spanish require supervision that is more intensive. The response of each student to working in such a situation will be unique and presents a challenge for the practice teacher to individualize learning. What is common to all of these situations is the development in students of the ability to work in the context of difference and to develop an understanding of 'local explanations' – a social work that respects differences. Hall and Senzere's (Chapter 9) account of work with a client and family, who explain his mental state in terms of bewitchment, provides a powerful example of how to work respectfully with difference.

There are particularly difficult tensions when social work is learned in a setting where it is a 'guest'. Bogo, Globerman and Shekter-Wolfson (Chapter 12) document the evolution of the organization of practice learning in a hospital setting. The impact of the decline of the Teaching Centre model, as a result of restructuring in the host organization, has heralded a return to individualized, fragmented and isolating placement experiences. The changes that they recount are a reminder of the fragility of social work as a relatively new profession. Theirs is a story about the local impact of global forces. It begs one of the significant questions, which emerges from the pages of this book: can we sustain diversity in practice learning?

Diversity and difference

There are many different 'mind maps' used around the world to help explain and understand practice teaching and learning. Even the term 'practice teaching' has different meanings from nation to nation. In the UK, it refers to the activity that takes place when students are placed in an agency as part of their social work course. In North America and Australasia, this would be referred to as 'field education' or 'field instruction'. To complicate matters, 'practice teaching' in a North American context has yet another meaning and refers to the teaching that social work students might receive about social work theory and method from a university or college based teacher. To help unscramble these complexities we have provided a keywords section near the end of the book.

There are other problems associated with the preparation of an international book using English as the language of publication. Despite its status as a world language, English has many different forms, particularly in respect of spelling and the meanings of words.[3] There is no basis for imposing a common standard, whatever that might be. We have, therefore, followed the spelling and grammatical conventions, which reflect the authors' region of origin – American English, Australian English and so on. We wish to respect the diversity of forms of communication and believe that imposing an editorial uniformity would not be in the spirit of this book. We have collaborated closely with those authors whose first language is not English to arrive at a final text in keeping with the authors' message.

Notes

1 The terms used to refer to various elements and roles within professional social work education are highly specific to particular countries and cultures. We would advise all readers to consult the keywords section near the end of the book.

2 The voluntary sector is sometimes called not-for-profit or independent sector.

3 There is also a problem in that English has only a gender-specific third person singular pronoun. Although not strictly correct, we have used the plural 'their' in such cases – this convention seems to be increasingly common.

PART I
SOCIAL WORK STUDENTS
A FORCE FOR CHANGE

Chapter One

University–Community Partnerships
Practicum Learning for Community Revitalization

Therese J. Dent and Alice Tourville

Introduction

Social work in inner-city communities is a growing and complex field of practice in the United States of America. Traditional social work practice learning has typically occurred through practicum (practice learning) placements within one agency, hospital or organization at a time. A shift to practice learning within a community as a whole presents a challenge to field educators to rethink the content and structure of their practicum programs (Allen 1998; Jarman-Rohde *et al.* 1997; Morrison, Alcorn and Nelums 1997). We are challenged to create practicum experiences that integrate direct practice learning involving individuals and families (micro practice) with simultaneous learning about local, national, community and institutionally focused policies, politics and dynamics (macro practice). How do political, economic and environmental situations affect community and individual behaviors and vice versa? How can one learn about the complex external and internal realities affecting community change while also learning to interact with the diverse individuals, families and organizations within the community? How can social workers assist the process of developing socially just community revitalization?

Community revitalization programs in the USA are evolving toward a concurrent focus on the social, economic and physical well-being of a community and its individual residents. They rely on an understanding of the dynamics of collaboration with entities and individuals both inside and outside the community. As field educators, our goal is to assist students through community-based practicums to develop the ability to think and work simultaneously in diverse micro through macro multidisciplinary practice arenas.[1] To promote the achievement of this goal involves building the capacity of students to integrate theoretical and practice learning in these disparate arenas.

The government, by funding university–community partnership projects, has encouraged universities to contribute to the revitalization of local depressed communities (Cisneros 1995, p.13). In responding to a request for proposals from the Department of Housing and Urban Development (HUD), the Washington University Medical Center Redevelopment Corporation received a five-year Joint Community Development (JCD) grant. As a component of the grant, the university's school of social work had the opportunity to develop innovative graduate level community revitalization-focused social work practicums. In addition to providing the students with knowledge, understanding and skills in a complex and rapidly evolving practice environment we, as field educators, are also challenged to structure our practicums to meet the needs of the community and the expectations of granting agencies.

This chapter describes a field education model developed within a newly proposed university–community revitalization partnership. We will discuss the dynamics of teaching and learning within an emerging practicum model. We will also describe how students experienced the challenge of learning to think and work simultaneously on multilevels of practice within a dynamic and emerging, sometimes conflict ridden, new university–community partnership.

University–community partnerships

United States urban policy is now encouraging the formation of local 'community empowerment' partnerships that simultaneously address physical, economic and social urban problems (Office of Policy Development and Research 1995). Implementation scholars (Pressman and Wildavsky 1979) pointed out that weak links between government sponsored funding sources and local communities were a primary source of failure of past government policy initiatives. In the HUD initiative described here, implementation of HUD, community empowerment, partnerships involves the process of blending (1) the requirements for university compliance to government policy guidelines with (2) the unique ongoing requirements demanded by a particular community context.

While the goal remains the revitalization of distressed communities, the role of the federal government shifted so as to be the catalyst and enabler of change rather than a top-down planner and source of implementation. HUD wants current urban revitalization strategies to be 'the result of community-based planning and decision-making' (Office of Policy Development and Research 1995, p.53). The distribution of federal grants evolved to promote this change and the Office of University Partnerships was created within HUD in 1995 to support the implementation of this new urban policy through the concept of university–community partnership building. Consequently, universities across the USA are becoming increasingly involved in the fate of their communities.

The community setting

The students' practicums are set in a culturally diverse, lower to middle income community of 4087 residents in 1555 households within an inner city 45-block area in St. Louis, Missouri (see Table 1.1). The community is isolated from neighboring communities as a result of being bounded by major limited-access highways on the north and south and by major city streets on the east and west.

Table 1.1 Residents' characteristics according to 1990 US Census Data	
Characteristics of community residents	
income less than $1000 per year	36%
income over $3500 per year	15%
minority (primarily African American)	68%
under 18 years of age	34%
single parent households	33%
adults over 25 without a high school diploma	45%
unemployed women	13%
unemployed men	25%

Significant social issues encountered in the community are unmet medical needs, high unemployment rates, a flourishing drug culture, and a lack of community educational and recreational facilities for youth. All school-age children are bused out of the community to 32 different schools because of school desegregation measures enacted in the city since the 1980s. The community is experiencing crime, violence, drug activity and shootings among youth gangs. The need for extended health and youth services is glaring.

Developing a practicum model

We designed our university–community social work practicums following the invitation from our university's medical center to assume responsibility for the social component of their multimillion-dollar Joint Community Development grant. While the other university–community entities in the partnership intensified their focus on the physical and economic aspects of community revitalization, the School of Social Work's Office of Field Education was specifically charged with improving the 'quality of life' for lower income residents (Washington University Medical Center Redevelopment Corporation 1995, p.1). Community needs and wishes dictated that we begin by focusing on medical, employment, and youth services. Social work students were taught to promote the empowerment of the community-as-a-whole while simultaneously working with residents and community leaders to help develop and deliver specific community-based programs. A multiracial inner city community became the students' client while they also learned to develop and provide one-on-one services with residents. The government's goal of community empowerment guided communication patterns and activities of social work practicum students. Kretzman and McKnight's (1993) book, *Building Communities from the Inside Out*, became the students' 'bible'. It provided a major theoretical framework that the students could use to assess community assets and work toward building community capacity and interaction. Each student was required to have simultaneous macro and micro practicum learning objectives, activities and responsibilities. These were outlined in practicum contracts written by the students and approved at the beginning of each practice learning experience by students' field instructors and the social work school's Office of Field Education.

Contrast with traditional models of practice learning

In the context of a community-empowerment-focused revitalization program, practicums differ in structure and content from traditional practice learning models. In traditional graduate level social work practicums in the USA, field instructors with a master of social work degree – employed by an established organization sponsoring the practicum – typically supervise students working within that organization. The field instructors, employed by an organization, teach students the interpersonal dynamics and skills necessary to fulfill the goals and responsibilities of their professional roles within their organizations. The content of practice learning does not necessarily extend beyond the boundaries of the organization's mission and work.

The lack of persons in the community available and qualified by the social work school's accrediting body to instruct graduate level practicum students required a new model of field instruction. Field instruction and supervision for practicum students was therefore obtained through grant-funded professionals from the School of Social Work and the wider practice community. These field instructors exposed students to the external and internal political and economic forces affecting community empowerment and revitalization as well as supervising their experiences in learning to work directly with residents.

Community-focused practice learning activities

The students learned a broad range of social work skills. To facilitate community empowerment, practicum students actively encouraged the lower-income minority population with whom they worked to participate in the community-wide revitalization planning meetings. Students worked with the community and local businesses to develop and staff a community employment referral center. They were involved in the development and delivery of summer and after-school youth programs. They worked alongside medical students on behalf of community residents and refugees in the newly created free medical clinic. They worked with local financial lending institutions to provide individual counseling and community workshops to educate and assist residents regarding planning for and accessing special mortgage funding for homeownership in the community. They initiated an outreach and support group to understand the dilemmas of female head-of-households and to work with them in advocating for individual and community services.

Weekly group meetings of all the practicum students in the community were held to supervise and coordinate their activities and to discuss the dynamics and interactive relationships of their learning. These meetings provided support and insight for students who often worked somewhat autonomously in difficult community roles. Such meetings enabled students to see and discuss broader aspects of community revitalization and how their activities fit into the process of community and individual empowerment. A snapshot of student discussions of their learning activities at a typical group meeting follows.

A weekly student group meeting

Heather began the meeting by discussing her work with the medical students in the recently established Saturday Free Clinic in the community. She reported that the overall number of patients continued to increase and expressed surprise at the number of immigrants from Middle-Eastern and Asian countries who were coming to the clinic. Heather discussed a need to establish a new-immigrants' network and speculated about where funding for such a network might be obtained.

Mara, a joint master degree student in social work and architecture who wanted to develop direct practice sensitivities and skills, discussed her home visits to several of the children's families in her church-sponsored after-school program. She was also excited about her work with the director/owner of a local pre-school to design the interior of the new building recently purchased to open a day care center. In addition, Mara reported about the issues and dynamics of the recent meeting of the community-based social service committee guiding the community activities of the students. (One of Mara's practicum responsibilities was to provide staff support for that committee.)

Esther, working to further develop the student-run employment referral center, discussed the upcoming Job Fair, an event in which employers would come to the community to interview residents for jobs. There were some unhappy feelings expressed about a local politician publicly taking credit for the Job Fair when the students in the employment referral center were doing all the work. Esther requested help from the other students to get Job Fair announcements to local organizations and churches and asked for volunteers to provide childcare for residents coming to the Job Fair. Esther was also arranging for the university to provide their university shuttle to transport community residents to and from the event.

Sue described the Job Club she was organizing at the employment referral center and the Job Readiness Workshops she offered to unemployed residents to prepare them for interviews with employers at the upcoming Job Fair.

Michael thanked the group for their help in making the Valentine party for the children in his after-school program such a success. He also had responsibility for arranging weekly field trips for children, in the upcoming summer programs in the community and requested help from his fellow students to select appropriate field trip sites and activities.

Mary discussed the homebuyers' workshop she was planning for next month and the dynamics of getting financial lenders and other providers to participate. She showed us the homebuyer's handbook she was developing for workshop participants and asked for feedback on the handbook and her plans for informing the community about the workshop.

> Juliane discussed the outreach program she developed that came to be called Bus-Stop Moms. Juliane and several other students were meeting with local mothers at their children's school bus stops on Friday mornings, inviting them to the employment referral center for coffee and donuts and discussing what the mothers wanted for the community and themselves. Through these contacts, Juliane said she was able to get some of the women to participate in the community revitalization planning meetings.

Integrating multilevel, multidisciplinary practice learning

An understanding of the interactions of multiple levels of professional practice was essential to students' learning while working within the community. Equally essential was the development of students' ability to work in multidisciplinary situations and to interact with diverse groups and individuals in a culturally sensitive manner. Sarah, one of the first practicum students in the employment referral center, described some challenging integrative aspects of her learning experience:

> One of the most valuable pieces of this to me has been learning to work with all of the stakeholders – presenting the employment program at the community meetings, working with the local politicians, recruiting employers and educational organizations to participate in the program, recruiting residents to use our services, and forming a mutually beneficial relationship with social service providers as well. Now that I look back on it, [the work] seems almost daunting!

While Sarah was helping to develop the community's employment referral center, she also participated in a grassroots community group that met to discuss (and often challenge at community revitalization meetings) the values and ethics driving the revitalization project. Sharing these perspectives with fellow students during group meetings contributed to their learning of the complexity of community revitalization issues. Her participation in this grassroots group added to an ur derstanding of community dynamics, the politics of community revitalization and the effects of disparate grassroots and institutional values on the progress of partnership building.

Supervision and coordination of multilevel (macro–micro) practice learning

An integration of learning about complex external and internal realities affecting community change, while simultaneously learning to interact with diverse individuals, families and organizations within the community, occurred within dual formats.

On the macro practice level, learning to understand the implications of federal policy, university, and community dynamics occurred in the previously mentioned weekly student group supervisory meetings in which the activities and goals of each student were discussed and coordinated. These meetings were held by the assistant dean for field education who had responsibility for the School of Social Work's participation in the partnership. On the micro level of practice, learning the subtleties of individual interaction with adults, families, children and youth, or unemployed individuals in the community occurred in one-on-one supervisory sessions with field instructors. Students received individual, direct service field instruction from professional personnel in the School of Social Work or from externally hired professional social workers with community or direct practice expertise.

Social work's role in building community empowerment partnerships

According to Schuftan:

> Empowerment is not a single event; it is a continuous process that enables people to understand, upgrade and use their capacities to better control and gain power over their lives. (Schuftan 1996, p.260)

The dynamics necessary for successful community empowerment, therefore, are inherent in social work values and practice. Maximizing self-determination, building on strengths and empowering people to participate in the decisions that impact their lives are basic professional values. The practice of social work involves efforts to help others clarify values and assess the relative importance of one value as opposed to others in a situation (Sheafor, Horejsi and Horejsi 1988).

The move to address physical, economic and social issues simultaneously can result in social service values and issues becoming a stronger component of the comprehensive community empowerment agenda. We can see the merging of empowerment as a social work practice principle with empowerment as our national strategy for community revitalization. We began to see that the practice values and skills of social work professionals could become essential to the success of HUD's new urban policy implementation strategy. Social workers can build bridges between the 'partner' with fewer resources and the university with less experience and skill in forming 'partnerships' with residents of distressed poverty-stricken inner city communities. Our challenge was to teach students to assume a partnership role with the community and the university in order to promote community empowerment and revitalization that included community participation and leadership.

Obstacles to partnership building

The involvement of universities in communities has often been fraught with alienation and mistrust on the part of the community and, frequently enough, elitism on the part of the university. The early teams of social work practicum students placed in the community found themselves in the middle of a dynamic reminiscent of the medieval town–gown schism. Within the context of our university–community partnership, two significant obstacles to partnership building were faced: recent history and communication across different worlds.

Recent history

Communities near universities have become accustomed to university students and faculty gathering data about their environment and lifestyle in order to complete class assignments, publish articles and obtain research grants. The experience of being 'used' for the advancement of academicians, who typically 'study' their situation and then leave the community, tends to establish an atmosphere of cynicism on the part of the community.

In this case, recent university strategies for working with communities became an obstacle to partnership building. The racially diverse working class community south of the university's medical center was asked to partner with the university that, during the 1980s and 1990s, successfully redeveloped the area north of the medical center, displacing some of the residents. Residents' fear that the university was going to 'take over' and 'gentrify' their community was rampant.

The university medical center, on the other hand, having previously experienced a successful redevelopment project using the old top-down strategies, was in a phase of adjustment to their federal grant's urban policy mandate of bottom-up community empowerment. Communication problems plagued the beginning of revitalization planning efforts as the university and community began to work through the process of following the joint community development grant's implementation strategies of community-based planning and decision-making.

Communication across different worlds

Communicating in the professional jargon of economics, real estate, and university disciplines can be easily misunderstood and alienating. Equally, a lack of sensitivity to the psychological and behavioral impacts of living in a distressed, sometimes violent, community can be a serious obstacle to learning how to communicate and work effectively together to establish commonly agreed upon goals.

Students, as they began their practicums, had to learn the importance of the manner in which they communicated with residents and other university–community partners. For example, students were expected to

- learn that the dynamics of their individual (micro) communication patterns had the potential to influence the dynamics of partnership building at the university–community (macro) level

- develop genuinely sensitive communication with residents to be able to understand their values and the source of behavioral dynamics in the community

- show respect for the opinions of diverse factions in the community in order to assist with problem-solving, planning and decision-making

- demonstrate and foster an attitude that the university and community can learn from each other how best to structure a relationship that results in community empowerment.

The next section will provide some aspects of students' practice learning within the health component of this community-focused practice model. The intent is to provide a feel for the work and the learning through a specific programmatic example.

Saturday Free Clinic: student learning

In the earliest months of partnership building, the community clearly described a major issue for poverty-stricken residents. Those who could not afford the minimal fees of the local government-sponsored community health clinic had no place to go locally for free healthcare. Thus, the initial program quickly established through the emerging university–community partnership was a Saturday Free Clinic located within the existing community health center that was not previously opened on Saturdays. A productive process of university–community communication and partnership building had begun.

Opening day at the Saturday Free Clinic provided a valuable lesson

Despite a disappointment, opening day of the Saturday Free Clinic provided an invaluable lesson in beginning to understand the interaction of macro and micro aspects of practice. The disappointment resulted from the fact that no clients appeared to take advantage of the free medical services requested by the community. By mid-morning, when it seemed likely that no patients were coming, the staff started questioning what went wrong. The opening of the clinic had been publicized by flyers, announcements in local churches and meeting places, and by word of mouth throughout the community. The clinic facility was clean and inviting. The medical students were eager to test their diagnostic and therapeutic skills and the attending physician was ready to serve as their guide, mentor, and supervisor. The social work student was poised to listen, to empathize, and to direct the client toward appropriate resources. The social work field instructor was trying to anticipate both the predictable and the unpredictable problems that the student might encounter. What then was lacking?

An explanation lay in looking at the big picture, the macro aspects of the endeavor, then searching to see how the Saturday Free Clinic, as a vital micro service component, would fit into the larger design.

Learning to see from the residents' point of view

The first and, perhaps, the most obvious factor in the non-attendance at the clinic was the weather. St. Louis, Missouri, always prone to extremes of hot and cold temperatures, had outdone itself that particular day. The mercury shivered at minus 2 degrees Fahrenheit. The sky was an ominous gray. There was no foot traffic on the streets and very few automobiles. The neighborhood appeared to be in hibernation. This is no surprise when looked at in the context of an economically depressed community. Transportation is a major problem. Older autos, especially those parked in unsheltered areas, often do not start in extreme cold. People who feel ill may well be reluctant to venture out on public transportation in inclement weather. Furthermore, the bus service is very limited in the area, especially on weekends.

Building trust

Over the years, residents of this neighborhood have been repeatedly reminded of their perceived 'deficiencies'. They frequently receive suggestions that changes in their employment status, their housing, their families, and their health should be made. Is it possible that potential patients stayed away because they believed health service providers perceived them negatively? Could a significant factor have been the ambivalence of the community due to their historical distrust of the university's motives for community involvement? Were they wary because the medical school of a major university was offering the medical services? Were there fears of being used as an experimental population, or merely to fulfill student educational requirements? The social work student, striving with sensitivity and empathy to understand the client's point of view, gradually learned that such provocative questions could not be ignored.

Student professional development in a university–community partnership

To assist in the development of university–community partnership building, a wide range of interprofessional sensitivity and skill development was required. Rebecca quickly learned in her practicum that her experience and openness to working with clients from a variety of social, ethnic, and economic backgrounds opened a window through which she could view, from a macro perspective, the struggles of the entire community. Because of its prevalence in the depressed community, her direct practice knowledge of substance abuse and its impact upon the health and well-being of both client and family was invaluable. Her command of medical terminology concurrently increased by studying vocabulary lists and reading charts. Rebecca found herself becoming both learner and teacher in this multidisciplinary setting. Interacting with physicians, medical students, nurses, non-professionals, and community workers, Rebecca soon found herself in a position of modeling professional conduct for some of the staff. The clinic practicum reinforced Rebecca's recognition of the need to set appropriate boundaries with clients and co-workers and to practice strict adherence to issues of confidentiality and ethics. Rebecca was continually reminded in her practicum of how the macro issues, (community fiscal resources, the legal system, leadership, politics) impacted delivery of healthcare on the micro level. She also learned that having some tolerance for bureaucratic delay served to lessen her own frustrations.

Maintaining a goal-directed focus and clear communication patterns

It was difficult for local residents, clients, and clinic staff to conceptualize the process of reaching ultimate goals for program development in the Saturday Free Clinic. They were frequently impatient with week-to-week difficulties and bureaucratic delay. Communication patterns that focused on goals of the clinic for patient care were important to avoid misunderstandings and unwarranted expectations. Medical students and physicians rotating through the clinic, coming from geographically and culturally diverse backgrounds, often had little time to acquaint themselves with the local culture before being thrust into the role of diagnostician and healer of this needy population. Rebecca, however, was a constant figure in the clinic on Saturdays as well as during the week for patient follow-up. The clinic's non-professional staff was usually drawn from the local community and they, together with representatives from local churches and other charitable organizations, were of enormous value. They taught Rebecca how to interact with the community and access local formal and informal resources. In this dissimilar gathering, however, it was not difficult to see how easily questions could go unanswered (or unasked), and rumors and misunderstandings develop. Rebecca gradually became a 'bridge', joining together the professional and non-professional staff, client and physician, client and community resource provider.

Diverse community needs require diverse practice skill development

Because the clinic is specifically designed to serve those who find that their very survival is a daily challenge, Rebecca soon learned to expect to be confronted by ongoing crises. Some clients are physically or mentally challenged. Some are elderly. Many have chronic diseases such as hypertension, diabetes, and heart disease. Many have been unable to work for years. Rebecca was often called upon to evaluate the adequacy of living arrangements, access to adequate food, and in some cases, the safety of the home environment. Prescriptions for medicine are filled in the clinic if possible but sometimes vouchers must be issued so the client can fill the prescription elsewhere. It was the responsibility of the social work student to determine how much, if any, of the prescription cost the client could pay. If medical tests not available at the Saturday Free Clinic were indicated, Rebecca had to find resources where those tests could be performed either free or at a reduced cost, affordable to the client. The student's ingenuity in making these arrangements was further taxed if clients had language barriers, hearing deficits, severe visual impairment, childcare issues, or transportation problems. Learning to understand and access local, state and federal resources for clients as well as to advocate for the needed development of clinic services became an important part of Rebecca's responsibilities.

Students reflect upon their community-focused practice learning

Perhaps the most meaningful assessments of the Saturday Free Clinic experience come from students after the completion of their practicums. Without exception, students say that they were struck by the grim reality of the world in which the clients live. One stated that although textbooks lay the groundwork for understanding, it is a hands-on micro practice experience that develops empathy. Students expressed admiration for clients who, while struggling with nearly insurmountable problems, were able to maintain pride and dignity and to express gratitude for even the smallest assistance. Often, students discovered that the person seeking treatment as the 'identified patient' was more concerned about the health of other family members. When assessing a client's needs it often became apparent that getting help with a utility bill or accessing a free air conditioner was of equal or greater importance than responding to the medical symptoms which prompted the clinic visit.

Students quickly came to appreciate that they were working with a population which is not only under-served, but also under-recognized. They found that many of the clients had been virtually invisible and the world of managed care with its health maintenance organizations, its complicated vocabulary and acronyms passed them by. They reported that most clients indicated never having had traditional medical insurance coverage and they do not expect that to change. Patient expectations of having their needs met, and those of their families, were bleak. Students often described life for clients as 'incredibly difficult', punctuated with losses and focused on survival. They concluded that community revitalization based on community empowerment needed to be built upon a foundation of responsiveness to basic individual human needs.

Review of practice learning from this initiative

This chapter reviews the development of a social work practicum model that responded to the circumstances of a new government-sponsored Joint Community Development initiative. The initiative supports the creation of university–community partnerships for the simultaneous economic, physical and social revitalization of urban communities from a community empowerment perspective. Of the five Joint Community Development grants awarded nationally, only the one discussed here included a social work component and the involvement of a School of Social Work. In contrast to practicums in established organizations where the role of the social worker is clearly defined, this practicum model was developed in the context of an emerging operational clarification of community empowerment within the partnership as a whole.

Critical issues for student learning

Critical practice learning issues encountered by students in this emerging university–community partnership include the following.

UNDERSTANDING THE COMMUNITY'S HISTORY, POLITICAL DYNAMICS AND ECONOMIC CIRCUMSTANCES, AS WELL AS THE BELIEFS AND DESIRES OF ITS RESIDENTS, BEFORE TAKING ACTION

Taking the time to familiarize themselves with their clients' view of their culture, circumstances and desires often conflicted with the students' desire to act upon their own (sometimes theoretical) perceptions of residents' needs. Students wanted to come away from their practicums with some satisfaction that they made a tangible contribution to the community. This laudable desire sometimes came in conflict with principles inherent in respecting the process of community empowerment – of working in collaboration with residents and community leaders to mutually clarify and achieve community goals. A student summarized this point by saying that she learned to take the soft approach and find out where people are coming from. She concluded that it often takes a long time to get things up and running when there is community participation in the planning and implementation.

DEVELOPING PRACTICE LEARNING EXPERIENCES IN SIGNIFICANT ASPECTS OF BOTH MACRO AND MICRO COMMUNITY PRACTICE

Through their interactions with community residents in the employment referral center, students identified a need for (and received) more clinically focused consultation and supervision of their work with individual clients. The focus of social work studies for these students had typically been in areas of social and economic development. Confronted with assisting individuals with substance abuse, a criminal record and severe poverty, the students wanted to learn more about the interpersonal dynamics of counseling individuals about possibilities for making changes in their lives. Conversely, students who were studying direct practice with children experienced how community and family dynamics affected the children with whom they worked. Consequently, these students wanted to learn more about how to collaborate with community leaders and disadvantaged families on behalf of the community's children. Thus, the practicum requirement that all students have experiences working directly with residents in a program setting, as well as with the community as a whole through program development efforts, increased students' desire for more depth and breadth in their practicum learning experiences. The impact of activities in one area of practice upon the other was more readily seen and understood by students in this type of community practice environment.

LEARNING THE DYNAMICS AND SKILLS OF COMMUNITY OUTREACH

Outreach to residents was difficult and time consuming. The effort involved in getting disenfranchised people connected to a community-driven revitalization process, however, enhanced individual and community empowerment. A student reflected that it takes perseverance to get people involved because so many residents are alienated. In the process, however, students learned the power inherent in valuing each resident as a person. When students and community revitalization leaders genuinely respected the integrity of each resident on the street and in community meetings, community collaboration and empowerment advanced.

HAVING SUPPORTIVE SUPERVISORY TIME FOR ACTIVE REFLECTION ON DEALING WITH UNCERTAINTY

Given the multidisciplinary semi-autonomous, fast-paced nature of the students' practicum responsibilities and activities, time for student reflection in individual and group supervision meetings was essential for integrating what students observed, experienced, and sought to understand. Within an individual student's practicum, one cannot necessarily see what's going on in the whole community or understand the multiple political and economic values and forces driving the action. It was very important for practicum supervisors to help students keep a focus on the macro dynamics of the 'big picture', as well as on practice skill development in their individual interactions with residents.

Keeping a journal of practicum activities, interactions, reflections, personal challenges, perspectives and questions facilitated an integration of macro and micro practice issues. It also focused learning within individual supervisory meetings. To help keep the big picture in mind and be able to focus on the long view, students suggested that they should keep a semester-by-semester log of the goals, process, difficulties encountered, and achievements. They felt that this would provide them with a sense that their time-limited role contributed to the long process of community revitalization and with a view of the challenges both faced and handled by students who proceeded them.

Critical issues for engaging in similar work

Several concluding recommendations are offered for those who may offer student practice learning experiences in similar community revitalization settings.

CLARIFYING GOALS AND STRATEGIES FOR COMMUNITY REVITALIZATION AMONG UNIVERSITY–COMMUNITY PARTNERS

In our case example, a working understanding of community empowerment among the multidisciplinary entities simultaneously addressing physical, economic and social problems in the community was not established at the beginning of the project. Doing so would have reduced communication problems and uncertainty about the role of the community leaders and residents in the partnership. It may have more clearly established the social component's role and funding requirements alongside those of the physical and economic components. In addition, it would have decreased the complexity of teaching students about community empowerment practice in an evolving multidisciplinary university–community partnership.

ENSURING COLLABORATION WITH THE COMMUNITY TO AGREE UPON GOALS, ROLES AND STRATEGIES OF PRACTICUM STUDENTS

As a resource for community empowerment, practicum students are most effective when the community knows what they are doing and has a clearly defined role in directing their activities. This is especially important because practicums are time-limited and have university-driven practicum learning contracts agreed upon at the onset of the practicum. We encountered a few situations in which residents or community groups wanted students (who already had contracts for clearly defined practicum activities) to take on additional activities that would have interfered with fulfillment of the previously agreed upon activities in their practicum learning contracts. By placing responsibility for decision-making about the roles and assignments of practicum students in a community-based human/social service subcommittee reporting to the community council, a sense of community control and decision-making for student activities emerged.

ESTABLISHING COLLABORATIVE UNIVERSITY–COMMUNITY SUPERVISION

More effective university placement and supervision of students occur when a community representative shares responsibility for design of the learning activities, on-site supervision, and grading of students. To work and learn effectively, students need both university and community support behind them. This kind of work in the real world of community revitalization is transforming for students. One student summarized his experience in the community by saying that he was proud to have had the courage to face the challenges. Another related that she had developed an appreciation for the complexity of social justice issues in community revitalization.

Acknowledgement

The work that provided the basis for this publication was supported by funding under an award with the US Department of Housing and Urban Development. The authors are solely responsible for the accuracy of the statements and interpretations contained in this publication. Such interpretations do not necessarily reflect the views of the US government.

Note

1   The usual plural of 'practicum' is 'practicums' although in the
    USA, 'practica' is increasingly being used.

Chapter Two

Social Work Placements in Police Stations
A Force for Change

Kalindi S. Muzumdar and Rashida A. Atthar

Introduction

Social work education has always emphasized the importance of the field placement for students. However, the field practicum, being a laboratory for learning, has an additional function; it can be used as a vehicle for social change or to initiate the process of such change. The following is a brief account of placements in the police station undertaken by students at the College of Social Work, Nirmala Niketan (NN), Mumbai (Bombay), India.

First, it is necessary to explain the term 'social worker', since it is used in India with various connotations. For example, the freedom fighters who participated in the Indian struggle for independence were also known as 'social workers'. They were revered by society. The current political parties 'inherited' this title of social worker and some of their representatives mingle with the public with the sole objective of securing votes during elections.

Then there are men and women who have philanthropic ideals, the 'do gooders'. They work instinctively and consider their work as charity. They do not undergo any training in social work and are content with the way they function. In addition, they make donations in cash or in kind to clients. There is another group of social workers who work voluntarily. These comprise college and school students, educated or non-educated youth and women from slums, middle class and well-to-do families. At times, professional social workers do become involved in voluntary social work. Most of them are sincere in their desire to help the poor, marginalized and victimized individuals and groups. However, most of these voluntary social workers are not trained and seek training at agencies that conduct short-term training programs for them.

Professional social work is distinct from the rest as it follows a body of knowledge and integrates theory, practice and research for problem solving. In India, professional training in social work was initiated by the Tata Institute of Social Sciences (TISS) in 1936. However, many Indians have yet to accept what is distinctive about the profession and there remains a strong feeling that social workers should not expect high remuneration for their work.

Ranade (1994), states that

> social work is concerned with the poor, the weak and the exploited. The World Bank, in its recent report, has forecast a bleak future for the poor of the country. What is the position that we, as social work educators, take in respect of these developments, and what role do we envisage for us in the new dispensation? (p.12)

Ranade goes on to suggest that social workers should be able to face the challenge of these world changes.

Rationale for the field placement

The poor, victimized and marginalized groups in Indian society are affected by various systems, notably educational, legal, healthcare and the police. In the context of the increasing violence against women and children, the role of the police assumes utmost importance (Dakshina Murthy 1999; *Times of India* 7 October 1999). In the ultimate analysis, it is the police whom the women and children approach for help in cases of kidnapping, wife battering, molestation, rape and other such assaults on human dignity such as making obscene remarks and gestures at women (known as 'eve-teasing': Balasubrahmanyan 1990; May 1984; Sanger 2000; Sharma 1999). Children too, who are lost or are sexually and/or physically assaulted, go to the police station. They may take themselves, or be referred there by social welfare agencies and like minded individuals and groups, or be apprehended by the police under the Indian Juvenile Justice Act 1986.

The treatment meted out to most women and some children in most of the police stations in Mumbai is not humane. Women who come to the police station with bruises and wounds are ridiculed and sent back with remarks such as: 'if your husband doesn't beat you, who else will?'; 'don't come to us with petty complaints, we have enough on our hands apprehending gangsters'; and 'we also beat our wives if they don't listen to us'. This inhumane treatment of women in police stations is widespread and is cited in several newspapers. For example, a tribal woman was stripped, raped and partially burned in police custody by a sub-inspector in Vadodara, in the state of Gujarat (*Times of India* 3 May 1998). Another example is of a 5-month-old baby who died in police custody in the state of Hyderabad because its mother was beaten and kicked while breast-feeding (*Indian Express* 19 September 1993). According to the police of the city of Delhi, 100 custody deaths occurred in the 5 years up to 1993 (*Indian Express* 19 September 1993). Drug addicts, too, are soundly beaten, locked up for a day or two and then released. Investigations in most of these cases leave much to be desired.

Upon observing this phenomenon, the College of Social Work (NN) initiated student placement in the police system in 1983. There was yet another strong reason for initiating this placement. In 1982, the police constabulary in Mumbai went on a strike. As is usual in such situations, some hooligan mobs looted a few shops and the police were held responsible for this. This strike was the last resort of the Mumbai police constabulary to bring their miserable living and working conditions to the notice of the authorities. The police system has been declared an essential service by the Indian government and hence the police personnel are denied the right to strike or resort to any such agitational measures. The College of Social Work (NN) took note of this strike and concluded that something was radically wrong in the police system. It recognized the need for social work intervention in the police system, in order to effect changes in the functioning of the police, by identifying their needs and problems, conveying these to the authorities, and consequently improving the police–public relations.

Initiation of the placement

The College of Social Work (NN) contacted the then police commissioner of Greater Mumbai, and secured permission in 1983 to work in the residential complex in south Mumbai of the constabulary and other police officers of lower ranks. The rationale for working in this residential complex was to observe the life of the police officers as householders and to identify their needs and problems.

In 1984 we again approached the police commissioner and sought his permission to work in one police station in Mumbai so that we could identify the needs and problems of the police at their workplace. More importantly, we could observe the interaction between the vulnerable individuals and the police. This would give us some direction as to which areas need our intervention in the police system. The police commissioner granted us permission to work at the Dharavi police station (Dharavi is the biggest slum in Asia). Later, in 1987, we secured permission from the then police commissioner to work in the Mahim police station in another suburb of Mumbai. In both Dharavi and Mahim, community riots are common.

Placement with the police

Objectives of field placements of MSW Part II students

Considering the complicated nature of the placement, only the senior postgraduate students were placed in the police stations. A team of four or five students was placed in each police station. The following are the objectives of the fieldwork for Master of Social Work (MSW) Part II students formulated by the College of Social Work (NN):

- develop an understanding of the systemic factors affecting the functions of individuals, groups and communities at micro and macro levels, and effect changes in policies at the micro and macro levels

- use a systemic approach to analyse the structure and functions of the agency to enhance and effect changes in policies at the micro and macro levels

- use different models of intervention selectively in relation to individuals, groups and communities

- function effectively as an administrator, using skills of management, supervision and training

- assume a leadership role in one's profession and in the interdisciplinary team

- enhance self-awareness leading to the promotion of growth in others

- appreciate the importance of professional responsibility and commitment in human rights issues

- use the field instruction to develop functioning as a professional social worker.

The broad purpose of the placement was to improve the police–public relations and the specific objectives were:

- to identify the needs and the problems of the police, especially of the lower ranks and communicate these to the authorities
- to create awareness among the vulnerable groups regarding their rights and responsibilities in relation to the police
- to plan programmes for police–public interaction
- to conduct a small survey related to the functioning of the police.

Procedure of placement in the police station

In the third year of the Bachelor of Social work (BSW) and second year of MSW, students can select their area of placement. Broad categories are offered to them for selection, such as health, education and community, rather than specific agencies. The field placement committee, comprising faculty members and the fieldwork coordinator, makes the placements. Prior to placing a student in a specific agency, the following major points are taken into consideration:

- the student's fieldwork experience in the previous year
- the student's fluency with the local or the national language
- the student's place of residence, since spending too much time in travelling is counter-productive to good fieldwork.

Timings and duration of placement

Fieldwork comprises 15 hours per week and the stipulated days are Thursdays (half days), Fridays and Saturdays (full days). There are fortnightly group conferences conducted with students in the same agency or across agencies with the same focus of work, in order to provide direction for future work. Senior students of the BSW (three years) and MSW (two years) programme work continuously for one month in a block placement in the same agency in the second term of the academic year, in order to acquire a feeling of being a professional in a social work agency. Students have one placement a year and, in addition, two weeks are used for 'educational camp' in which all students are taken to rural or tribal areas for 15 days to expose them to different projects.

Tasks assigned to students in the police station

In the initial stage:

- observe the functioning of the police station
- study the administrative set-up of the police station
- study the Bombay Police Act and the Indian Penal Code (IPC) with special reference to laws affecting women and children
- understand the problems of the police in performing their duties
- begin to handle cases of non-cognizable (NC) offences, which are offences for which the police need a warrant to investigate
- establish professional relationships with the police personnel as well as with the public
- plan meetings with constables and officers to discuss social issues and the roles of the police
- plan lectures along with discussion sessions for police and school students, women's organizations and the youth of the slum community.

In the middle stage:

- independently handle NC cases and non-legal aspects of legal cases
- organize meetings of constables and officers separately, to discuss social issues such as street children, the problem of dowry (a practice in India in some communities, of giving gifts in cash or in kind, to the bridegroom as a condition for marriage), prostitution and child sexual harassment and the role of the police in respect of these; emerging social problems, such as the impact of AIDS, are included in these discussions
- conduct a small survey on any one aspect of the police functioning or on the perception of the public regarding the police
- conduct training programs at some of the training centres for the police in Maharashtra, with the help of the faculty adviser and the team
- organize talks by the police in the surrounding slums, schools, colleges, women's organizations and youth groups.

In the termination stage:

- terminate all the work at the police station including the cases handled and refer the incomplete cases to the police personnel

- write a report of the work done in the entire year and submit it to the police commissioner to effect policy changes

- write summary recordings of the work done during the entire year

- prepare a plan of work for the following year's students.

Reactions of the police to the students placed in the police station

Initial reactions

Given the context outlined in the introduction to this chapter regarding the place of the social worker in Indian society, the entry of students into the police stations was seen as an unnecessary intrusion. The police viewed them as representatives of political parties seeking votes and their reaction varied from anger, hostility, doubt and sarcasm to condescending acceptance. Some police officers were apprehensive that the students would catch them taking bribes and report the incidents to the higher authorities.

The students were obliged, therefore, to explain to the police personnel the concept of professional social work and its objectives. The reaction to this explanation was at times skeptical and hostile and at other times positive.

Reactions in the middle and terminal phases of student intervention

The initial hostility gave way to positive working relationships. The police willingly began to refer cases to students and to cooperate with them in all the programmes organized by them (e.g. training sessions). Duty officers (DO), who are police personnel of the rank of sub-inspector who are designated to register the first information report (FIR) of the complainant, would actually ask the NC cases to come on students' fieldwork days. The constables and officers began to involve the students as observers in their investigative procedures; for example, registering the dying declaration of a burn victim. Of course, there remained a few police personnel who continued to be doubtful and indifferent to the students' work, despite students' efforts to change their attitude.

These students were given a lot of freedom which they used judiciously, for example in reading the registers of NC cases and the FIR of clients whose cases the students were handling. Significantly, a few policemen and policewomen began to seek assistance from the students in their personal problems.

Methodology of working in the police station

Most of the 74 police stations in Mumbai are located in large slum complexes. The new students and the faculty adviser/field instructor sat in the duty room where complaints are registered with the duty officers and observed the process of registering and handling complaints. These observations indicated that more than 85 per cent of cases referred to the police station were of non-cognizable offences. A large number of these pertained to petty quarrels at the public water taps and conflicts between two or more women. Until 1983, wife beating and physical and mental torture of women at home were not considered offences. The women complainants were thus driven away from the police station by some police personnel. There were a few who listened patiently to them, but said they could not assist since they were civil cases.

With the advent of Section 498A of the Indian Penal Code, there has been a gradual change in attitudes and behaviour towards women, especially by the police. Section 498A was introduced as a section of the IPC in 1983 and came into effect in 1985. It states that physical and mental assaults on a woman by her husband and/or his relatives is a cognizable crime, punishable by three years' imprisonment. The intervention of women's organizations and of the two colleges of social work in Mumbai (the College of Social Work and Tata Institute of Social Sciences) has played an important role in changing the attitude of the police. This work is continuous and students play an important role in it. Section 498A gave a leverage to all those who deal with the police in relation to women in distress.

One of the major objectives of work with the police was to improve their communication skills and interpersonal relationships. It was observed that these are the most important skills necessary in order for them to be able to coordinate work with each other and increase their efficiency. An example of how this was done is shown in Table 2.1.

End

Means

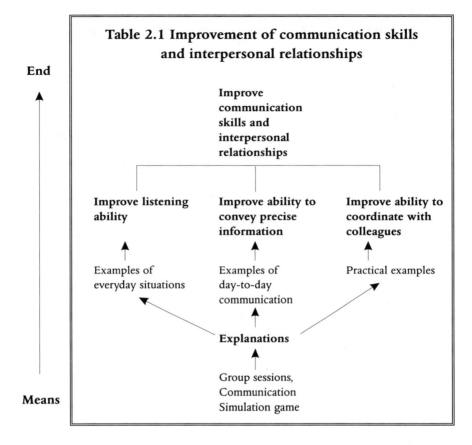

Table 2.1 Improvement of communication skills and interpersonal relationships

At times, the students were assigned cases by the police and challenged to do 'a better job than us'. As the students handled these cases, they were watched closely, especially by the inspectors and sub-inspectors. In most cases, the NC cases were resolved and the police had to acknowledge the contribution of the students, though condescendingly. The students' success was largely due to their efforts to use the integrated approach to problem-solving (Table 2.2). They paid home visits, conducted family interviews, involved the neighbours (with the consent of the clients) and simultaneously worked with the slum community and non-governmental organizations (NGOs) to alleviate their common problems. They involved the police in all their work.

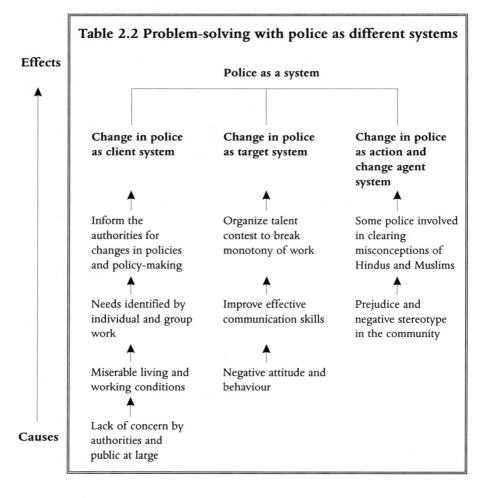

Table 2.2 Problem-solving with police as different systems

Effects

Police as a system

Change in police as client system	Change in police as target system	Change in police as action and change agent system
Inform the authorities for changes in policies and policy-making	Organize talent contest to break monotony of work	Some police involved in clearing misconceptions of Hindus and Muslims
Needs identified by individual and group work	Improve effective communication skills	Prejudice and negative stereotype in the community
Miserable living and working conditions	Negative attitude and behaviour	
Lack of concern by authorities and public at large		

Causes

A summary of the students' work in the police station

The students performed a variety of tasks. The following is a summary of their work during the placements.

Individual and family work

Students handled cases of family conflicts (e.g. between siblings, mother-in-law and daughter-in-law, and couples). They also handled cases of drug addiction, alcoholism, gambling, eve-teasing, physical and mental ill-health, love affairs and elopement of teenagers. Most of the clients lived in the large slum complexes in which the police stations are located.

These cases were self-referred or brought by relatives and friends. The duty officer has the responsibility of talking to the complainants and then requesting sub-inspectors to register these cases. The services of the constables are used to bring the culprits to the police station (e.g. the husband who beats his wife), to escort complainants to the hospital and other such jobs.

Students took the complainants aside with the permission of the DO and conducted the interviews. It is important to note that it is not possible to have any kind of privacy in the police stations, since there are often four or five complainants being interrogated by the police at the police station at any one time, which is extremely noisy. Therefore, the students took the complainants into the small compounds of the police stations and interviewed them. These interviews helped the complainants to feel at ease at the police station and to speak freely to sympathetic listeners. At times, the culprits also were interviewed in a similar fashion, again with the permission of the police. Complainants who may have violated the law themselves (e.g. drug addicts and eve-teasers) were the most reluctant to talk to the students. It took quite some time for these people to have confidence in the students and to relate their problems. As already mentioned, the police used to perceive various types of addicts merely as criminals and it has taken some years for students, social workers, psychologists and doctors to help the police realize that substance abuse is a mental illness and requires long-term treatment. Our students made continuous efforts to drive home this point. They informed the police regarding the de-addiction agencies in Mumbai and sometimes accompanied the police and the addicts to these agencies. They followed up these cases as long as they could, helping to motivate the clients' families to continue the treatment. There were a few who refused to be involved in the treatment process, but their families were adequately motivated to keep up their efforts.

Cases of marital conflicts were handled by students to prevent litigation and to strengthen family bonds. However, in cases of extreme torture, the clients, especially women, were enabled to seek legal advice.

Interviews at the police stations often necessitated home visits. The concept of confidentiality had to be adapted appropriately to the type of cases and the culture of the slums. Very often, neighbours surrounded the students while they were in the clients' homes. Generally, in slums, neighbours volunteer information regarding the clients' problems and the clients willingly accept this. There are rarely any 'secrets' or privacy. Given this situation it was doubly difficult for students to conduct family interviews. Yet with the theoretical input in the classroom and the guidance of the faculty adviser, the students managed such situations quite well, and often involved the police as observers.

Cases of 'love affairs' and elopement are quite common. At least once a month, one such case is referred to the police stations. The youngsters, usually in their teens, are overwhelmingly influenced by the film media. The most popular Indian films among the masses are those that depict love at first sight between the hero and the heroine, their song and dance numbers, the sudden entry of the villain and the ultimate victory of the hero. Elopement is eulogized and most Indian films depict the consent of both sets of parents in the end. Given this ideal-ized model, cases of elopement are common. The parents of the couple lodge a complaint and request the police to catch the 'rebels'. When the couple is brought to the police station, the parents sometimes request the police to beat these youngsters and 'to put some sense in them', and both the police and the parents of the couple have been known to resort to physical assaults. The police frequently ignore the laws relating to physical assaults on offenders.

When students established their credibility, the police respected their requests, including the ones to stop beating the young couples. The couple and the parents would be counselled by the students separately first, and jointly at a later stage. The goal of this counselling was to bring about a compromise between both parties. Students observed a lack of knowledge of existing laws among clients as well as among police personnel of the lower ranks. Hence, they had to educate the police and the clients regarding the laws affecting them in specific cases.

Groupwork and community work

Students used groupwork techniques to form new groups or work with existing groups in the slum complex. The objectives of groupwork were as follows:

- to enable the group members to handle petty problems so as to avoid referral to the police stations

- to educate the groups regarding various police procedures, such as FIRs and the *panchnama* (a statement by witnesses of the offence)

- to educate groups also about registration of dying declarations, and individual rights *vis-à-vis* the police; for example, women and children cannot be asked to report to the police stations after 7: 00 p.m.

In Maharashtra, there are several religious festivals celebrated with a great deal of enthusiasm. One such festival is the Ganesh festival, which lasts for ten days and is celebrated publicly. The local youths, both boys and girls, are actively involved in organizing various programmes of dance, songs, plays, mimicry and lectures. Some of the students placed in the police stations used this opportunity to organize lectures by the police personnel to large audiences regarding the police procedures and rights of the citizens. Students faced problems of 'red tapism' and administrative hierarchy when arranging such lectures.

Generally, the police are viewed as baton-wielding, corrupt demons by the citizenry, especially by the slum dwellers (Deshpande 1990). Students used various methods to change the behaviour of the police personnel, as well as the misconceptions nurtured by the slum dwellers. One such method was to organize informal sessions with the police and school children, women's and church organizations and other NGOs.

Students also tried to network with NGOs in Dharavi, as they interact often with the police, but these attempts were not successful due to the varied ideologies, objectives and functioning of these agencies. In times of crisis, however, all the NGOs got together and worked diligently along with the students. One such crisis was the communal riots of 1993 in Mumbai between warring Hindus and Muslims. Houses and shops were looted and burnt and people were murdered mercilessly. The College of Social Work (NN) kept the college closed for two weeks and staff and students plunged into relief work and rehabilitation programmes organized by the state government. Later, the work continued in the riot-stricken areas and was considered as the students' fieldwork.

Learning gains for students placed in police stations

In addition to the general gains in fieldwork, such as problem-solving skills, students placed in police stations gained specific knowledge and skills. They learned to function as professionals in a very significant yet regimented system affecting all citizens, and more especially the victimized, exploited and marginalized groups. They learned close observation of a system responsible for law and order and how to identify its needs and problems. The students overcame their initial apprehension, skepticism and doubt regarding the police department. They functioned as a liaison between the citizens and the police, and also as a vigilant group to monitor the proper functioning of the police personnel. Other important learning gains included: organizing meetings and training programs for the police (made difficult by 'red tapism'); educating the citizens regarding their rights *vis-à-vis* the police; communicating with the police authorities (including the police commissioner); and giving social work inputs in the training centres of the police in Mumbai and districts of Maharashtra.

The research study

As part of the studies for the MSW, the co-author conducted research about policewomen in greater Mumbai (Atthar 1987).

Specific objectives of the study

- the socio-economic and educational background of the policewomen and the factors that motivate them to join the police force

- the role performance of the policewomen

- the type of training the policewomen received and its impact on them in the performance of their duties.

Assumptions of the study

- policewomen have an important role to play in society as agents of social control

- the role of policewomen is not yet institutionalized, despite having been inducted into the service in 1948

- the policewomen's role is yet to be established in the more challenging functions of the system, like work in the police stations and investigations.

Hypotheses of the study

- majority of policewomen come from low socio-economic backgrounds

- the major motivating factor of the policewomen to join the police force as a career is economic need

- training imparted to the policewomen for their role performance is not adequate.

The sample comprised 80 policewomen, which comprised 15 policewomen officers (inspectors and sub-inspectors) and 65 policewomen head constables and constables. The research design used was the survey design and data collected using the interview schedule.

Major findings of the study

The findings of the study were consonant with the first two hypotheses. Most of the respondents (75) had low socio-economic backgrounds. The majority of respondents (51 or 64 per cent) joined the police force due to their economic need. Policewomen were asked about the adequacy of training in confrontation skills, knowledge of legislation, and working with people in need. The level of education was negatively correlated with adequacy of training.

It appears that the police service is an employment agency to accommodate the less educated and deprived women of society at constabulary level. Informal talks with the policewomen revealed that they play a peripheral role in the police system and their training did not equip them to take up challenging tasks. They are assigned tasks of a social worker without any training in social sciences. There was a discrepancy in the training of policemen and policewomen.

The study recommended that the College of Social Work (NN) should assist in formulating the curriculum for policewomen, with college staff as a resource for the training programmes. The study also recommended that cases of women and children be handled solely by women police at the police stations and lock-ups. An article based on the study was published by the *Times of India*, the leading national daily newspaper in all its city editions.

Subsequently, other surveys and research studies carried out by students have played a role in trying to bring about positive changes in the police system: for example, the 1994 cohort conducted a survey of all the police stations in Mumbai and submitted the report to the police commissioner and to the state government. Consequently, there have been regular efforts to improve the physical condition of the police stations. The students of the 1998 cohort conducted a study on the familial and work problems of the women police, which was appreciated by the police department.

A brief analysis of the placement

It is generally understood that the police system in countries like India has lost its credibility. The image of the police is sullied on account of their ineffectiveness and corrupt practices. Yet, the police system affects everyone. The profession of social work is committed to social justice and human rights and, therefore, it cannot ignore malpractice in the police system. Student placement seems to be an entry point to effect meaningful change in the system.

Malaise in the police system in India is due to miserable living and working conditions, as well as inadequate training in the humane aspects of the work.

Hence, the students concentrated not just on the slum dwellers who faced a great deal of difficulties in the police stations, but also on the police personnel themselves. They also worked with various groups in the slums, schools, women's organizations and other such institutions regarding their rights.

In the ultimate analysis, when a nation expects its police force to be effective, it has to focus both on the needs and problems of the police personnel as well as the citizens and their mutual responsibilities. Students can play a crucial role in achieving this goal.

Conclusion

Over the years, there have been positive changes in the living and working conditions of the police as well as their interaction with the public. The College of Social Work (NN) has played its part in these changes, as has the Tata Institute of Social Sciences, various women's organizations and the police personnel themselves.

The College of Social Work (NN) was the pioneer in initiating student placement in the police system in Mumbai in 1983 and has been able to establish the role of the social work profession in the police system. College staff are often consulted and approached to conduct various types of training sessions for the police and are involved in the Mahila Dakshata Samitis (women's vigilance groups), formed by the police department. We can feel confident that the decision to place students in police stations has been successful.

Chapter Three

Integrating People and Services

A Practice and Learning Experience
through Field Instruction

Anna Y. L. Leung, Heidi S. K. Hui and Frances Y. S. Ip

Introduction

That field instruction plays a crucial part in determining the quality of training
and education for social workers is obvious and not contentious. Field instruction
provides a practice and learning experience for social work students – giving an
opportunity for students to understand agency structure and service delivery; use
concepts to interpret situations and map out goals and courses of action; try out
techniques in practice; acquire self-awareness and professional identity and to
develop their own personal style of work (Berengarten 1961; Butler and Elliott
1985; Department of Social Work and Social Administration, University of
Hong Kong 1997; Kerson 1994; Tsang 1983; Urbanowski and Dwyer 1988).

However, field instruction has other functions that perhaps do not occupy as
central a position as the educational dimension but are nevertheless, significant.
Typically, field instruction is carried out in organizations providing various types
of social services. As indicated by Bogo and Vayda (1998), field instruction takes
place in the context of two institutional settings – the school and the field.
Various authors have commented on tensions that can exist between the school
and the field. Such tensions arise from differences in orientations and expectations. For example, the school may strongly emphasize the importance research
and knowledge building, coupled with a future-oriented perspective and an
abstract, general approach to social work. On the other hand, the field is likely to
emphasize factors such as practice competence and efficiency of service delivery.
The field approach to social work is specific and concrete and it is more focused

on the present. Where there is an insufficiency in communication and mutuality between the school and the community is not a desirable state of affairs. Field instruction may be regarded by both parties as a venue through which the two parties can interact, collaborate and attain mutual understanding and benefits (Munson 1987; Raskin et al. 1991; Vayda and Bogo 1991). Therefore, besides the purely educational function, field instruction has an important role in acting as a bridge between the school and the community.

Moreover, field instruction has yet a third function. Through the placement of students in agencies for direct practice, field instruction also offers opportunities for staff and students to experiment with new theories, try out innovative ideas and develop pioneering projects. The advantage of the field placement as a venue for experimentation is that it can blend together 'education', 'research', and 'practice' (Rapp et al. 1989). In addition, McClelland (1991) pointed out that field education has provided leadership in:

1. applying new approaches of social work practice for existing settings and

2. developing new settings in which social workers can practise.
   (McClelland 1991, p.182)

This chapter describes and analyses a field instruction project carried out by the Department of Social Work and Social Administration, University of Hong Kong, that attempted to exploit the multiple opportunities offered by field instruction and student placement, as described above. This was an experimental project to explore ways of developing integrated service delivery in a public housing estate, known as Shek Wai Kok, in Hong Kong. Reflecting the three functions of student placement and field instruction as elaborated above, the broad objectives of the Shek Wai Kok integration project were

1. to provide a base for the practical training of social work students

2. to facilitate agency–school collaboration

3. to experiment and develop ideas in service delivery.

The project: conceptual basis

Social service planners and social work practitioners have always been fascinated with promises of the prospect of 'service integration'. Achieving high levels of service integration are regarded as a means to eliminate fragmentation, prevent service gaps and avoid unnecessary duplication. All of which leads to improved service delivery (Gans and Horton 1975; Guetzbow 1966; Kamerman and Kahn 1976; Maxwell 1990). The Hong Kong government, for example, published a White Paper on social welfare service development that called for 'an integrated approach of service delivery' which was seen as a means to help to 'overcome the difficulties created by the compartmentalising of clients' needs and the fragmentation of service provision' (Hong Kong Government 1991, p.16). Yet, as poignantly pointed out by Kagan: 'In reviewing the history of service integration, one is struck by its nobility of intent, its tenacity of purpose, and the ineffectiveness of its implementation' (1993, p.ix).

The difficulty with 'service integration' as an ideal is that the reality is hard to achieve. Moreover, the meaning of 'service integration' is open to many different interpretations (Redburn 1977). Hence, for instance, Agranoff and Pattakos (1979) suggested that there could be four levels of integration:

1.   client-centred integration aiming at meeting the multiple needs of clients with a multidisciplinary approach

2.   programme-centred integration to link up discrete services into a multifaceted delivery system through means such as joint planning and budgeting mechanisms and information sharing systems

3.   policy-centred integration at the central government level that called for an integrative mindset in assessing needs, setting priorities, allocating resources and monitoring outcomes

4.   organization-centred integration that aimed at the reorganization of agency structures into super or mega agencies.

The Hong Kong government could be assumed to be concerned with integration at the policy and organizational level when it pleaded for an integrated approach of service delivery. On the other hand the Department of Social Work and Social Administration at the university was more interested in exploring integration at the client and programme level: i.e. at the point of contact between service and people, 'where things really happen'. In particular, to explore the processes and means by which the integration of people and services in a community could be facilitated through social work intervention. It was hypothesized that, operationally, the integration of services and people in the neighbourhood could be achieved through improving the responsiveness of the services to the needs and achieving a better 'fit' with the characteristics of the residents.

The concern for the specific needs of people in an identified neighbourhood suggested another meaning for the term 'integration' – to add to the confusion about the use of this term. Hence, in the field of rehabilitation, there has been a recurring debate about the virtues of an 'integration model' versus a 'specialization model' in serving those in need (Haring and Lovett 1992). 'Integration' in this context, is concerned with issues of normalization and the right of people with special needs to a safe and meaningful life in the community.

Like service integration, the integration of people with special needs into the community has been given great emphasis by the Hong Kong government, and is used as a guiding principle for setting the aims of rehabilitation services (Hong Kong Government 1977, 1995). The Disability Discrimination Ordinance was enacted in 1995 to provide legal protection to disabled persons against discrimination. In reality, the ideal of community integration is hard to reach. A great barrier to progress has been the resistance of residents, not only in passively avoiding contacts with people with special needs, but also in actively opposing the setting up of rehabilitation services in their community (Li 1993).

Through an experimental project in one neighbourhood, the department aimed at exploring means of doing social work that would build up the inter-agency and inter-clientele networks within the given resources of this neighbourhood, and in the process, to facilitate both 'the integration of services' and 'the integration of people'. A *networking approach* was proposed as the primary means of engineering the integration process. The *integration of people* was to be achieved through the promotion of mutual help, encouragement for volunteering and other modes of networking which sought: the relaxation of rigid boundaries between different client groups; the enhancement of their sense of belonging toward the community; and the building up of informal support networks to complement formal services. All of these measures helping to bridge service gaps and thus to realize the goal of community care (Bulmer 1987; Froland 1981). The *integration of services* was attempted through developing a network among service providers in the neighbourhood to help facilitate communication and cooperation, sharing of information, and pooling of resources. In the process, it was envisaged that the traditional rigid boundaries of services defined both by specific target groups and agencies and specific functions would be relaxed. While a service network would be established through which a person with a service need in the neighbourhood could get the necessary information and assistance to enable them to locate suitable services.

To summarize, the Shek Wai Kok integration project was based on a belief in the principle that 'clientele integration' and 'service integration' could go hand in hand with each other. Ideally, the loosening of 'clientele boundaries' and the loosening of 'agency boundaries' would act upon each other in a reciprocal way.

Through these processes, elements of communal support would be increased, releasing potential for mutual care in the community.

The approach to this experiment was 'learning by doing'. There was no pre-defined course of action or implementation steps to be followed. Initial ideas were implemented tentatively, and further plans and actions evolved after monitoring and analysing the community's responses to those tentative initiatives. Such an approach is appropriate in situations when the goals of a project are clear but the pathway to reach those goals is not (Sabel 1994)!

The project: more background information

Shek Wai Kok is a typical public housing estate with eight big housing blocks and a population of around 27,000. By Hong Kong standards, it is a small estate, with a range of social services, including centres for children and young people; services for older people; services for mentally handicapped people;[1] kindergartens, primary and secondary schools and also a public library. This estate was chosen as the location for the project for very practical reasons: its manageable size, and the friendly relationship that the department had established with some of the agencies operating in the neighbourhood. The project involved three non-governmental organizations. These were large-scale, well-established, multi-centred agencies operating units in the neighbourhood serving respectively, young people, older people, and handicapped people. The project spanned a period of 28 months. Altogether 30 students worked on it, during five periods of placement.

The Department of Social Work and Social Administration at the University of Hong Kong adopts the faculty-based field instruction unit model (Urbanowski and Dwyer 1988) in administering its field education programme. This model has students supervised by staff directly employed by the university, the majority being part-time field instructors. The students are placed in social work agencies of various types, including governmental and non-governmental organizations, in primary and secondary settings – all serving a variety of target groups.

Shardlow and Doel (1996) have identified eight models of practice learning in social work. These are the apprenticeship model, the competency-based model, the growth and development model, the managerial model, the academic model, the articulated model, the loop model and the role systems model. Based on this categorization, the model adopted by this department in its approach to practice teaching is a combination of the competency-based model and the articulated model. Much emphasis is given to the outcome of practice training. An elaborate form with over 70 behaviourally defined items has been designed to record and measure students' performance at the end of each fieldwork practice. On the other hand, the integration of academic and practice learning is also regarded as a core element in practice training. During their field practice, the students are explicitly expected to apply the skills and knowledge learned from various components of the programme to practical situations.

The project: development and results

The project went through three phases (Leung, Hui and Ip 1995a): *exploration*, *implementation* and *consolidation*, summarized pictorially in Figure 3.1 (for more details of the development of the project, please refer to Table 3.1 at the end of the chapter).

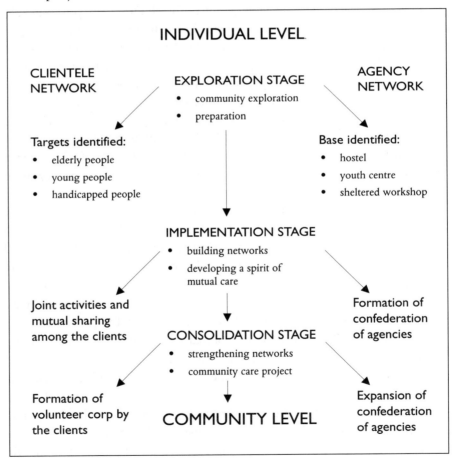

Figure 3.1 Levels of project development

Exploration phase (May 1992 to August 1992)

The aim of this phase was to gain an understanding of the community, and to identify and establish a base for the project, through agency visits, community walks, talking to potential service recipients, observation of community dynamics, discussion and analysis of the data obtained. Eventually, three agencies, operating three different services, namely, a youth centre, a hostel for older people and a sheltered workshop for the handicapped, were identified as the 'base agencies' for experimenting integration work.

Three client groups, served respectively by the three agencies, were identified as having needs and potential that could be linked up through integrative activities that would facilitate them to use their potential to serve others and have their own needs fulfilled. These were older residents in the hostel, handicapped people working in a sheltered workshop and the members of the youth centre. The first step was to facilitate the participation of the handicapped workers in the activities of the youth centre, and to develop the abilities of the three groups in serving each other and the community. These three client groups hence formed a core around which the inter-clientele network was to be built.

Implementation phase (October 1992 to August 1993)

The implementation phase was constructed on the groundwork laid during the exploration phase. Further efforts were made to break the boundaries, develop the inter-clientele as well as inter-agency linkages, and strengthen the sense of communal well-being in the neighbourhood.

Various programme activities were used to promote interaction and mutual exchange among the client groups. Perhaps the most significant event was the completion of a community survey through which households with singleton elderly, mentally handicapped or physically handicapped persons were identified through the efforts of the three client groups serving as volunteers.

This process consolidated the development of the inter-clientele network. Mutual caring relationships were built up among different groups. Moreover, improvements in social skills and the development of more positive self-images were observed among the clientele. At the inter-agency level, as the agencies saw the benefits of 'integration' on their clients, commitment toward the project was strengthened. Importantly, at the end of this phase, a confederation was formed with these three agencies as founding members, with a view to extend membership to other agencies in the community.

Consolidation phase (September 1993 to August 1994)

The objective of this phase was to strengthen the inter-clientele and inter-agency networks, and to build up structural support for the further development of the integrative work in anticipation of the withdrawal of student placements. This withdrawal was considered to be a necessary step to allow the community to take full responsibility for this development, as up until this point students on placement had provided an important developmental resource.

A special feature of this phase was the launching of a community care project involving the three groups as volunteers, backed up by the assistance of the three agencies, to provide support and care to individuals and families with special needs, who were identified through the community survey conducted previously. This project was a means of strengthening both the inter-clientele and inter-agency networks. Moreover, it encouraged the participants to actualize themselves through serving the community.

Meanwhile, the membership of the confederation of agencies was expanded. The objectives of this confederation were clearly spelt out as follows:

- to maintain linkage among the cooperating agencies

- to provide continuous support and stimulation to the volunteers

- to develop and strengthen 'community care' in the neighbourhood as a focal point for both 'clientele' and 'service integration'.

To summarize, the project began with modest attempts to build an inter-clientele network among three client groups: young people, handicapped workers and older people. The encouraging effects of clientele integration gave impetus to service integration through the building up of an inter-agency network. As 'integration' became a feature of the work of the agencies involved, a further step was taken to develop the potential of the 'clients' into resources who could provide informal care to serve the community.

Analysis: attainment of objectives

Previously, it was stated that the Shek Wai Kok project had three objectives: to provide a base for the practical training of social work students, to facilitate agency–school collaboration and to experiment with ideas in service delivery.

The unique experience for field instruction offered by this project will be discussed in detail in the next section. Meanwhile, the extent of attainment of the other two objectives will be briefly examined.

Experimentation

As an experiment in integration at the neighbourhood level, with the aim of exploring ways of doing social work that will contribute to the development of inter-agency and inter-clientele linkages within the community, the project can claim some success.

The uniqueness of the Shek Wai Kok development is that it has evolved out of a process of responding to clients' needs and characteristics. It is a people-based project, carried out with a bottom-up approach in which the initiative and control have come 'from where the people and the energy are' (Shearer 1986, p.197). The positive impact that the project had on the three core client groups was well recognized by the centre supervisors (Li 1994; Wan-lau 1994; Yau 1994). Their self-image was raised, their social skills improved and their sense of belonging to the community strengthened. Besides, the project created opportunities for the people in the neighbourhood to meet and mix with handicapped people and to observe their abilities. This was the best way of developing understanding and acceptance of people with special needs.

As for the intervention methods: this approach requires intensive efforts by the social workers first, to feel the pulse of the community and then to act as a catalyst helping to release people's energy for growth and change. It also calls for a deep level of involvement and collaboration among participating agencies. On the other hand, it should not be forgotten that all of the programme activities used to promote 'integration' in this experiment were within the service spheres of the agencies involved. In other words, these activities were in line with the agencies' philosophy and objectives, and could be assimilated into the regular work of the agency.

However, a project of such nature probably has little chance of success in a large community. Even within the Shek Wai Kok neighbourhood itself, the impact was limited and confined mainly to a relatively small number of people. Therefore, the contribution of the experiment lies mainly in identifying a process through which social work methods can be used to bring about some of the people-related benefits that 'integration' promises.

Agency–school collaboration

This project required close cooperation and communication between the agencies and the school at both 'headquarters' and 'front line' levels. As all three centres were operated by large, multi-centre organizations, it would not have been possible to use them as the base for the project without approval from their respective headquarters. Representatives from the headquarters level or mid-management level of the agencies regularly joined the entire project team of unit staff, student social workers and faculty members to review the progress of the project, clarify issues and exchange expectations. This brought about a much closer relationship between the faculty and the agency staff than was customary.

At the front line level, the ideas and direction of 'integration' developed out of discussion with the workers of the participating centres, in groups or through individual interviews. However, the actual implementation relied heavily on the student social workers. They designed the programme activities after gathering the information and suggestions from the parties concerned and observing the clients' responses – and did most of the implementation work. The involvement of the agency workers, however, increased steadily during the later part of the project as they prepared to assimilate the integrative work into their regular work. Regular exchange and close communication between agency workers and student workers was essential. After all, the success of the experiment depended not only on the effectiveness of the student workers in carrying out their work, but also (and perhaps even more so), on the attitude of the agency workers, on their being convinced of the worth of the project, on their commitment to participate. The experiment would have been a failure if it was seen by the agency workers as 'their' and not 'our' project.

This example of incorporating experimentation and research in student field-work placement shows how the school and the agency can collaborate not only to provide challenging field practice opportunities, but also to meet their respective objectives in knowledge building and improving service delivery. Neither party would have been able to do it alone. The school lacked a service base and community contacts, while the agencies had limited resources. The student workers not only provided extra staffing resources, but also had the advantage of not having to work within predefined areas of responsibilities. They could afford the time to study the characteristics of the community and enjoyed the freedom to experiment with programme design. Moreover, as a neutral, third party in the neighbourhood, they were in an excellent position to play a mediator role among the participating agencies in order to bring about greater integrative efforts across community divides (Maxwell 1990). Moreover, the fact that this was an 'experimental project' carried out under the name of the school, gave allowance for mistakes and failures. The agencies were 'protected' from any political or resource consequences should the project prove unsuccessful.

Analysis: the practice–teaching–learning experience

As a location for student fieldwork placement, the Shek Wai Kok project presented the following special features (Tong *et al.* 1994):

- The working and learning environment was 'unstructured' in the sense that there was a lack of examples, operational guidelines, previous practices, established procedures etc. that the students could follow. Therefore, there was a corresponding abundance of uncertainties, ambiguities and conflicting expectations (Leung 1996; Wong 1994).

- As the project was based in the neighbourhood, the students not only learned to work within one agency and to serve one specific client group, but also learned about the characteristics of the community, the inter-agency relations, the local community networks etc., as well as the needs, characteristics and potential of the three client groups targeted for integration.

- The students enjoyed greater freedom in designing the work assignment and shaping the practice and learning experience than those placed in regular fieldwork settings – where students' choices might be restricted by conventional practices and policies. In this project, the students had the opportunity to try out different social work methods to fulfil objectives that they themselves had defined, to meet the needs that they themselves had identified.

The field learning experience

The unstructured nature of the setting, the experimental nature of the assignments, the involvement of many parties in the project, and the initial confusion, scepticism and even resistance among agency staff (and students as well) toward the idea of integration, made placement in the Shek Wai Kok project a substantial challenge for students. It was for them both a physically and emotionally exhausting experience. The students went through doubts, frustrations, disappointment, a sense of inadequacy and lack of control, as illustrated by the following quotations from the students' logs.

- After hours and hours of discussion all of us were still hopelessly lost as to how to integrate the three clienteles. We had confusion about the direction of the placement, and our expectation on the outcome of the project.

- The general attitude of the agency staff toward the mentally retarded was negative. They thought the project was a waste of time.

- The workload is terrible. I really feel exhausted, I need a break.

- This was our seventh meeting. We discussed the items in detail but could not decide what to do because there were so many different opinions. The atmosphere was not harmonious.

- These days, our temper is not so good. We are overworked, and the work situation is always changing and out of our control.

To summarize, the students' 'learning pains' were as follows:

- They had to take greater initiative and exercise more imagination than their fellow students in attempting to operationalize the concepts of integration for practice since there were no ready-made models that they could follow.

- The lack of concrete guidelines and a well-defined work assignment meant that students had to spend extra effort and time to identify needs and design programmes appropriate to the aims of the project.

- Due to the involvement of many parties in the project, great demands were placed on the students' time, patience, understanding and use of skills to arrive at consensus among themselves, gain agency staff's support for their proposals, and work through the delicate inter-agency and interpersonal dynamics to put their ideas into practice.

Where there are pains, there are also gains. Compared with conventional modes of fieldwork settings, placement in the Shek Wai Kok project offered the students

- wider exposure through experiencing different: services; agency structures; clienteles and modes of intervention

- more learning about teamwork and the skills of relating and working with people, such as communicating, organizing, leading, exerting influence and negotiating

- greater challenge to use self-reflection as a means of learning; the skills of analysing, evaluating, and drawing lessons from experiences were greatly strengthened

- more varied interpersonal experiences through which they could develop greater social maturity, learn to be more flexible, more realistic, with an increase in the capacity to empathize with others, to consider issues from different points of view, and to handle frustrations.

In the students' own words:

- This fieldwork project is novel and challenging. From the experience, we learned to be more flexible and to be brave in experimentation. Since the project involves three agencies, I got to know the different styles and philosophies of three agencies. I feel happiest that I have learned all three methods, casework, group work and community work. This has been a great opportunity.

- In this placement, we had the freedom to do what we wanted to do under supervision. We learned to identify clients' needs. We were more willing to take initiatives and more committed to our work.

- This placement had given me a lot of stimulation through getting to know the three clienteles and understanding their needs. We had much freedom to make plans and changes. It had given me an excellent opportunity to experience the whole process of planning and implementing a programme. Moreover, through the joint project I learned how to cooperate with others in work, and to be more assertive in expressing my ideas. Most important of all, the project proved that 'integration' among the three clienteles is possible. The way they could learn from each other and the joy they got from mutual caring gave me great satisfaction.

- I had many opportunities to learn teamwork…how to get along with my field-mates and be assertive…the importance of communication. The placement had enhanced my interpersonal relationship skills and widened my perspective.

In retrospect, students who did their placement in the Shek Wai Kok project were observed to have a more innovative spirit and a more critical mind. They had a deeper understanding of the social work mission and a more imaginative approach as to how that mission could be realized.

The field teaching experience

The success or failure of such an experimental project in field practice training pivots upon the efforts of the field instructors involved. The experience of the field instructors who participated in the Shek Wai Kok project and the strategies that they used in overcoming difficulties can be explored in terms of the roles they had played. These roles comprised three aspects: managing, teaching and helping (Kadushin 1992; Leung, Tam and Chu 1995b).

THE MANAGER

As a manager the field instructor's tasks have been identified as falling into three major clusters (Leung *et al.* 1995b): preparing the student for placement, negotiating the 'goodness of fit' between the student and the placement agency and planning and monitoring the student's work. As an experimental project the Shek Wai Kok fieldwork environment was fraught with uncertainties. The students had to be very thoroughly prepared for the lack of concrete guidelines and the likely state of confusion they would experience, particularly at the beginning of each placement period. On the other hand, students often harboured great expectations about the project and became disheartened when they recognized some of the project's limitations. Hence it was necessary to discuss with them, before going on placement, their expectations, provide them with a full picture of the constraints and possibilities, so that, as far as possible, they would approach the project with a realistic, balanced attitude. The field instructor also has to make extra efforts to mediate between the agency and the student workers, since in the absence of well-defined guidelines and models, the progress of work depended heavily on effective communication and close collaboration of the involved parties. This situation also demanded the field instructor pay close attention to monitor the students' work, making sure that all parties were well informed and updated about the progress and obstacles.

THE TEACHER

As a teacher, the field instructor is expected to teach the students how to apply theory to practice and how to use practice skills (Leung *et al.* 1995b). In the Shek Wai Kok experiment, while a lot of knowledge taught in class was relevant and useful to the students in both understanding the community and designing and carrying out intervention attempts, there was no ready-made, well-defined 'integration model' that could be followed. Together teachers and students engaged in a process of learning by doing through which they tried to translate the concept of theoretical integration into practice. The field instructors found several teaching strategies useful (Tong *et al.* 1994). For example, students were asked to write detailed logs about their experience. In-depth analysis and discussion of these logs often resulted in insights concerning client needs, service gaps and alternative forms of action. Students worked in small groups and were encouraged to learn through group processes. By learning to accommodate different opinions and to resolve conflicts, their perspectives were widened and their inter-personal skills improved, while brain storming in groups was an effective method to generate new ideas. Team supervision sessions were also held from time to time. Such sessions included all the students engaged in the project and faculty members not directly involved in the daily supervision but responsible for the overall design and coordination of the project. It provided a forum to clarify concepts, compare perspectives, assess the feasibility of alternatives, and evaluate progress.

THE FACILITATOR

The field instructor's third major role is that of a helper, a facilitator, whose chal-lenge is to support the students through the working and learning experience, and to encourage the student's self-reflection (Leung *et al.* 1995b). In the Shek Wai Kok experiment the field instructors were called upon to make extra effort to support their students as they struggled through the uncertainties, ambiguities and disappointments experienced during the progress of work. It was not infre-quent that students experienced frustrations and a sense of not going anywhere. At such times, they needed a great deal of encouragement and support from the field instructors. It was essential that the field instructors conveyed understanding and acceptance of the students' feelings of inadequacy and even failure, and in turn gave them assurance that setbacks, mistakes and lack of progress were accept-able and expected – an unavoidable part of the learning and discovering process. Also the experience of participating in such a project challenged the students to make reflections that were more philosophical in nature. Situations of conflict, uncertainties and competing interests among different parties often aroused intense and negative emotions in the students. The field instructors not only had to assist the students to recognize such emotions and handle them constructively, but also had to seize the opportunity to enable the students to clarify their own values, assumptions and objectives, in the context of the underlying value assumptions about social work.

A summary of the findings of the project is presented in Table 3.1:

Table 3.1 Summary of the Project Development

Phase	Aim	Programme means/activities
1. Exploration, May 92 to August 92	• gaining understanding of the community • identifying and establishing a base for integration work	• community study • arrangement made for placement of student social workers in three agencies in the neighbourhood • formation of an elderly volunteer group • community education programme
2. Implementation, Oct. 92 to August 93	• breaking down of boundaries • building up of inter-agency linkages • evolution of a sense of 'mutual care'	• consolidation of the three groups formed in Phase 1 • 'drop-in' sessions in the centre for handicapped youths • joint social/recreational activities • environmental enhancement project (with three groups serving as volunteers) • community survey (with three groups serving as volunteers)
3. Consolidation, Sept. 93 to August 94	• strengthening of inter-clientele and inter-agency network • building up structural support for further development	• continuation of joint activities • completion of the community survey started in Phase 2 • community care project involving the three groups to provide support and care to needy persons/families through friendly visits • 'spring cleaning operation' • fun day for needy persons/families

Development		
Clientele level	Agency level	Community level
• three target groups identified: the young people, the handicapped, the elderly	• three agencies identified to provide a base for integration work	• the community's attention to the existence of groups with special needs and abilities aroused
• improved self image and social skills, particularly for the handicapped and the elderly • greater mutual understanding and caring, particularly between the elderly and the handicapped • greater understanding of the community, a 'spirit of care' gradually developing	• gradual acceptance and normalization of the participation of the handicapped youths in the Youth Centre activities • closer cooperation among the three agencies • inter-agency network formed through the setting up of a confederation among the three agencies	• more organizations took an interest in the project and assisted in the activities • greater understanding of community needs
• strengthening of mutual care spirit • development of the potentials of the three groups into resource in informal care	• expansion of the confederation of agencies to include other agencies serving the neighbourhood	• initial devlopment of informal caring networks in the community

Conclusion

The Shek Wai Kok project demanded a high level of investment in terms of time and energy from students, teachers and agency staff. Was it worth the effort? As an innovative attempt in social work practice, the project has made some interesting discoveries, even though the scale of the work was too limited to result in any significant impact. As an experiment to improve school–field collaboration and provide a challenging, unique opportunity for student fieldwork practice, the effort has been well spent. Nevertheless, the project has its limitations. From the practical point of view, social work schools and departments under pressure to produce the greatest number of trainees with the least amount of resources may find it too costly to emulate such a project. As a placement setting, it is not suitable for students who need clear structures and specific instructions in order to learn effectively. Moreover, students placed in such a project it may lack opportunities to learn about more 'conventional' modes of working in and negotiating through social service bureaucracies. On the other hand, it is always important that in planning the students' field training programme, every effort must be made to understand their individual learning needs and characteristics so that an appropriate 'match' between student and setting can be made; and to ensure that the programme offers them a sufficient variety of experiences to put them on a good track for future practice.

Note

1   'Handicapped' as a term is used in Hong Kong; in the UK, for example, this term would not be acceptable to many service users.

Chapter Four

Learning Opportunities and Placements with Asylum Seekers

Dee Underhill with Claire Betteridge, Ben Harvey
and Karen Patient

Introduction

Social work students in England follow a training curriculum prescribed at national level. This is organized around six 'core competencies' and students must gather and present evidence of their abilities in each of these competencies in order to achieve the Diploma in Social Work or DipSW (Central Council for Education and Training in Social Work (CCETSW) 1996). Practice teachers are based in social work agencies and provide support to students by arranging opportunities for practice learning, teaching students, and ensuring adequate supervision of the quality of students' work with service users. Sometimes the day-to-day supervision of work is provided by a work-based supervisor and the practice teaching is provided off-site by a qualified practice teacher. Students have two periods of practice-based learning; the first placement is 50 days long and the second is 80 days. College-based tutors provide coordination between the student's class-based and practice-based learning.

Practice learning in England is funded, so that agencies receive an agreed income from student placements. Some agencies use this income to employ people to coordinate and develop practice learning opportunities. This has meant that the finding of placements has become less the responsibility of the university and more that of the agencies, in partnership with the educational establishment.

This chapter is written from the perspective of a practice learning coordinator employed by a social services department (a public agency of local government) in the east of England. However, its authorship acknowledges the particular significance of the students in this project, and the perspectives of other participants are also incorporated in the chapter. One of the main responsibilities of a practice learning coordinator is to provide and organize practice learning opportunities for Diploma in Social Work students. This work is shared with their partner university, which also employs a practice learning coordinator, in this case to take responsibility for placement provision in the independent and voluntary sector.

What follows is a reflective account of the development of practice learning opportunities for DipSW students with people seeking asylum in England. It is set in the context of local and national reactions to a highly politicized situation. In addition, this was a complex situation because of the need to ensure adequate opportunities for the students to meet the core competencies in a relatively experimental situation. The chapter also provides a reflective account from those directly involved, the students, the project coordinator, the practice teachers and the supervisors. It is always enlightening to learn the views of service users about students' work (Shennon 1998) and an account from the asylum seekers themselves would make the picture complete. Unfortunately, this was not practical because of the speed with which they moved on; and it was perhaps not appropriate at the time of their applications for asylum. One student remarked:

> When feedback was sought from the asylum seekers during the placement, my experience was that my perceived role as someone who had control over how their basic needs, food, clothing, etc. were met had a great impact on the way in which the clients would speak of us. The issues around power, both for the client and ourselves, provided much material for the module on Power and Responsibility in Social Work.

Background

In late 1999 the numbers of people requesting asylum across the UK began to increase dramatically, a situation perceived as resulting primarily from the conflict in the Balkans. The numbers arriving in person at some social service departments made increasing demands on teams, especially 'duty' social workers (that is, social workers who are on duty to receive newcomers and emergency work, sometimes called an intake team). With no major arrival points in Cambridgeshire, there was speculation that the large numbers of asylum seekers might have resulted from the fact that it was the first refuelling stop for lorries driving from the English east coast ports.

At this time, people actively seeking asylum in Cambridgeshire and who would otherwise be destitute were directed for assistance to the social services department where the prime responsibility was to provide support under the National Assistance Act 1948 or the Children Act 1989. If it could be established that they had relatives or friends in other parts of the UK, applicants were issued with travel passes to join them. Limited resources could be provided for those remaining, if they fulfilled the criteria. Many of these people held professional qualifications as doctors, teachers, students, etc., but their status prevented them from working in the UK for the first six months, and thus they were not entitled to benefits.

The system to assess and process asylum seekers was protracted, with a two to three year wait for formal applications for asylum to be processed by central government. In 1999, 71,160 people applied for refugee status (Home Office asylum statistics); while awaiting assessment, hundreds of applicants were being detained for lengthy periods, even though they had committed no crime. The situation in Cambridgeshire necessitated a sensitive and speedy response to deal with a growing and complex situation.

Social work response

A senior manager in Cambridgeshire Social Services Department was appointed to establish an asylum seeker project. An ex-police officer with previous experience of similar work was appointed as project leader, to coordinate and supervise the day-to-day work of the project. The project was charged with the task of being proactive in assessing and working with existing and new asylum seekers in the county. The project understood its aims as relatively short term, since forthcoming legislation would remove the social services department's responsibility for new asylum seekers, but not until August 2000 for new asylum seekers and September 2000 for families where benefits had been removed. Unaccompanied children would always be the responsibility of social services (Immigration and Asylum Act 1999 – the Asylum Support (interim) Regulations 1999.)

It was considered that the project might provide appropriate learning opportunities for students embarking on their second (80-day) placement, particularly if there were a group of perhaps three students, supported by a team of practice teachers, on-site supervisors, college tutors and project managers all working together.

Involvement of the practice learning coordinator

The practice learning coordinator's first responsibility was to identify practice teachers and on-site supervisors for each of the three students and establish their placement location. They needed to have a base in a social work (fieldwork) office with access to administrative and social work support, and to be willing and able to travel out of the office to research accommodation for the refugees, visit asylum seekers locally and across the county and have regular meetings with the project leader at his office. These placements were already due to start, so the timescale was very tight.

The DipSW course is based on a curriculum with specific 'learning outcomes', which incorporate the six core competencies referred to earlier, and a list of explicit social work values. In the second placement, there are twelve learning outcomes. For example:

Core Competence: Social Work Intervention

- explore the responsibility to make decisions where there are competing claims, and demonstrate antiracist and anti-discriminatory practice

- contribute to promoting the rights of children or adults at risk or in need.

Core Competence: Assessment and Planning

- assess and review people's needs, rights, strengths, responsibilities and resources in the context of antiracist and anti-discriminatory practice

- work in partnership to develop and manage packages of care, support, protection or control.

A key concern was the possibility that the urgent and dramatic nature of the work might overshadow the need for the placement to be an environment for practice learning, where students could meet all of their learning objectives for the DipSW award. Integrating the students' learning needs with the needs of the project would be essential to the success of an innovative and proactive experiment in placement provision.

All the interested parties met to identify practice learning opportunities and to agree the designated practice teachers and on-site supervisors. Three students were enthusiastic to take part and volunteered themselves from a larger group.

They were not asked to complete a learning styles questionnaire (Honey and Mumford 1986) but, with hindsight, 'Activist' learners were the ideal. It was decided that two of the students would remain in the fieldwork office with their practice teachers, and the third would be based in the project office, with an off-site practice teacher. Although he had no previous experience of social work or practice learning, the project leader was keen to meet everyone's needs and offered all three students weekly supervision and guidance. He planned to divide the work of the project up into three sections: working with new applicants; monitoring existing accommodation facilities and researching new ones; and completing formal reviews of existing applicants. It was planned that each student would have the opportunity of working in each of the sections in turn.

The social work curriculum calls for 'Assessment and Care Management', and these were not explicit elements of the work with asylum seekers. There were different interpretations and tensions, with some who considered that most of the students' work would implicitly be a form of assessment and care planning, and others who wanted more explicit opportunities, perhaps by having the students spend part of their placement time with fieldwork teams, doing specific assessment and care management work.

The students would certainly be fulfilling an extremely useful role within the project, but doubts remained as to whether this could meet all of their learning needs.

The placement began and the involvement of the practice learning coordinator would normally be expected to be minimal. However, at this time, the asylum seeker situation became international news and the spotlight was turned on the work of the project in this quiet corner of eastern England.

Reflective accounts from the students

In evaluating this experimental placement, it is important to understand how the students became involved in this new project and how they experienced it as a place for learning practice. What was their understanding of the role of the various practice teachers, and were they able to make connections with college-based learning? In short, what were their reflections on this placement?

Karen

Karen had expressed an interest in joining the project from the very beginning, but found the volume of work initially overwhelming. She understood the role and responsibility of the project was to provide basic humanitarian aid (food, accommodation, warmth) and she linked this with the baseline of Maslow's hierarchy of need (Maslow 1970). Karen found the links between practice placement and college-based learning unclear and admitted to feeling slightly 'divorced from college'. However, as the placement progressed, she became able to make several considered connections with her learning, though there was little specific input on the course about this client group. She was sure that Communication Skills (a core competency) were of primary importance, and noted the range of nationalities of asylum seekers, who included Afghan, Bela Russian, Colombian, Estonian, Georgian, Iranian, Iraqi, Kosovan, Russian and Sudanese. Karen described the Interpreting Service as 'responsive and sensitive' and felt she learnt much from the interpreters, particularly in relation to anti-discriminatory practice; for example, an awareness that within the Kosovan culture, it is not deemed correct for a Kosovan woman to speak directly to a male who is not her husband and, therefore, the provision of a female interpreter is required.

Completing the initial application form and the life history of each asylum seeker was sometimes traumatic, upsetting or disturbing. Karen quickly learnt to be selective in what and how she asked details of 'how you arrived here', what family remained at home, contacts here or elsewhere. Often journeys had been harrowing, with family members lost or dead, and few or no contacts in England. A range of resources and actions were offered depending on each applicant's particular status and circumstances. In general, students followed through their work with each individual applicant, but this depended on other pressures. Karen would have preferred to have had a full-time practice teacher on-site, as she was aware of the heavy existing workload of her practice teacher who worked part-time. She had to be innovative and imaginative in meeting the Assessment and Care Planning learning objective and would have liked a more specific opportunity to do so.

In conclusion, Karen's learning was considerable and she felt privileged to have taken part in the project. Her strongest memory was how well the group gelled and how closely the team worked together.

Claire

Claire felt that the early stage was one of 'conscious incompetence' (Reynolds 1942), as she struggled with the various personalities, roles and value bases of those involved in the project. Claire's practice teacher was able to put these feelings into context and in particular to help her look at power imbalances both within the project and, more importantly, in the work with asylum seekers. Claire's previous experience and knowledge of working with disability provided her with transferable skills and, as she embarked on the day-to-day work, she felt more confidence. She remembers all the students feeling overwhelmed by the volume of applicants. However, rather than 'sinking', each student became autonomous and proactive. They made decisions about workload division between themselves on a daily basis, while reporting back to the project leader regularly for advice and direction.

Claire described her early panic and fear about the nature of the project, approaching the work with some trepidation. She remembers the experience of interviewing an asylum seeker who had no idea of where he was, believing himself to be in Canada, not England. She recalls asylum seekers with professional qualifications, but no status to work here, those who had undergone harrowing experiences prior to leaving their homes and families, others whose relatives had died on the journey here, refugees who arrived in only the clothes they wore, with no documentation or possessions.

Claire spoke eloquently about her learning on the project, in particular about communication skills and anti-discriminatory work. 'It really clued me up and made me aware, made college-based work live for me.' There was a further dimension to her learning when she, herself, was subjected to oppression and discrimination by a male asylum seeker. Cultural competence became a reality rather than something to read about (Cross *et al.* 1989; Doel and Shardlow 1998, pp.165–176). Claire acknowledged the 'brilliance' of a practice teacher who helped her to make sense of all this experience. By the midway point of the placement her confidence was restored, the work was less stressful and she was now conscious of her own competence (Reynolds 1942). In addition to relating the placement to learning outcomes, Claire also reflected that she had learnt a huge amount about herself and had grown personally as well as professionally.

Tea with the director

As the students embarked on their placement with asylum seekers, the British press and media headlined what they described as a huge increase in asylum seekers. A moral panic was unleashed, with exaggerated claims of the demands

Ben

Ben had the advantage of having his first placement in a local independent refugee organization. After qualification, he hoped to work as a social worker in this specific setting. He described the first few weeks of the placement as chaotic, with a heavy workload and a huge backlog. 'We were rushed off our feet, running with lunch in our mouths; we would plan work and within half an hour need to re-prioritise and change tack.'

Moreover, although there is literature on practice methods within a crisis intervention framework (Coulshed 1991; Dattilio and Freeman 2001; O'Hagan 1994), the project had no agreed model of practice on which the students could base their work. There are interesting accounts of groupwork with refugees (Ajdukovic, Cevizovic and Kontak 1995; Tribe and Shackman 1989), but there was no time to plan anything of this nature. In particular, Ben found it a very stressful tension between wanting to help vulnerable people over time and the transitory nature of the work, so that he was often not able to take the work through to its conclusion. Ben experienced the dilemma of asking vulnerable, alienated people to share personal and painful histories, only to find himself unable to support many of them beyond a day or two, as they moved on. Ben never became immune to the tragedy of the asylum seekers' stories, finding them regularly traumatic and sometimes almost too much to bear.

Ben enjoyed the challenge and impact of the work and particularly the evolution of the project team. He identified the need to be enthusiastic, resourceful, think on your feet, be autonomous, make decisions, and take independent and collective responsibility all necessary for the success of the project. As the placement progressed, the volume of work created its own demands, despite the project co-leader's original plan for the work to be clearly defined between the students. Ben took much of the work with new asylum seekers, Claire worked with families and developed local accommodation resources, and Karen worked across all areas, being 'ruthlessly efficient' with the paperwork. Ben felt that the class-based modules on Communication Skills, Law and Mental Health were particularly relevant to the placement, but was unsure of the relevance of the Ethics and Values module to the project. Ben felt strongly that Assessment and Care Management should be a compulsory module on social work qualifying courses and that students should have explicit experience of this in their practice learning opportunities.

being made on the UK's resources, reinforced by regular images of street beggars. In particular, the legitimacy of the asylum seekers' right to asylum was called to question and they were vilified as 'bogus'. At this time, an aeroplane was hijacked and landed at an airport in a neighbouring county. On board were over 100 Afghan passengers, who were allegedly asylum seekers. This, too, became national news, feeding the general panic. The whole issue of asylum became highly charged and polarized, with truth and reason the major casualties of inflammatory rhetoric.

Social work is a publicly sanctioned job, 'at the crossroads between help and control' (Doel and Marsh 1992, p.10). It is no stranger to controversy and often finds itself defending those who are marginalized and discriminated against, while trying to maintain public confidence in it as a profession. A difficult circle to square. The students and their colleagues in the project were in the thick of such a controversy. A county-wide intranet 'talk-room' facility attracted much attention, with many comments unfortunately being judgemental, discriminatory and incorrect (and anonymous!). There was concern about the possible effects that this critical climate would have on the students. However, they subsequently remarked how the pace of the work kept them so busy that 'it all went over our heads really'. The practice teachers and supervisors made public statements about the students: 'I would like to further affirm that they are dealing not only with practicalities, but are having to listen to stories of torture and hardships that any very experienced worker would find difficult to hear. They are a credit to their chosen profession.'

Contact was maintained between all those involved in order to monitor whether any supplementary supports were needed for the students. The social services director formally and publicly invited the students to meet with her to share their experiences. Despite initial reluctance to step into the limelight, the three students recounted the genuine regard shown by the director both for their own work and for the project overall. She also expressed interest in their views of placement provision and their perceptions of working for the department and their future career plans. They helped to raise the profile of practice learning and social work education at a time when agencies are preoccupied with surviving the daily demands of service provision.

The project leader's perspective

With no previous experience of working in a social work setting, the project leader experienced the establishing and supervision of the project as a steep learning curve. The process of becoming a team had been complex, discovering what the needs were:

> to find out other working practices in other teams across the country and also overseas, to be familiar with and use the internet, to look at existing and planned legislation, national policies and codes of practice – all alongside coping with the growing work demands of the project itself.

The weekly meetings were important to allocate and discuss work, to consider individual stresses and to develop a sense of shared involvement in the project.

The project leader was concerned that he would not be able to assist the students in meeting their specific learning needs. He was mindful that, from the students' perspective, the project was a placement, and their specific and explicit learning objectives were central to their part in it. Some imaginative and resourceful methods were needed to ensure the students met these, particularly the Assessment and Care Management learning outcomes. His judgement of the students was unequivocal: 'The students left the project unquestionably more competent and knowledgeable. They were three very special people who contributed hugely to the project's success'.

The practice teachers' perspectives

The views of practice teachers and supervisors were sought several months after the completion of the placement.

Ben's practice teacher had some management responsibility in her team and had an overview of the sudden and dramatic increase in the number of asylum seekers arriving in person at the team office or through the duty (intake) system. She described this as a point of crisis for the team and regarded the asylum seeker project as unplanned and reactive, 'reflecting the national situation'. The team gathered in the office weekly, so she had an overview of the students and their progress and had firm views about the student learning in particular. She felt that the qualities required of the students were to be mature, proactive, problem-solving and adaptable. Fortunately, this was the case with the three students, but less able students would not have been able to cope with all the demands made on them. She was resolved that the starting point should be the student's learning needs, and felt there had been no problem finding the evidence once Ben had spent some time doing specific Assessment and Care work with a colleague.

The practice teacher witnessed the impact of the students on the project as one which was energizing. 'We all loved it!'

Karen's placement supervisor was a member of the duty (intake) team in the same office and she reported similar views to those of Ben's practice teacher. As far as the placement supervisor was concerned, the students' help had been invaluable.

Karen's practice teacher also had first hand experience of the increasing demands being made on the duty (intake) team by asylum seekers. He believed

> Until the asylum seeker project was set up, we were able to provide the bare minimum in terms of our statutory and legal requirements, and as the referrals increased dramatically we were wondering if we would be able to cope. Once the students and the team were in place, we do not know how we would have coped without them. The students were able to provide a social work service. They could do more in-depth work, take a proper history, listen to the stories, assist and enable the asylum seekers with their housing, health, dentistry, etc. in a more appropriate and sensitive manner, using interpreters where necessary and staying with the process longer.

the placement had been poorly prepared and was a reaction to immediate pressures, describing the situation as 'mushrooming', with a lack of clarity of role. He felt it was fortunate that the students were of a high calibre, able to rise to the challenge. He felt he should have given more continuity to his student than he could as a part-time worker and that specific Assessment and Care planning experience should be made an intrinsic part of any future practice learning experience with asylum seekers. However, he believed there were transferable social work skills from the placement.

Claire's practice teacher was 'off-site' and not involved in the day-to-day work of the project or duty (intake) teams, which gave her a different perspective on the practice learning opportunities for the student. She was aware of the work demands made on Claire and the importance of the practice teaching sessions in helping Claire make sense of the learning objectives. Time was also spent on values, ethics, cultural awareness and anti-discriminatory practice. This practice teacher connected the student's work with crisis intervention models of practice and her work was greatly appreciated by Claire (Coulshed 1991; O'Hagan 1994).

The team manager's perspective

Although the interview with the team manager occurred several months after the placement, she could remember clearly her concern about the impact of the increasing numbers of asylum seekers on her team. She felt the duty team was already over-stretched and these increased demands were leading the team to feel overwhelmed. She felt that the team lacked both resources and specific expertise in this area, and she was keen to find a solution. However, she was also cautious about involving students and clear that their own learning needs should be the main priority.

She felt the students' enthusiasm, openness and commitment helped them to integrate well. The students' ability to challenge and be challenged, coupled with their growing expertise led to the whole social work area team becoming a centre of excellence, to which other teams referred for help and guidance.

The manager witnessed anti-discriminatory practice becoming a real and live issue in the team, with much discussion around attitudes and values. This engaged not just those directly involved in the project, but all the members of the team. It was an opportunity for everyone to consider their own value base.

The project leader continues to hold weekly meetings in this team's office, and the manager is confident that the strong links formed as a result of this unique practice learning experience will prevail.

Conclusion

It is evident that much of the project's success is due to the competence and commitment of the social work students. In addition, the determination, skill and flexibility of all those involved in practice teaching and supervision has also been significant. The students have each spoken about their strength as a group, and they became close with each other and with the project leader. They are aware of the unique nature of this placement opportunity, and have expressed a sense of privilege in taking part in such a memorable example of practice learning, with such an impact on practice. All three students are now qualified practitioners. Karen and Claire are social workers in English social services departments and Ben is working with asylum seekers nationally.

This was an innovative practice learning opportunity. Set against the enormous media interest in this issue, it was possibly a unique placement experience for qualifying students in the UK. There is much to be learned by all of us engaged in practice teaching and learning, nationally and internationally. A number of themes have emerged.

Planning

The greatest threat to the success of the project was the lack of time to plan and prepare fully. Planning becomes all the more crucial when there is a mutual reliance between project and students. A longer lead-in would have helped to consider other kinds of arrangement for practice teaching, such as group supervision (Brown and Bourne 1996).

Coordinating

Coordinating the early stages of a new project can be difficult because of the number of participants and the variety of their ideas, responsibilities, expectations and agendas. Roles and responsibilities need to be clarified at the planning stage, especially in order to protect the student role. The practice learning coordinator has an important role in emphasizing the learning component.

Contextualizing

However good the planning could have been, larger events can have a major and unforeseen impact. Decisions around asylum seekers were especially high profile during this placement, but we are all reminded that social work practice touches areas of controversy and high emotion. It is true that students need adequate protection from the glare of publicity, but it is interesting to speculate how social workers are to learn the art of communicating with the wider public?

Innovating

There is a tension between the learning needs of students, the demands of social work agencies and the service needs of users. Relatively prescriptive curricula, driven by learning outcomes tied to competencies, make it difficult to experiment. Of course, students should never substitute for poor resources, but they can derive much learning from enjoying the scope to innovate and develop services.

Postscript

In view of the major change in national legislation for asylum seekers (Immigration and Asylum Act 1999), the department's current responsibility is towards existing applicants for asylum. All new applicants will be assessed on a national basis by an agency of central government (National Asylum Support Service or NASS).

The project is now well established and the leader has a small permanent staff. However, his positive experiences with Karen, Claire and Ben have led him to continue offering a practice learning opportunity for Diploma in Social Work students on their second placement. He considers the qualities needed for future students as motivation, maturity, adaptability, and a commitment to the work of the project.

It has been possible to place two further social work students with the project, with the involvement of one of the original practice teachers with students. We hope that time and events will allow this placement to continue to offer students a unique and creative practice learning opportunity.

PART II
SOCIAL WORK LEARNING
MODELS AND METHODS

Chapter Five

Student Supervision in Context
A Model for External Supervisors

Jane Maidment and Pauline Woodward

Introduction

Finding opportunities for practicum learning is a problem faced by many programmes in different parts of the world. However, that was not our particular problem. While we could locate the number of placements that we needed, we still had a dilemma. Unlike many programmes that struggle to access student placements, we had plenty of requests from agencies to take students. However, these were made by small community agencies that did not necessarily employ qualified social work staff. We wanted to be able to utilize the wide-ranging learning opportunities available in these agencies, but at the same time ensure that students received quality supervision – our dilemma how to achieve this standard of supervision using the placements that were offered to the university. In this chapter a model of external supervision is presented that has developed from experiences of providing 'long-arm' student supervision from the Department of Social Work, University of Canterbury, New Zealand. This is a two year post-graduate programme, where approximately a third of the students are mature aged and have worked in social service work prior to undertaking social work education.

Although much material has been published on supervising both workers and students in the social services (Bogo and Vayda 1998; Kissman and Van Tran 1990), little of this material has focused specifically on the role of the external supervisor. We discovered that although both in-post and external supervisors needed to address similar issues with students and within agencies, the particular emphasis given to certain tasks and processes differed.[1] We found that recasting supervision within an ecological perspective helped explain the reasons for these differences, as well as account for the increased complexity inherent in external supervision arrangements.

In this chapter, some of the formative ideas in relation to the literature pertinent to student supervision are discussed, and these are related to our experience of using an external supervision approach. Next, an analysis of external supervision from an ecological perspective is outlined using a model format. Examples of common student–agency–supervisor dilemmas are illustrated and related to the ecological model. We summarize in tabular form ways in which the model can most productively be used in student preparation and reflection on field placements, and in field supervisor training (Table 5.2 on p.107). In conclusion, some limitations of the model are discussed posing challenges for future theoretical development in field education.

Linking the literature with the experience of providing external supervision

Student satisfaction studies on supervision have yielded valuable results in terms of identifying supervisor attributes that positively influence the teaching and learning encounter. Not surprisingly, these factors include the quality of the supervision offered (Fortune *et al.* 1989); having theory–practice links clearly articulated (Fortune and Abramson 1993); supervisor enthusiasm and knowledge about practice (Marsh and Triseliotis 1996); and receiving ongoing feedback about performance on placement (Kissman and Van Tran 1990).

Additional literature on the desired roles and characteristics of the supervisor has been published in the form of guidelines for practice teaching. These guidelines are generally in keeping with particular educational pedagogies such as facilitating reflective learning (Gould and Taylor 1996), ensuring competent practice (Cooper 1992) or using a particular model of supervision (Shardlow and Doel 1996).

Although both research on student satisfaction and publications on practice teaching have been useful for developing strategies to provide quality external supervision, we have found supervisor credibility impacted significantly on the teaching and learning encounter when external supervision was used. The notion of credibility will be discussed in more depth later in the chapter.

Contextual influences

The impact of the agency setting on student learning outcomes is readily acknowledged in the literature. This attention has resulted in the development of practice models that situate field learning within context specific environs (Walker and Boud 1994), and examine workplace learning, using a socio-political analysis (Hughes 1998). The macro-context for welfare delivery in New Zealand is inevitably linked with economic rationalist ideology (Cheyne *et al.* 1997). Social workers have documented the impact of current neo-liberal ideals on the delivery of health, welfare and education services in New Zealand (Henderson 1998; Rennie 1998). The new managerialist paradigm that dominates practice has resulted in social work being defined by agencies in terms of inputs, outputs and fiscal efficiency (Randal 1994).

Although these socio-political factors make up the broader context in which student field education occurs, the micro-environs of the agency setting have considerable bearing upon the teaching and learning encounter. In particular, students benefit from being able to access contributions from a number of agency practitioners, both where social work role models are on site (Secker 1993) and where students have an opportunity to do work that is perceived as 'useful' (Nixon *et al.* 1995).

We learned that the external supervisor must both have a clear understanding of the agency culture, and be aware of the potential for student socialization into practices that are not necessarily consistent with social work ethics, values and standards, particularly in agencies that were not staffed by social work professionals. The external supervisor, unlike an in-post supervisor, needs to spend time clarifying agency beliefs and values, as stated and practiced. This may necessitate making several visits to the agency and meeting with a range of personnel. Without this understanding, it is not possible for the external supervisor to assess the student's awareness of practice and agency issues as they arise throughout the placement. In addition, the external supervisor needs also to have an understanding of the client group being served by the agency in order to facilitate meaningful casework discussion.

Attention to process

The need for clear communication between the student and supervisor is emphasized in social work literature on supervision (Bogo and Vayda 1998). However, the external supervisor needs to attend to process and communicate on three levels, with the student, with the agency and with the school of social work. In addition, the supervisor has to engage differing levels of administration within the agency setting (Homonoff and Maltz 1995), including agency management, the 'team leader' and the individual who will be most closely associated with the student's daily work, the task supervisor. In these discussions roles and responsibilities for each of the parties are clarified, along with identification of any known agency changes, frictions and potential or real difficulties that may influence student learning. Liaison, negotiation, consultation and advocacy are all required on behalf of the student with the agency. Much of this work is completed even before the placement begins.

Having completed this groundwork, the external supervisor can negotiate a learning agreement between the student, agency and self with some knowledge of contextual influences specific to the particular placement setting. Throughout the supervision process the external supervisor needs to be responsive to informal cues such as comments made by agency workers, or non-verbal behaviours noticed during agency visits, and these cues need to be assiduously followed up and queried.

Clearly, the supervisor who is external to the agency does not have the benefit of being an 'insider' who can tap into spontaneous learning opportunities as they arise. The external supervisor therefore has a role in raising awareness in the agency about how unexpected learning opportunities can best be utilized. Hence, several of the process skills used by the external supervisor are similar to those used in performing the school faculty liaison role (Faria, Brownstein and Smith 1988; Fortune *et al.* 1995; Raphael and Rosenblum 1987).

By not having access to the day-to-day workings of the agency, the supervisor is greatly reliant on the supervision encounter and staff feedback to facilitate student assessment. Much of the current literature on practicum assessment gives emphasis to observing student practice (CCETSW 1991; Tanner and Le Riche 1995). While such direct observation is a requirement for student assessment in the UK, New Zealand does not yet have a similar system of standards for practice teaching. However, we found selective observation of student practice was imperative to the external supervisor in assessing student performance. Since the external supervisor does not have the benefit of being on-site to co-work or observe the daily interactions between the student, workers and clients, provision must be made during the contracting phase for the supervisor to directly observe student practice. This may take the form of sitting in on interviews, or using audio-visual technology to record interviews, groupwork or family meetings. Clearly both sitting in, and using recording mechanisms require client consent, and negotiating this consent is part of the student learning process (Maidment 2000).

Using a range of assessment tools is necessary to validate opinions and develop student critical thinking and reflection. A useful matrix for understanding depth of student learning has been developed in British research (Gardiner 1989). Gardiner identified graduated levels of learning including content, process and finally meta-learning where students acknowledge and demonstrate a range of learning strategies that integrate aspects of both content and process. We have found in order to work with the student towards meta-learning, diverse teaching, learning and assessment tools need to be utilized by the external supervisor. Student written work (including an agency analysis, file notes and letters), team presentations, client feedback and student self-assessment adds depth to the assessment process. In addition, attention needs to be given to how the student manages the work, relates to others in the team, and liaises in a constructive manner with outside agencies. These considerations all form part of the assessment process. During the contracting phase, the external supervisor needs to negotiate with the student and agency, how feedback will be secured from agency workers, clients and outside agencies regarding student interaction. These measures are then included in the contract – using explicit terms and 'time-frames'.

Stakeholder interest

Facilitating field learning involves a complex interplay between a number of stakeholders who have an immediate interest in the student placement. We have noted these parties in the model presented in Figure 5.1. Practicum teaching and learning exchange needs to be influenced by the student's preferred mode of learning (Davenport and Davenport 1988; Fox and Guild 1987). However, other factors also affect the process of providing external supervision. These include the degree to which the agency feels supported by the school of social work (Fellin 1982): the level of client satisfaction with the student work; agency emphasis regarding duty of care requirements (Zakutansky 1993); and the nature of input provided by the faculty liaison into the learning exchange (Fortune *et al*. 1995).

Together, these interests, along with the personal style that the external supervisor brings to learning exchange, will influence the placement outcomes for each stakeholder. Although attention in the literature has been given to stakeholder interest in field education – on both an individual and partnership level

(Bogo and Globerman 1995) – little analysis of the dynamic interchange between contextual influences, stakeholder interest, and supervision process has occurred.

We found that conceptualizing external supervision using an ecological interpretation facilitated such an analysis of practicum education.

Examining external supervision from an ecological perspective

Ecology is the study of relationships between organisms and their environment (Germain 1991). In order to understand human development Germain has reconceptualized behaviour within an ecological framework, where behaviour is understood as the outcome of interactions between individuals and their environment. These outcomes are referred to as transactional relationships, whereby both entities, the individual and environment, are shaped as a result of an ongoing reciprocal exchange (Germain 1991). Living systems work towards maintaining a good fit between themselves and the environment, but stress arises as a result of life transitions, environmental pressures and interpersonal pressures (Payne 1997).

This framework serves as a useful tool to investigate the notion of external supervision for a number of reasons. First, it acknowledges the centrality of environmental influences on the teaching and learning exchange. In our model we have identified the following as contextual influences, including the current socio-economic climate; Aotearoa New Zealand Association of Social Workers (ANZASW 1992, 1993) Competency Standards and *Code of Ethics*; university field education requirements; agency policy and procedures and student family, social and work commitments.

Second, an analysis of transactional outcomes is inherent within an ecological framework. These transactional outcomes are derived from the concepts of adaptedness and adaptation, stress and coping; acknowledgment of power and oppression; with a focus on human relatedness, competence, self-direction and self-esteem (Germain 1991). Thus, the impact of the external supervision arrangement can be examined on a number of levels. The focus of such an examination may be the way the student develops personally and professionally while on placement. Alternatively, how the relationship between the agency and the university is grounded in formal and informal contractual arrangements may be equally important elements to explore. Client perceptions of student work or agency service may be considered in light of intervention outcomes, or the role of the agency task supervisor may change as a result of providing mentorship during the placement. Each of the stakeholders with an interest in field learning will be affected in different ways as a result of the student undertaking the placement. The notion of transactional outcomes can be used to explore both the positive and negative effects of the external supervision arrangement on the stakeholders involved in the process.

Third, an ecological framework provides clues for understanding the roles and tasks involved in conducting external supervision. The placement process presents a challenge for students negotiating the role transition towards the development of a social work identity. The role of external supervisor is to assist the student with progressing through this developmental transition, using the skills of enabling, teaching, facilitating (Payne 1997), and assessment, to guide the process.

Managing the interface between the student and contextual influences that impact upon the learning is integral to conducting external supervision. In this regard the supervisor needs ably to assess the student's social networks and aspects of the agency physical environment, and intervene where necessary in terms of providing mediation, advocacy and a degree of placement organization (Payne 1997). From our experience of using this model, we have also discovered that the skills of motivating, communicating and negotiating are critical to providing external supervision for students.

Assessment of the student's performance on placement presents a particular challenge for the external supervisor who is 'once removed' from the immediate practice context. Agency staff and client input, as well as using audio and video recordings of interviews are integral to the assessment of student performance in the field. A strong emphasis on relationships within and between the individuals and systems underscores an ecological approach to supervision and assessment. With this in mind, a range of agency stakeholders have a role to play in the assessment process. The supervisor first briefs these parties about student competency expectations and the process of how assessment of competencies will occur during the placement. It is critical that the student is aware from the beginning of the placement that a systemic approach to assessment will be used and the timing of these assessment activities. In keeping with an ecological approach the external supervisor is particularly interested in finding out how the student relates to co-workers and clients and demonstrates an ability to network, engage and communicate with a range of agency stakeholders.

The ecological paradigm acknowledges difference in terms of culture, power, spatial and temporal understandings, and interpretations of territory (Germain 1991). In this way it is a framework that serves the supervisor, student and agency staff in understanding how each stakeholder may interpret verbal, non verbal and written information, cues and behaviour differently. Understandings of assessment, privacy and confidentiality, definitions of family and kin will differ depending on whether the student, supervisor or agency staff are Maori, Pakeha or from another ethnic background (Bradley 1995; Selby 1995).[2] In this way, the ecological framework can be used as a reflective tool to guide the teaching and learning process, and further understanding between placement stakeholders.

Figure 5.1 shows how we have conceptualized external supervision from an ecological perspective. It illustrates competencies needed by external supervisors, the range of stakeholder interest in field placements, contextual influences that impact on the student practicum, and processes used to facilitate teaching and learning in the field.

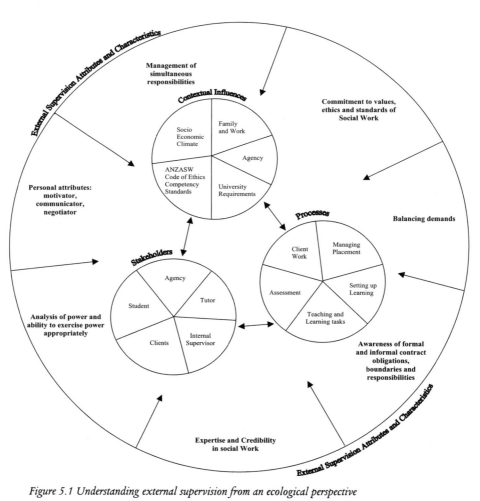

Figure 5.1 Understanding external supervision from an ecological perspective

The model is made up of four discrete parts that interrelate, creating the teaching and learning milieu in which the student and supervisor interact. External supervisors ideally need seven key attributes to perform this role:

- expertise and credibility in social work practice

- awareness of formal and informal contract obligations, boundaries and responsibilities

- ability to balance demands

- commitment to values, ethics and standards of social work

- ability to manage simultaneous responsibilities

- ability to motivate, communicate and negotiate

- an analysis of power and the ability to exercise power appropriately.

The task of providing supervision from within the agency also requires the supervisor to demonstrate similar attributes and characteristics. However, the context of the arrangement significantly differs due to the supervisor's role being external to the agency daily functioning. The aim of the external supervisor is to facilitate an open system of communication and exchange between themselves, the student, the university and agency personnel. It is at this point in the process that the notion of credibility plays a critical role. We found that people providing external supervision needed to have particular professional standing in the social service community. Credibility was important to agency personnel who were opening their doors to scrutiny by a worker from outside the agency setting. The credibility of the external supervisor was also important to the student, who wanted to be assured that they would not be 'short changed' through having an external supervision arrangement.

The need to guarantee standards and ensure credibility led us to formulate a checklist of 'person specifications' for the external supervisor. These 'specifications' are listed above and appear around the outer circle of the model. Drawing upon these attributes, the supervisor facilitates placement teaching and learning as well as ensuring agency, university and professional requirements are met. We found over time that individual external supervisors developed areas of expertise, such as supervising research placements, practice in small community agencies or in agencies that traditionally did not employ social workers, such as industry settings.

The contextual influences on practicum learning, as noted above, may be at a macro or micro-agency level. Of particular significance to New Zealand social work is the desire to facilitate teaching and learning about social work in a way that demonstrates commitment to Maori / Pakeha bicultural practice. This commitment is mandated through the *Code of Ethics* (1993) and Competency Standards (1992) of the Aotearoa New Zealand Association of Social Workers. Durie (1995) outlines the goals of biculturalism in public service using a continuum as illustrated in Table 5.1.

Table 5.1 A bicultural continuum				
Cultural skills and knowledge	Better awareness of the Maori position	A clearer focus on Maori issues and Maori networks	Best outcomes for Maori over all activities	Joint ventures within agreed upon frameworks

Source: Durie 1995: 3

Some students will therefore be placed in agencies where simply learning skills and knowledge specific to working with Maori may be emphasized. Others will be placed in agencies that adhere to an overtly proactive political and indigenous agenda.

Further contextual considerations include the need for accredited social work courses to fulfil requirements as outlined by the New Zealand social service industry-training organization, Te Kaiawhina Ahumahi (1997). This affects field supervision in that courses must demonstrate that the practicum promotes indigenous models of education. In countries other than New Zealand, those governing social work education will have different requirements; nevertheless, their influence will form part of the context in which field education and external supervision occurs.

Student family and work commitments are a second feature of the context that may impact on the way that student, external supervisor and agency staff work together during the placement. Supervisors need to take account of the multiplicity of demands in adult students' lives, including the need to juggle placement, employment and childcare responsibilities. The role of the external supervisor is to negotiate and monitor placement management, to ensure that university requirements, agency and student needs are each being met.

The agency will have its own culture that forms a substantive part of the context in which student learning occurs. Some of this culture will be expressed overtly in terms of codes of conduct and ethics, policies and procedures. Students and external supervisors however need to be mindful of the less obvious aspects of culture, such as where informal power rests in the agency, and the nature of the 'unspoken' rules. This is an area where the external supervisor is at particular disadvantage until a firm relationship has been established with the agency. The task supervisor in the agency is best situated to inform the student and external supervisor about these matters. However, such disclosures require the development of a relationship based on trust between the parties involved.

The school of social work (or university) will have requirements that the student, agency and external supervisor need to fulfil. These are usually set out in the learning contract that is drawn up between the parties at the beginning of the placement. Most schools have their own benchmarks in terms of the type of course and emphasis they bring to social work education. This may include special priority being given to bicultural delivery of service, social policy or direct practice, and these areas of emphasis will determine the direction and process used for supervision.

How client work is accessed in the agency, the process used for assessment, and agreement about what learning opportunities will be made available to the student, are all influenced by the nature of the relationship the external supervisor is able to establish with the agency. The interests of different stakeholders in the work of the agency, and student teaching and learning, will influence both the content and process used to conduct external supervision.

Figure 5.2 shows a 'map' of how a placement scenario and the role of the external supervisor might be understood using an ecological perspective.

Katrina

Katrina is a single parent on placement. She cannot afford to pay for childcare and has no family in the immediate area. For these reasons Katrina is unable to participate in agency groupwork during the evening. Her task supervisor in the agency is disappointed because the groupwork would be a good learning opportunity for Katrina, but also the agency has a policy of co-working only in evening groups, for safety reasons. With Kartina unable to be one of the evening facilitators, another person would need to be paid to co-work. The agency is not well off financially.

Agency finances and Katrina's family commitments form the context in which this particular dilemma is situated. The stakeholders most affected by Katrina's absence are Katrina herself and agency staff (who want her to participate). The external supervisor needs to negotiate with both Katrina and the agency to ensure that Katrina may access sufficient client work in her placement to meet course requirements, and to ensure that daytime learning opportunities in the agency are maximized. The context, process, stakeholder interest, and supervisor attributes will each impact on how this problem is resolved.

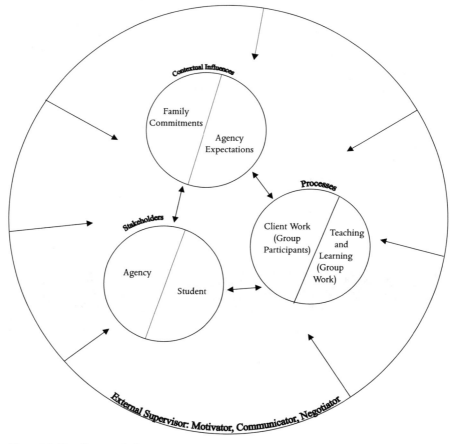

Figure 5.2 Map for scenario 1

Figure 5.3 shows the map for a second scenario, focused on using an agency analysis as a learning tool.

Bill

The external supervisor asked Bill to complete a written agency analysis and present his work in an agency team meeting. The external supervisor attended the student presentation in the meeting. During the presentation the student noted how the client statistics were 'rigged' to show multiple attendances in order for the agency to receive a higher rate of funding for services provided. The student did not question this process, but had accepted agency staff rationale that it was the only way to get sufficient funding to keep the service running and provide client services.

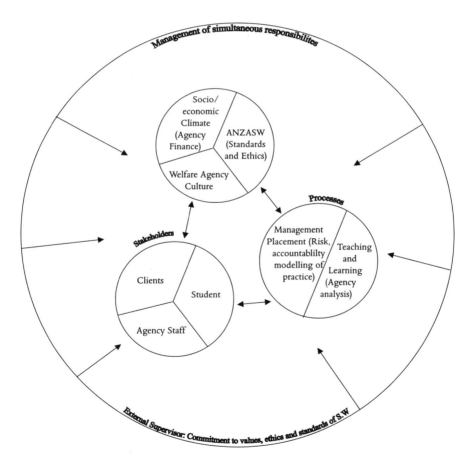

Figure 5.3 Map for scenario 2

In this scenario the student adopted an unethical practice that was occurring within the agency setting. The rationale provided for 'rigging' the statistics was of a contextual nature, and related to the economic cutbacks for welfare provision. However, the agency culture and the standards of practice as outlined by ANZASW (1992, 1993) were in direct conflict. In relation to process, the incident was revealed through a teaching and learning task (the agency analysis). This revelation impacted on the future management of the placement by the external supervisor. Stakeholders in this scenario were the agency clients, the student, and agency workers.

The role of the external supervisor in this situation was to raise awareness of the ethics, values and standards of practice in social work. Within this role the external supervisor has to be mindful of accountability to the profession, to the university (as an employee), and to the student in terms of demonstrating competency and ethical practice. Thus the external supervisor is required to manage simultaneous responsibilities in working between the university, student and agency systems.

Utilizing the ecological model for external supervision and student preparation and field educator training

In our work with educators and students we have found the model a useful tool to diagrammatically illustrate the multidimensional nature of relationships, influences and personal characteristics that impact on the teaching and learning process. In Table 5.2 we have summarized how the model may be applied to student practicum preparation and reflection, and field supervisor training. The transactional outcomes of interaction between individual students, field educators and the environments in which they work form the basis for the critical questions.

Table 5.2: Utilizing an ecological perspective for external supervision

Target group	How the model can be used	Critical questions
Student pre-placement preparation and post-placement reflection	• to help prepare students for placement • to illustrate the micro and macro influences on practicum teaching and learning, and agency functioning • to identify dilemmas in practice • to identify stressors during the practicum • to raise awareness about what the student may expect from the external supervisor • to illustrate different forms of accountability, and where they lie in field learning	• How do you feel about going out on placement? Have you felt like this before? Under what circumstances and why? • What challenges do you anticipate you may have to address on placement? • Which contextual influences most impacted on your learning and why? • How did your perceptions of social work change during the placement? • What elements of power and/or oppression did you witness or experience yourself on placement? • Which type of learning tasks and processes best facilitated your learning and why?
External supervisor training	• to illustrate the range of stakeholder interest in practicum education • to raise awareness of the multidimensional nature of providing external supervision • to identify field educator attributes for providing external supervision • to identify the processes in facilitating practicum learning • to promote the use of diagrammatic techniques in student supervision • to identify areas where providing external supervision differs from that of in-post supervision	• How do you define your role as an external supervisor? • What do you anticipate will be the major challenges for you being an external supervisor, and how might you prepare for these challenges? • Have you had difficulties in demonstrating any of the attributes identified? If so why? What strategies might you develop to address these areas? • How will your knowledge and experience of power and oppression inform your work as an external supervisor?

Clearly the ecological model can be used by students and educators to help guide the external supervision process. However, we have also identified some limitations in its use, which suggest the need for a more sophisticated representation of process issues.

Limitations of the ecological model for understanding external supervision

First, an ecological perspective provides the means of organizing a thematic discourse on external supervision. It does not, however, provide explanations that can be used to understand why parts of the system relate in the way they do. This shortcoming may be addressed by incorporating a more comprehensive analysis of open, closed and nested systems within the ecological framework. While we have not as yet explored this possible development, the inclusion of this analysis may help explain the changing nature of relationships between stakeholders in the placement process.

Second, although the model includes some broad attributes and characteristics needed by the external supervisor, it does not incorporate specific tools to negotiate conflicts of interest, or include a range of theoretical positions to inform the facilitation of learning. In this regard the external supervisor needs to be familiar with the traditional field teaching and learning techniques used in mainstream supervision, as well as having mediation, negotiation and advocacy skills to support the student learning in the host agency.

Third, the model as it stands includes assumptions that are firmly rooted within notions of adult education and demonstration of professional competencies. Not all social work supervisors or educators agree with using these particular paradigms to guide field learning (Dominelli 1997; Humphries 1988).

Hence we currently view this model as a first stage in the development of a more sophisticated framework for understanding the diverse pressures and influences on those engaged in an external supervision arrangement.

Conclusion

There are few theoretical frameworks and models of practice pertaining specifically to the practicum. In this chapter we present a model for external supervision in the field, based on an ecological interpretation of factors that impact on learning. Supervisor credibility, following up informal cues within the agency setting, and observing student work are all critical aspects of providing external supervision. A model for understanding the multidimensional nature of relationships and influences in field education is presented, including particular emphasis on required supervisor characteristics and attributes. In the current economic climate where a scarcity of training and professional development resources prevail external student supervision can often be a weak link in the chain for social work education. Through development of this model we have endeavoured to highlight the specific attributes needed by the external supervisor for this arrangement to work effectively. These attributes include expertise and credibility in social work practice; awareness of formal and informal contract obligations, boundaries and responsibilities; ability to balance demands; commitment to values, ethics and standards of social work; ability to manage simultaneous responsibilities; ability to motivate, communicate and negotiate; an analysis of power and the ability to exercise power appropriately. Problems in using external supervision with students can be minimized by engaging experienced, insightful field educators who have excellent communication and engagement skills. These qualities are imperative for the supervisor to be able to gain the trust and commitment from agency staff while remaining once removed from the daily practice context.

Nevertheless more work is needed to devise methods of analysing the changing nature of communication and relationships between stakeholders in the placement process. The challenge remains to develop a more sophisticated theoretical understanding of this aspect of the student and external supervisor's teaching and learning milieu.

Notes

1   In-post supervisor: supervisor employed by, and working within, the formal structure of the placement agency. External supervisor: supervisor working externally to the placement agency and contracted by the university to provide student field supervision.

2   Maori: indigenous population of New Zealand. Pakeha: New Zealand inhabitants primarily of European descent.

Chapter Six

Student Practice Placements as Gatekeepers to the Profession

Sigrún Júliusdóttir, Steinnun Hrafnsdóttir
and Bjarney Kristjánsdóttir

Introduction

Social work education has a professional and ethical responsibility to train students to give quality service to consumers. The quality and acknowledged status of education is an indicator of the social worker's professional competence where tutors as well as practice teachers act as gatekeepers to the profession. In this chapter, the assessment process will be explored in relation to the concept of gatekeeping in general, using social work education at the University of Iceland as a frame of reference.

It is argued that the evolution of the notion of professional competence is dependent on the structure of education, the academic setting and the infrastructure of the programme. Carefully selected practice agencies and appropriate tools of assessment are also central (Skovholt and Rönnestad 1995). In that context the process, training and recruitment of competent practice teachers is crucial, as we describe in this chapter.

The institutional context paves the way to professional competence

In modern society the emphasis on knowledge and professional skill defines the traditional role of social workers (Júliusdóttir 1999). Therefore, graduate programmes in social work benefit from being located in an academic setting where there is an imperative to provide students with substantial theoretical knowledge with training in research work and with an ability to link it to the real world. There are, however, both pros and cons in an academic setting for social work education, and these deserve some discussion (Júliusdóttir 2000).

The cons for the academic setting are not so easily analysed as the pros, although some can be mentioned. There may be a conflict within the profession itself that weakens its position in the broader family of social sciences. This relates to the 'invisible loyalties' to the past, for example historical roots of charity and to political commitment. This in turn creates uncertainty, which prevents social workers from standing up for their own case and take their place as a discipline in the social sciences; it can create resistance and defensiveness. This sense of 'not fitting in' with sister disciplines might cause one to argue for special non-academic settings which advocate practical connection rather than theoretical emphasis.

The pros for placing social work education in academic settings relate, as mentioned, to the emphasis on theoretical knowledge, academic discipline and research orientation, which we believe has been neglected in social work for too long. Initially, the emphasis on positivistic methods and traditional research in the social sciences did not generally appeal to social workers and was seen as antithetical to their basic philosophy and ethics. As a result, social workers preferred practical work to scientific activity, staying true to a professional attitude based on strong ethical basis and integrating the micro and macro perspectives in its psychosocial approach (Hollis 1964). In the latter part of the twentieth century, social work's theoretical concepts and systemic thinking gained more clarity (Payne 1997; Pincus and Minahan 1973).

Now, as the social sciences develop rapidly towards more open and varied approaches, there is also room – even a need – for disciplines such as social work (Trevillion 1997; Gulbenkian Commission 1996). Social work has contributed considerably to the social sciences. Indeed, there are many ways in which social work may strengthen the position of the social sciences; acknowledgement of values, the practically based contextual understanding of social phenomena and the direct experience which is gained through contact with clients and colleagues in different settings through the field. Vice versa, it benefits social work to join and identify with other related but better theoretically established disciplines.

In an academic setting it is possible to work towards the coalition and application of theory, research and professional skill. Thus, the academic competence of the becoming social worker is assessed and guaranteed through the standards set by universities.

In order to assess practical skills and professional ethics the enhancement of practice placements remains of utmost importance. In practice placements the students begin to develop a professional identity and there lies the core component of evaluating their non-academic skills and professional competence. The implementation of the assessment process is, however, a difficult and controversial task, both in terms of what criteria to apply and which parts of the performance of students should be assessed.

The infrastructure of education: a framework for assessment

The practice placement is a significant component in the gatekeeping of the social work profession and social work programmes should aim at developing a model of the most efficient structure of placement, providing high-quality placements in selected agencies with specially trained practice teachers, and providing practice teachers with assessment tools (Júliusdóttir 1996).

The structure of practice placement in the educational process may fulfil two goals: offering practical training while, at the same time, serving the gatekeeping function. This twofold goal may be obtained by a model of two practice placements periods distinguished by their different goals and objectives.

Practice Placement I

Practice Placement I has the main goal to give an overview and a broad general understanding of the professional field of social work, its role and tasks. This broader kind of placement is often for a shorter time, but benefits from being stretched over a whole term, with for example two days a week in the field integrated with three days of theoretical studies in the school. Cases from the practice placement are presented, analysed and discussed in small group seminars where a teacher from the university conducts the group work. There, the students get training in connecting real cases to theoretical discussions and also to discover interesting research areas.

As an example, practice placement in the social services and general hospitals would be suitable organizations to serve this goal. In this placement the practice teachers receive guidelines from the school to carefully select cases for the students. The students have an opportunity to be introduced to more complicated cases that have been referred to the practice teacher.

It is important to arrange this placement in the early part of the education as it helps the student to realize through direct experience and client contact, if they have chosen the right profession. At this stage, the student may also be helped through close supervision to work out some of their personal doubts and concerns. It subsequently encourages students to be more goal-directed and conscious of electives in their coming studies, as well as for future career planning.

Another advantage of this model is that teachers can at this early stage simultaneously assess the students' various abilities:

- How suitable are they for the role of a professional helper?

- How capable are they of integrating theory to practice?

- Do they have the skill to translate academic knowledge to social context?

- To what degree do they have maturity and insight to see how different services and settings need to be activated for different goals in different systems? (Pincus and Minahan 1973 p.51–61)

In this placement the focus in assessment is on personal competence and personal qualities while the focus of assessment in the second practice placement is more task-oriented, although personal development is also emphasized.

This two-stage model also shapes better conditions for a meaningful second placement. The experience of the first placement confirms (or otherwise) the students' commitment to the profession, so they are more likely to complete the second part of their education assertively and in due time.

Practice Placement II

In Practice Placement II the main goal is to provide a more specialized knowledge and training in a selected area through placement at a more specialized institution or field of service. When coming to this placement the students have gained theoretical knowledge of social work as a profession and its historical development. They have knowledge of policies and services, human behaviour and intervention strategies.

The second practice placement is planned for the second half of the education programme, close to graduation. Similar to Practice Placement I, it is stretched over a whole term, but for a block of three or four months. The focus is now on direct preparation for the professional role and on research and professional development. Integrating their own research work to their practice placement helps to shape a more positive attitude to research and 'research-mindedness' beyond graduation (Doel and Shardlow 1998).

At this stage in their education, the student can be assessed in relation to their professional developmental phase in the learning process and in their personal development (see below). In this second placement the practice teacher continues to have a gatekeeping responsibility but it is on a higher level, so to speak. It has not to do with the question 'to be or not to be' a social worker, but the restrictions the student has to face and deal with to be able to develop further in the learning process.

A practice model of this kind promotes the consciousness of a close linking of theory and practice, making social workers more conscious of theory in their approach.

Evaluation

A study to evaluate a model of this kind was conducted at the School of Social Work at the University of Iceland. It covered students and practice teachers' expectations and experiences before and after the first two years of implementation of this model (Thorsteinsdóttir and Júliusdóttir 2000). The results revealed positive expectations about this educational model among both third and fourth year students who were entering it. Most students and practice teachers answering the questionnaire and participating in the interviews expressed positive experiences regarding that kind of structure for the education. There was a significant difference between the groups of third and fourth year students. Those who were in their fourth and last year had more positive expectations of the model. The overall experience of the students and teachers participating in the programme two years later was in general positive.

The following quotations from open questions regarding 'linking theory to practice' reflect their views of the linkage with university:

> 'One of the main advantages is having the school as immediate support behind you.'

> 'It was good to meet the other students and share the experience simultaneously in the school, even though it is at the cost of losing contact with the practice placement on those days.'

> 'It gives continuity and a close linking to the theoretical part which makes it easier to apply scholarly thinking in practice.'

> 'It is valuable to relate fresh examples from field experience to content in the lectures and have it worked out in the group.'

A few of the students stressed heavily the disadvantages of breaking the week and losing the opportunity to follow regular activities (the other three days) in the practice placement. The practice teachers were generally more sceptical than the students and stressed the disadvantage of disruption with comments such as:

'The student is not so concentrated when they are occupied with theoretical linking and their studies next day.'

Nevertheless, the majority of the practice teachers were positive:

'Stretching it over a longer period is an absolute strength; it is easier to assess the students' qualities and process over a 12 week period than 6.'

'The seminars were rewarding and it was supportive to share experience with other practice teachers.'

'The seminars strengthened the relationship to the school.'

'It was exciting to follow the student's theoretical studies and be so involved in what they are doing in school.'

'The old model was demanding but not productive, neither for the student nor the institution.'

High-quality placements in selected agencies and trained practice teachers

There are different ways to develop high quality practice placements and an effective model of cooperation between the academic institution and the service institutions. The central themes to build upon are recruitment of placement, evaluation of cooperation and continuity. These three concepts are interwoven and relate both to the selection of agencies for placement and the production and stability of practice teachers.

Recruitment of placement opportunities

There needs to be wide enough choice of agencies in order to make arrangements and placements in accordance with the different aspects and requirements of the two practice placements.

The recruiting process may be enriched through several specific activities:

- a strategic introduction of the school and the educational programme to practice agencies

- inviting professional leaders and administrators to visit and to participate in different activities within the university

- highlighting the possibility of screening competent professionals for future employment may appeal to employers

- mutual interests, such as in research, can be emphasized

- signing a mutual formal contract which serves as a commitment, where both parts are guaranteed some benefits.

These all help the development of the placing process. Roles and tasks of both parties are defined and mutually acknowledged and this makes the practice placement more effective.

Evaluation and continuity

Organizational changes and turnover of professional staff render agencies rather unstable in nature, for good and for bad. Therefore, there is a need for an initial and a continuous evaluation of their lasting suitability as locations for training. Valuable tools are the students' evaluations of both practice teachers and the agency itself at the end of the practice placement.

Another way of evaluating agencies and social workers as educators is through introductory courses and continuing training programmes for practice teachers arranged by the educational institution.

The continuing replacement of qualified practice teachers is a necessity, but safeguarding the stability and continuity of them as a group is still more important. By developing a considerable number and variety of practice teachers it is possible to match the right person for the right student at the right time. This shapes the most favourable condition for a functional and fruitful assessment process, both at the individual and the group level.

Different methods have proved helpful to prevent dropout from the group of practice teachers and enhance their growth:

- respecting the need for a break and not taking a student every year

- giving positive feedback and reinforcement

- offering support and new stimulating cooperation through joint professional projects

- participation in practice-seminars, where there is both theoretical input from the educational institution and a dynamic analysis of the learning process

- jointly developing new assessment techniques

- suggesting research areas, offering research supervision and/or jointly working on research projects (Rosenfeld 1989; Yng 1998).

Despite these endeavours, the problem of finding sufficient practice teachers is common in Iceland, as elsewhere.

Assessment: a dynamic process and a concrete tool

The assessment of students is a continuous process throughout the practice placement. It is important that there is an agreement of the educational goals and objectives of practice placements and that this is shared between students, practice teachers and the academic institution. A shared agreement is more likely to be gained by providing training and seminars for practice teachers, seminars for students and by providing assessment scales and a detailed practice curriculum.

However, it must be emphasized that the assessment is not a simple process. As several commentators have argued many difficulties are involved in assessing students such as defining a satisfying level of competence for social workers, what should be measured and how (Hughes and Heycox 1996; Morell 1980; Shardlow and Doel 1996). Despite this fact, it is necessary to develop a procedure that can simultaneously assess students' competence and enhance their learning opportunities in the field. It is important to be able to measure the skills and personal abilities of students to become social workers. Both students and practice teachers find it more reliable to have special guidelines and assessment tools to aid in this process, rather than relying on the subjective opinion of the practice teacher alone.

An educational model that uses a multi-tiered, systematic approach to assess students is one way of organizing the assessment of placements more effectively (Júliusdóttir 1999; Nai-Ming Tsang 1993). In their training, practice teachers learn to use various tools of assessment; they are informed about the learning process of students, and their educational role and the role and expectations of the academic institution. It is also useful to provide practice teachers with seminars on a regular (monthly or weekly) basis throughout the practice placement period. In the seminars, the academic teachers can support the practice teachers in their roles, provide them with some theoretical input and the practice teachers can share their experience, compare and assess the process of their students in a dialogue (as quoted in the study above). In the shorter practice placement the practice teachers fill in a short assessment form of the students, while in the longer practice placement they write a more detailed and comprehensive assessment of the students.

Additionally, it is important to provide the students with seminars, as mentioned above, throughout the practice placement, so they can discuss and compare the development of their practice learning. This also gives the academic institution an opportunity to support the students and monitor their progress. The students write a thorough report in both practice placements. In this report they describe the placement organization and their work and also explore their subjective experience, together with a self-assessment of their strengths and weaknesses.

Assessment of students over time

It is the role of practice teachers to organize the practice placement, and to allocate relevant work to the students, in order to facilitate their learning and to assess their competence. It is important that the practice teacher and the student in the early phase of the practice placement set a baseline for the student, and agree a short-term and longer-term plan for the whole practice placement period. In this plan the goals and tasks of work are stated clearly and within specific time limits. Weekly supervision sessions are obligatory.

It is important to assess the students according to their developmental phase in the placement. The practice teachers must be able to diagnose the learning stages of the students and assess them accordingly with different assessment tools (Gerdman 1989; Killén 1992; Kristmundsdóttir 1985). It is helpful for any practice teacher, and should be a professional obligation and pride for a social worker, to use Berta Reynolds' (1942) learning phases as a frame of reference. She divides the learning process into five stages; we will explore the first three of them, since students usually reach only the third stage before qualification (Killén 1992; Nisivoccia 1990).

In the first phase students are often acutely *self-conscious* and insecure about their competence. In this phase, it is important for the practice teachers to explore the expectations of the students, introduce the organization and allocate simple work. The need for structure and direct advice and guidance are often strong at this stage.

The middle phase is sometimes called the *sink or swim* phase. More demanding tasks can be allocated to the students in this phase. The students are increasingly occupied with their client and how to work effectively with the client system. The students should be able to work more independently and be more secure in their role as students. This often appears in students' eagerness to perform and 'verify' themselves. At this stage, students often need confronting with the reality of what is possible, while not dampening their enthusiasm. In turn, the practice teachers often need much help from the school. Through the regular seminars, where there is a support from the group leader and the other practice teachers participating in the group creating a feeling of mutual trust and security, they are able to work out the various problems in a constructive and efficient way. The different phenomena that may appear and need to be dealt with in this phase are also resistance, transference, parallel processes and some of the well-known defence mechanisms. The working through of the process in this phase is most often quite as demanding for the practice teacher as for the students.

The school has a major responsibility to guide and support the practice teachers and even help them to work on their own feelings of ambivalence with the supervising role.

In the third phase, the students are more secure. They are more *conscious* of the learning process and are able to relate theories to practice in an uncomplicated and more adequate way. The phenomena of separation, differentiation, dependency–independency and the difficulties ending a situation and the transition to something new, all need to be explored, evaluated and worked through. The role of the practice teacher is to guide the student, relate theory to practice and give critical feedback and positive reinforcement. This is usually an easier and more rewarding stage for practice teachers.

Concrete tools used in assessment

Practice teachers observe students' progress on an ongoing basis to evaluate competence, values and integration of knowledge. In order to achieve a satisfactory picture of the abilities of the students, it is important to make systematic use of various assessment methods.

Many practice teachers and students find it quite effective to use an assessment scale in combination with other methods. It is important to emphasize cooperation with the practice teachers when developing the scales, and the use of an assessment scale should not be an end in itself. This is true of the whole assessment process, where evaluation serves both as a purpose and as a technical tool.

Assessment scales have been developed in schools of social work in various countries and it is important for the academic institution to look at the development in other countries in this regard. Although there are difficulties in deciding what criteria should be used in measuring competence of social work students, the following broad themes seem to be used as indicators in various assessment scales in many educational settings (Júliusdóttir and Hrafnsdóttir 1992; School of Social Work, University of Leicester 1990). At the University of Iceland, the following items make up the assessment scale:

- the student's ability to use the supervision session (preparation, self-reflection)
- the daily cooperation with the practice teacher and the supervisory relationship
- the ability to look at themselves critically, to assess their own strengths and weaknesses
- the extent to which the supervision sessions build into a continuous developmental process
- the general ability to absorb instructions or criticism
- the sensitivity to register various messages in the agency and adapt to them
- the ability to distinguish between emotional responses and the professional evaluation of the client's problem
- practical organizing skills, record and report writing and other paperwork
- methodological skills in analysing and making assessments
- interview techniques and therapeutic skills
- the ability to apply scientific knowledge, integrating theory with practice.
- cooperation and partnership with clients, social workers and other organizations; ability to follow rules and adapt to the working culture of the practice placement agency
- ethical behaviour; the ability of the students to respect the clients, their rights and different values and a sense of equality. In general, to apply the ethical standards of the social work profession, show professional loyalty and responsibility.

Specific indicators may be developed under each of the themes on a scale from 1 to 5. By using the scale as a discussion base and filling it out, preferably jointly, at certain time intervals (such as at baseline, mid-term and final stage evaluation) it is possible to measure the student's changing behaviour over time and get a picture of their progress during the practice placement as a whole. Practice teachers are often reluctant to apply scales, especially in the beginning, perhaps because of a tendency to be protective towards the student and wishing to understand rather than analyse or make any demands on them, as in the case of a client. In work with social work clients, self-responsibility is acknowledged and an obvious requirement. Analysing through evaluation and establishing a baseline is, however, a prerequisite for successful progress in the practice placement. It also helps the practice teacher to recognize the learning phase that the student is experiencing and to make demands in accordance with that.

The other methods that have proven helpful to use in relation to the assessment scales are various. According to Hrafnsdóttir's (1995) study of practice teachers in Iceland, it is most common for them to use the regular as well as specially selected supervision sessions to evaluate students (100 per cent). Also many (83.3 per cent) use observation of the student conducting a client interview and assess the student's record and letter writing (80 per cent). The methods least used are role playing (33 per cent) and audio-tape (20 per cent), despite encouragement from the school.

Assessment in the different practice placements

Practice Placement I

In this first placement, the role of the practice teacher is to organize the placement according to the aims of the university and to serve the gatekeeping function. The student should receive clear information about the practice agency, the service it is giving and the connections to other agencies and the community it serves. Students are expected to develop a clear insight into the everyday work of the social workers and their collaboration with co-workers and other professionals. Most of all, the student has an opportunity to experience the role of the social worker for the first time. The practice teacher's role is to facilitate the student's contact with real issues in the social worker's profession and to promote learning by practice tutorials. As has been discussed, the role of the practice teacher in this practice placement is to assess the student's suitability for the role of a professional helper. The main assessment tools that are used are written reports from the student, reflections in the practice tutorial and an assessment scale, which is useful to point out concerns that must be addressed. The student's ability to relate theory to practice is assessed in the group work at the university, where they present real cases.

Most students come to their first placement with great expectations and willingness to master the skills and working habits of the experienced instructor. They are also strongly motivated to learn about the clients' situations and beliefs and may easily identify with them. It is very important that practice teachers carefully prepare the arrival of students to the agency. They need to organize the practice placement to facilitate the learning process so the student will have an appropriate time schedule. It is also important that co-workers are prepared. A careful preparation will make the assessment process easier.

As an example of assessment in Practice Placement I, consider the following case:

Anna

Anna's first placement was in a Family Department of the social services. The main tasks in the agency were children's welfare and financial assistance. Anna was in her late thirties and had practice experience from working in a financial organization where she was giving financial advice to people and also from having a disabled person in her family. She knew what it meant to fight for resources for a minority group. This experience was mostly connected to finding solutions for other people and that affected her beliefs about the social workers profession and her first tasks in the placement. She believed that the social worker's main issue was to solve the client's problems for them and it took some time for her to understand how important it is to help clients to find their own solutions.

Anna said that she wished to become a social worker because she wanted to make herself useful to the clients and she had ideas about what they needed from society. One of the cases that were allocated to Anna was a family with three children seeking financial and housing assistance. In an interview with the family, they seemed quite defensive and were not willing to talk about their personal situation. Later it turned out that the family had been through many problems because of illness and alcoholism but at that moment they were not ready to work on those issues.

This was an opportunity for Anna to experience the significance of basic interviewing techniques, such as showing respect, active listening and positive reframing, in exploring the client's situation, and the importance of distinguishing between the client's ideas and thoughts and your own. Anna presented this case at the university and got support and assistance from the teacher in relating theories of psychological processes and interview techniques to this particular case. This helped Anna greatly in understanding the family's persistance and helped her to develop her interviewing skills. She was also able to discuss this case in the supervision sessions.

'How come people go so far until they ask for help?' Anna said, when she realized how complicated client problems could be. In the first practice placement it takes time to help the student not to get overwhelmed by the client's difficulties and to experience how empathy is more useful than sympathy. As a result, students often start to question if this is the right career for them.

Anna began to doubt if that way of working suited her personality and her confidence was somewhat diminished, as she felt that she was not mastering the skill. She seemed to be somewhat disappointed in not being able to solve the problems of the clients immediately and of the complexity of people's situations. In addition, Anna found it difficult to face the frequent shortage of resources and she considered why social workers do not use more time to develop new services instead of seeing clients all the time.

During the first weeks of the practice placement Anna was somewhat reluctant to accept advice and critical remarks from her practice teacher. She wanted to solve the problems herself and avoided asking for help. However, during the later phases of the placement she said that she trusted the practice teacher more and was willing to discuss this problem.

It is very important that the student gets an opportunity to reflect on these issues in order to find out what is the reality of the social worker's world – what are the possibilities and what are the limitations. The supervision sessions were time for such reflections, and there was an opportunity to reassure Anna that those feelings were quite natural in that phase of learning. By using the assessment scale it was helpful to point out concerns and also areas of strength, so she was able to win back some of her confidence. Subsequently, she was more realistic in her role and position as a social work student. At the end of the placement Anna felt secure about her choice in becoming a social worker.

At the close of the first placement, the practice teacher provided a written report for the school with these recommendations for Anna and her practice teacher in Practice Placement II.

Anna needs to develop her understanding of the complexity of the clients' problems and not to jump to conclusions about the nature of these. She has also to develop further her image of the social work profession. However, Anna was very enthusiastic, related well to clients and staff and has the potential to become a good social worker.

In Practice Placement II, as in the first placement, the practice teacher needs to organize the practice placement and facilitate learning, as well as serving as a gatekeeper to the profession. The learning process and professional development of the student is evaluated at the supervision session, held weekly during the whole period of 3–4 months. In addition to the supervision sessions, regular assessment interviews are performed together with teachers from the university.

In the first part of Practice Placement II, the reading of chosen records and reports and observing meetings are useful for the students to grasp the scope of the services. It is possible to let the students provide written summaries of the working process in different cases, or of certain aspects of meetings to assess them in this phase. In later phases, it is important in a systematic way to assess the different competencies that are stated in the practice curriculum and in the assessment scale. In this regard, examples of record and report writing, role-play and process notes are useful. Also, joint work so that the practice teacher can observe the student directly in action and give feedback on performance. Increasingly, technological methods, such as video or audio taping is used in assessing students, with the permission of clients.

At this stage it is important to assess the student's ability to relate to the clients and the quality of their interaction. In the supervision sessions, practice teachers and students can discuss the performance of the students and the practice teachers can give feedback on various aspects of interview techniques, communication, etc. The ability of the practice teacher to recognize the student's learning phase is vital, to prevent unfair assessments from being made (Killén 1992).

As an example of the assessment process in the second part of the practice placement we shall again follow the student, Anna. Her second placement was at a social service agency in a specialized division, handling foster-care. At the end of Practice Placement II, the practice teacher also gives a written report to the School, though it is different from the first. In the first practice placement the report primarily serves as an assessment to be used for establishing a baseline for the second practice placement. At the close of Practice Placement II, the written report is a final evaluation of the student. It can be useful for the student when seeking the first job and it is useful for the school in making the final assessment and credit setting in graduation. It is then the responsibility of the practice teacher and the academic organization together to decide whether the student is sufficiently competent.

During the first weeks of Practice Placement II, Anna was reading records and reports, attending meetings with the practice teacher and observing the practice teacher interviewing clients. In the supervision hours she got an opportunity to reflect on what she had read and experienced, and she was interested in finding out how she could relate this practice reality to theories. Her relationship with her co-workers developed satisfactorily and she seemed satisfied with the possibilities the placement could offer.

Later, Anna started to see her own clients and the interviews were carefully prepared. Some hypotheses concerning the problems were discussed and role-play was used in training. At this stage, some problems appeared in Anna's attitude and she had difficulties accepting advice and proposals from her teacher. For instance, Anna said that she did not find it useful to write down her interviews and she became defensive about admitting that she did not know what to do in some cases. She also said that she found it difficult to present herself to the clients as a social work student. She mentioned that she might have difficulties in asking for assistance when she started to work on her own and she also found it hard to express and explain her beliefs in a larger group. On the other hand, it seemed to be easy for Anna to create confidence, both with co-workers and clients. She identified strongly with clients in the beginning but found it difficult to face phenomena such as sexual violence to children and adolescents. Gradually, she realized that professionals must work on their own prejudices and feelings in order to be able to help other people.

The practice teacher was able to handle these matters in a constructive way as she knew that these mechanisms were likely to appear according to the information she had from the previous placement of Anna. The practice teacher also got support from the seminars at the university of how to work through these problems. These things were discussed with Anna in the supervision sessions and also at the assessment meeting with the teachers from the university. The assessment scale was used from the beginning, and it proved quite helpful in working with Anna through her concerns about her confidence and mastering skills. When using the assessment scale over some time, the process becomes clear. When Anna started writing down the interviews she began to realize how useful this was. She also said that introducing herself as a social work student and telling the client that the teacher was standing behind her made her more relaxed about her own performance. She was also able to trust the practice teacher and use the supervision sessions in a constructive way, working with inner feelings and her defensiveness. As the placement unfolded, Anna seemed to experience this profession more and more exciting and giving her many possibilities. Her professional skills had developed considerably and she was increasingly aware of her strengths and weaknesses in the social worker role.

Guidelines for the assessment of marginal performance

Despite the care taken in the selection of students and the planning and recruitment of placements, situations can arise when there is a doubt or concern about the performance in practice placement. These kinds of difficulties can be various, such as temporary personal problems, poor professional skills, unprofessional behaviour, lack of skills in communication and cooperation, issues of role boundaries, inability to relate theory to practice, inability to internalize social work values and an inability to relate to the clients.

The practice teacher has the responsibility to guard the gate and learn to read the warning signals, responding quickly to any concerns. To be able to do so, it is necessary that the university develops a specific strategy and procedures to use in marginal cases. This enables effective support to be offered to students and practice teachers. Relevant indicators of trouble are identified and the guidelines on how to respond when there is a concern are made explicit. These guidelines are often used together with assessment scales and the curriculum for practice placements.

It is important to contact the tutor at the university immediately when there is concern about a student's performance, so that the relevant discussions can take place. By assessing the problem in its earlier phases, it is possible to give more support to the practice teacher and the student with regard to handling the situation and setting clear and realistic objectives for the remainder of the practice placement.

Practice teachers should make concerns explicit to the student from the beginning and keep careful notes with illustrations of the student's work. This makes it easier to document the reasons for their concern over students' performance. It is preferred that the assessment scale is used from the beginning of the placement, because it is an effective instrument to measure the progress and competence of students.

A meeting is held with all parties (a representative from the university, the practice teacher and the student) where different options are explored. A written contract can be made where it is stated which aspects in the placement the student has to improve and the deadlines for meeting those requirements. The parts which each person has to play are documented, when to re-assess the situation and what future actions are necessary. During this process, and especially in the beginning, it may be seen as useful to get a second opinion from someone who could be a social worker or a team member from another discipline.

At this stage it is recommended that the practice teacher increases the supervision sessions to two times a week at a minimum and gives the student special work assignments. In some cases independent counselling is recommended for the student. The representative from the university meets with the student and the practice teacher at regular intervals.

Where these methods are used and the student does not make progress, the following courses of action are possible:

- The practice placement may be extended in accordance with the students' need and circumstances.

- The student may be placed in another placement with another practice teacher in order to test practice ability further.

- The student may have to end the placement or take a break (intermit) for further contemplation and revision of the situation.

- The practice teacher and the representative from the university fail the student.

In several cases students have used the process described above successfully to progress to qualification. There are examples, too, of students who do not proceed. Sometimes there is a need for crisis work by the practice teacher and the school. This can release new and more appropriate solutions for the student. We will illustrate this with the case of Sara.

Sara

Sara was 24 years old. She had some experience working with disabled people, supporting and guiding teenagers. During the first two years of her university studies she used to work with adolescents at a voluntary organization. In the reference letters enclosed with her application to the social work course, both referees confirmed her involvement and gave her their best recommendations. Her grades were a little below the average.

In Practice Placement I Sara did well, according to her practice teacher, who was rather inexperienced. However, she wrote in her report to the school that she had found it 'pretty hard to come close to Sara in the supervision sessions'. She wrote, 'Sara was somewhat arrogant in her attitude and seemed insecure as she frequently referred to her experience stating: "I don't need this critique" when she was corrected'. She recommended that Sara should get a 'tougher' practice teacher in Practice Placement II and that the focus should be directed more towards her personal limitations. The practice teacher at the school thought that the pairing might have been unfavourable and found a senior social worker at a social service agency as a practice teacher for the second placement.

During the first two to three weeks in Practice Placement II, Sara seemed content and eager to learn. However, gradually she started to argue about most tasks and methods. She obviously had a complicated relationship with authority and difficulty with the student role. She took initiatives in inappropriate ways and once she lied about her position as a social work student. After two meetings over two weeks at the school, together with the practice teacher, she continued to behave in the same manner. In addition, she had been absent several days because she 'had to do some important errands' or 'was ill'. A special plan was made for her over the next three weeks. Simultaneously, Sara was recommended to seek support and work with herself in therapy, to which she reacted positively.

In the last meeting with the school it appeared that Sara had not implemented any of the suggested interventions. On the other hand, she expressed her disappointment with her studies and said that she had found out through sincere discussions with her practice teacher that she was more interested to take a job she had been offered as a youth leader.

In this example, the practice teacher at the social services felt strong responsibility for Sara and empathized to win her trust. Through some extra supervision sessions she succeeded in encouraging Sara to talk genuinely about her anxiety towards authority and formal responsibility. Sarah felt pressure from her family to gain promotion to higher professional status, but she herself thought she would be more satisfied with work as a youth leader, at least for the near future.

By providing indicators of minimum standards and a system for handling students with marginal ability, the university emphasizes the importance of the practice teachers' gatekeeping role. It seems to be that practice teachers are very reluctant to fail students and do not contact the university unless there is serious doubt about the competence of the student. Morell (1980) suggests that considering the personal involvement that develops between the student and the practice teacher and the pressure in higher education to give an award of some kind, this is not surprising. It is, therefore, of utmost importance for the university to provide clear guidelines in these cases and to support the practice teacher and the student in what is a very difficult situation.

Conclusion

As we have described, there are various aspects to consider when organizing the practice placement component of social work education. No other part of the study programme gives more natural access to evaluating the student's ability to work with the difficult and demanding ethical nature of social work. The practice component must be developed in direct connection with the overall structure, framework and goals of the study programme. As described in the beginning of this chapter, organizers of social work studies need to create the conditions for practical training of high quality, no less than for the theoretical part.

We have stressed the fact that social work educators have the responsibility of gatekeeping, guarding entry to the social work profession, since 'they are responsible for the products that they help to produce' (Moore and Urwin 1990). A good and well-organized study programme can contribute to a sense of professional empowerment and avoid burnout and a feeling of low status in the working place. In turn, this will have a positive influence on professional collaboration and respect for colleagues in other helping professions. More specifically, social work training programmes are responsible for ensuring their graduates have a strong position in a competitive professional labour market.

Chapter Seven

Becoming a Social Worker
Using Student Job Descriptions in Child Care and Family Support Placements

Nicoleta Neamtu with Silvia Cioaza

Introduction

The reinvention of the social work profession in Romania began in the middle of the year 1990, as part of the new political changes following the removal of totalitarian communist regimes in eastern Europe. Romania experiences many social problems which have been neglected or denied under the old political system.

Social work education was completely abolished in 1969. There were higher education institutions in the social work domain organized at college level between 1929 and 1952. After that, only the post-high school level of training in the field of social work remained until 1969. Since 1990, social work education has been restarted and integrated into human and social sciences schools in the main academic cities of Romania: Bucharest, Cluj-Napoca, Iasi and Timisoara. Besides these, there are theology-social work schools in almost each county capital city. The new social work in Romania has received particular assistance from the European Union, Unicef, Peace Corp, and a number of American universities and organizations.

Social work training in Romania is organized at the undergraduate and graduate level. The bachelors can be obtained after studying four full-time years, at which point the students may call themselves social workers, and the masters takes one further fifth year. The failure rates are around 10–15 per cent. The social work schools are accredited and evaluated by a central national body for higher education.

Generally, public education is free, though there are a few, separate places occupied by students who are paying for their education in public universities. The best students in each year of study receive scholarships financed by the state. Social work education is offered in Romanian and Hungarian and there are quotas reserved for Hungarian and Gypsy minority students to study social work.

Once qualified, social workers are overwhelmed by a great number of dramatic and tragic cases arising from the new economic, social and moral challenges facing the population of Romania. In the transition from totalitarism to democracy, poverty and unemployment are on the increase and corruption seems to be a great barrier to a healthier society. In addition, some social workers have had to deal with the refugees from former Yugoslavia. The children and families component could be considered one of the most advanced areas of social work practice in Romania.

This chapter focuses on the selection of activities for social work students made by the practice teacher in a public administration setting working with children and families services. We use the student's 'Job Description' to consider each of the five years of study (three years of generalist practice, one further year of specialist practice and a fifth year for those 15 – 20 per cent who go on to their masters). We follow the changing role of the student from observer to co-worker to independent worker, from working with a few relatively simple cases to a large and more difficult caseload.

The specific features which recommend placements in the county Child Protection Department as interesting for practice teaching and learning are the social work mission of the institution and the variety of services offered to the target population. These include prevention of child abandonment, residential childcare, reintegration of children to their biological families, short and long-term foster care, national and international adoptions, and protection for abused or neglected children. The methods of work used by the organization cover the full range of individual, family, groups and community organization at a start-up level. The geographical area served is urban and rural covering the whole of Cluj county and students have three placements in the same institution. A number of the students who are placed in the Cluj Child Protection department go on to find employment there.

First year: observation placement

The first placement follows the initial semester, when students are expected to have passed social work theory and methods (part one) and law for social workers. It is largely one of observation and consists of four hours of practice experience once a week for fourteen weeks and six hours per week for three weeks during the summer practice. The students write a detailed analysis of a favourite social work agency visited (see Table 7.1), relating it to specific legislation and analysing the recording style of cases in different agencies. At the end of the semester the students must be able to write practice reports and pass an oral examination.

Table 7.1 Dimensions for analysing a social service organization or institution	
Dimensions	Students' comments
1. Organization mission statement	
2. Agency legal status	
3. The major problems of its clients	
4. Services provided by the organization	
5. Clients' needs, how are they determined?	
6. Clients' rights expressed by the social work law and other internal and international laws	
7. Social work methods used by the organization to satisfy clients' needs, social workers' roles on service delivery	
8. Variety of clients in percentages	
9. Cost of services: total cost for the past year, the budget for each program	
10. Funding sources of the agency, how much and what percentage of funds are received from each source	
11. Type of clients refused by the agency	
12. Other agencies that provide the same services in the county	

13. The organizational structure of the agency, organizational chart	
14. Power and influence within the organization: informal relations in decision-making, the roles of first line social workers on major policy decisions	
15. Leadership and management bodies: members' background	
16. Employees' moral and work satisfaction from different levels of the organizational hierarchy	
17. Major unmet needs of the agency, difficulties of any kind, organizational barriers	
18. Personnel policies and procedures	
19. Public image of the agency in the community	
20. Rate of turnover among staff in the last two years, reasons for leaving the agency	
21. Organizational outcomes, effectiveness and efficiency, social programs evaluation procedures	
22. Conclusions: overall impression of the student about the agency	
23. Improvement suggestions for agency functioning proposed by the student	

Source: The table is a combination of the general guidelines used by Zastrow (1995)

Visits are organized under the direct guidance and supervision of the practice teacher who chooses the agencies to be visited, taking account of the students' interests and wishes and the need to select a variety of clients, programs and agencies at different stages of organizational development. Agencies employing social workers are better able to teach the professional role for the students.

Second year: direct practice placement

At the end of the first year of study the student is more aware of what social work is and whether they are suited to it. The professional journey continues for those students who want to and in the second year they are offered the opportunity to work with people who are socially disadvantaged. Students have to put into practice the principles of casework (Biestek 1957): individualization of help, purposeful expression of feelings, controlled emotional involvement, acceptance of clients with their own reality and dignity, non-judgmental attitude, self-determination, and maintaining confidentiality. All key values for the entire social work training.

Field instruction for the second year students consists of direct practice with four to six cases and is centred on collaboration with agency employees as colleagues, working with a variety of different agencies concerned with children. The second year student needs to possess knowledge and skills of social work methods with individuals and families for a successful completion of their general duties. At the end of this stage of learning the student is expected to

- practice individual interviewing and counseling with not too difficult cases
- demonstrate case recording skills
- assess family functioning
- perform entry-level care planning
- evaluate their own practice learning
- demonstrate increased self-awareness.

At the beginning of the placement the agency supervisor encourages the students to name and list their anxieties regarding practice learning. Many of these are linked with how they will apply social work theories and methods learnt at school. At the end of placement students are asked what they suppose their concerns would be if they were placed in the same agency next time, and these show a radical change in how they perceive practice learning. The final list is more pragmatic as a result of the practical challenges the students have faced in the mean time. Typical of these challenges are the situations described below.

> A social worker and student had to see the family of a child who was to be adopted. When the social worker knocked at the door somebody inside was screaming. The door suddenly opened and the child's father, drunk and nervous, lost his self-control, grabbed an axe and made threats. The social worker and the student ran away as fast as they could, worrying about their personal safety. It was a sad experience for the student, demonstrating the strong hostility of some of the people with whom he would have to work.

On another occasion a social worker was accompanied by a female student on a visit to a Gypsy family. All the members of the small community were curious and gathered to watch them, especially since the student's fair skin looked strikingly different. After some discussion the leader of the Gypsy community came near the student and suddenly he kissed her. The student was scared and confused, but the social worker advised her that in the Gypsy's culture this meant good luck. The encounter had a happy end and they left the community in good spirits.

Students are likely to need to develop skills in working with different Gypsy communities. There is a common pattern where absence of identity cards means Gypsies cannot take advantage of some of their civil and financial rights. The majority of the children in public care in Cluj county are from Gypsy communities and students learn at first hand about the oppressiveness of the state towards these communities. Students also learn the importance of making home visits to the clients together with another social worker, who can support them or sometimes to ask for assistance from others such as the police in situations which can be risky.

The students' responsibilities and tasks in the second year of study are gradually organized from relatively simple to more difficult and complex. They are expected to work with four to six cases. After they have learnt the social services network in Cluj county they are expected to refer people to the appropriate service and to liaise with other agencies as appropriate. Working together with an agency employee in the duty system enables students to be aware of the diversity of cases and how are they allocated. A step forward in their learning is their participation in the initial assessment of needs and resources in very different cases. The majority of students engage well with the agency's mission and enjoy taking part in the educational programmes of counseling for family planning offered for the general public to prevent child abandonment. They are less enthusiastic about learning recording procedures and the legal jargon used in record-keeping which, nevertheless, provide important legal evidence about clients' lives.

At the end of this second placement the students have to know about family functioning and to be able to design action plans. The student, practice teacher and practice coordinator (the liaison person) write the final evaluation at the end of the student's second year of study. Those students wishing to train in areas of social work practice other than child care and family support do so after the second year.

Third year: more advanced direct practice

The learning journey becomes more complex for third year students, as they are expected to be more involved in direct work with service users and to develop new competencies. Their field instruction is framed by this job description:

- Supervision is one and a half hours per week for 17 weeks.

- Work performance is reviewed in line with professional standards, agency standards and the guidelines of the social work school.

- The student is expected to work closely with agency colleagues and to possess knowledge of child protection legislation.

- Students continue to develop individual interviewing, counseling and recording skills, but the emphasis is on assessment and intervention with prospective families for permanent, voluntary and involuntary placement

- The students need to demonstrate new skills, such as working as an agency worker and evaluating practice.

An example of work at this stage is described below.

A case selected by the supervisor for practice learning was of a single mother with 3 children by 3 different fathers. The maternal grandparents were caring for the elder boy and another family had adopted the sister and younger boy. The elder boy was 10 years old and achieving good results at school; however, the maternal grandmother contacted the social worker to say that the boy had refused to go to school and was aggressive and disobedient.

The social worker and the student arrived at the house to find the old lady weeping. The children's mother was asleep in the house, after heavy drinking. When she suddenly woke up she threatened all the people gathered there and the boy was so scared that he was ready to jump over the balcony of the house and was refusing to talk to anybody. The social worker managed to talk to the mother and learned that, because of her behaviour, the child was becoming more and more frustrated, violent and refused to attend school.

The student participated in the discussion with each member of the family, trying to arrive at a plan to support the whole family. It was an example of a complex situation. The solution for the best interests of the child is not immediately evident — whether to support him at home with his mother, to place him in kinship care or, if that is overwhelming for the grandparents, to arrange a placement with other people. This case was an opportunity for the student to do a brief assessment of the biological family as a whole and to focus on an individual assessment of the child as well.

Students' anxieties and workload are discussed in the weekly supervision session and the entire group of students placed in the same agency do a brainstorm after the midterm period to compare the current list of anxieties with the one from the beginning of the semester. Some of the students' anxieties disappear as they better understand the expectations of the agency and practice teacher. Student anxieties are also alleviated by sharing concerns and how they have been solved with the previous group of students.

The responsibilities and tasks of these junior social work students include the assessment of potential foster families for children who need permanent custody procedures, family placement and entrustment, initial home visits, home studies for assessment to collect references about the family and to record initial home visits and home studies, developing their record-keeping skills further. By the end of the third year of study the students have to know how to assess biological families of the children in need and make action plans for children who need permanent family placement or entrustment. The areas covered are adapted from 'Looking after Children' forms used in England (Department of Health 1995).

Students are beginning to feel more like an agency worker by making referrals for additional services when indicated and coordinating these services (e.g. welfare benefits, Medicaid, disabled care, legal and transportation services). They will have worked with five to seven cases and they are encouraged to develop their critical thinking by monitoring the effectiveness of the social work intervention in the cases assigned to them. Another source of information is the feedback obtained from their peers about their practice skills. At the end of the third year (sixth semester) and a total of 216 working hours, the students are involved in the year's summative evaluation meeting together with the practice teacher and the faculty liaison person (tutor).

Fourth year: networking skills

The students are already well over halfway through their practice learning journey and are piecing together the whole puzzle of competencies needed to become social workers. Their learning experience will go further by developing past achievements and obtaining some macro practice skills in the final year of their general training. To start the next stage of their learning journey the students need to possess both the practice experience from the third year and the knowledge and skills of Community Organization and Management in Social Work. The job description of the senior generalist student (fourth year student) placed in the Child Protection Department of Cluj county is:

- build on the skills developed in previous placements
- liaise with national and international foundations and associations specialized in offering financial support to the non-profit sector
- develop good connections with private funding organizations
- cultivate links with the local and central institutions responsible for the administration of funds in the child protection field
- write effective grants proposals for different types of social problems.

In the senior year the student is expected to work with about ten cases and their responsibilities and tasks combine micro and macro practice skills. Part of the student's work is the assessment of individual, community and agency needs. The student needs to use methods of data collection and analysis and to be familiar with information technology for obtaining relevant statistical data. One of the favourite activities for students at this stage is to search the internet to find funding sources in the child protection field and also to help some non-profit organizations to design their web pages, which will add new assets to the local community. Students are also aware by now of how many funding opportunities have been missed by different organizations because they did not know how to write a successful grant proposal. Some students consider their participation as organizers from the beginning to the end of a fundraising campaign as the most exciting task of their practice learning. Usually they are surprised and proud of the results of their fundraising campaign for good causes.

Acting as clients' advocate, especially to take action on behalf of children who are seeking help to protect their rights, is another significant activity at this stage. Child abuse and neglect cases are often those used in this placement for the acquisition of advocacy skills by senior students. New anxieties appear for the students who deal with these cases, arising from the ambiguous role of the social worker. It is difficult to resolve these cases for many reasons, and social work professionals can be really worried about how far to intervene in a case because they are left largely unprotected by Romanian legislation if a child's parent intends to sue them. One of the cases used for the practice learning purposes is described below.

The Department of Child Care and Family Support was informed about a girl of 13–14 years old living alone with her divorced mother. The mother was an ex-lawyer who suffered from progressive schizophrenia and she sometimes locked her daughter in the part of the house without windows or heating. The girl was taken home by a family who saw her sitting under staircases in a local building and the family wanted to adopt the girl. The social worker and the student went to visit the mother to discuss the situation. She was afraid of them, locked the door and threatened them with violence if they came any nearer. The student realized that they needed the help of the police. Social workers must be prepared for all kinds of menacing situations, including the presence of fierce dogs, and they have the right to ask for assistance in order to protect children's rights.

At the end of the placement, after a total of 112 working hours, students are expected to evaluate their own practice and to take part in the summative evaluation having effectively written the final practice report. They use the information from Table 7.2 to assess the functioning of the institution where they have been placed.

Table 7.2 Organizational assessment tool						
Functions	Sub-category	Stage of organizational development				Recommend-ations
		Start-up	Developing	Expanding	Sustaining	
1. Governance	1.1 Board					
	1.2 Mission					
	1.3 Constituency					
	1.4 Leadership					
2. Operations and management systems	2.1 Management of information systems					
	2.2 Documentation of procedures					
	2.3 Personnel					

	2.4 Planning					
	2.5 Administration					
	2.6 Program development					
	2.7 Development of procedures					
3. Human resources	3.1 Staff roles					
	3.2 Work organization					
	3.3 Performance management					
	3.4 Salary administration					
	3.5 Conflict resolution/team development					
	3.6 Communications					
	3.7 Diversity					
	3.8 Volunteer management					
4. Financial resources	4.1 Accounting					
	4.2 Budgeting					
	4.3 Financial control					
	4.4 Audit/external financial review					
	4.5 Fund management					
	4.6 Resource base					
	4.7 Legal status					
5. Service delivery	5.1 Sectorial expertise					

	5.2 Community ownership					
	5.3 Impact assessment					
	5.4 Program management					
6. External relations	6.1 Public relations					
	6.2 Constituency relations					
	6.3 Government collaboration					
	6.4 NGO collaboration					
	6.5 Local resources					

So, the students have arrived at their destination as qualified social workers.

General issues

Some general issues concerning the organization of practice learning:

- Practice for all placements is only one day a week, apart from the fifth year, and the students are not able to carry on to the end of the work with a client.

- Practice teachers are not paid during the summer practice and so the students miss their professional supervision; on the other hand, some social services organizations offer the resources of their agency to maintain supervision. Practice teachers receive the same payment (money per hour) as university lecturers or assistant university lecturers, depending on their qualification and experience. In general it amounts to no more than 7–8 per cent of their annual salary.

- All placements are on a group basis, except the summer practice which can be on an individual basis, and the practice groups are too big for an effective social work practice. Sometimes there are 10 to 13 students at the same time in one agency.

- There are no seminars available for practice training before and during the placement.

- The practice supervisors are not always trained to do this job; the training of trainers is an important issue to be solved in Romania.

- The links between the School of Social Work and practice placements need to be improved regarding the agreement of both partners on the content, standards, quality and quantity of appropriate practice learning. The pattern of placements is evolving and changing from year to year.

Fifth year: block placement at masters level

In the fifth year of study, at masters level, there is an opportunity for a block field instruction in a specialized area of practice, taking a total of 336 working hours. The students need to build on the practice experience already gained in the previous years and to learn new procedures and skills and to collaborate with new institutions. Below is the job description for masters students (specialist social work students) doing their field practice at the Cluj Child Protection Department:

- Collaborate with the same professional people as in the third year of study.

- Expand on the functional relationships with the same organizational structures as for the second year of practice experience and with some new authorities specific to the specialized area of practice (such as the Romanian Committee for Adoptions, Government Child Protection Department and county law court).

The general duties for the specialist social work student are focused on working directly with children and young people, knowing the legal framework of foster care and adoption, understanding the childcare system and working in a multidisciplinary team. The students are expected to work more independently than at the undergraduate level, and to act as co-worker on duty with another team member. Most of the time of the specialist student is spent in direct client contact. Participation at the staff meetings, supervision and formal evaluation meeting is also important for the development of a critical thinking and professional growth.

In the fifth year of study the students learn to give the necessary information for prospective substitute families. Staffing the phone in recruiting campaigns for professional foster carers or adopters is another responsibility assigned to the specialist student. Co-working in groups for the preparation and selection of prospective professional foster carers is one of the advanced tasks required in the fifth year of practice experience, along with making arrangements for the proposed placement of children. The masters social worker is involved in formal evaluation meetings.

The following cases illustrate learning in the fifth year about assessment of adoptive families and the support needed in a foster care placement as a first step for adoption process.

The social worker met with a couple where the woman was unable to conceive children as a consequence of a septic abortion when she was a teenager. At the second meeting the social worker asked permission for the student to join them and they all met at the family's home, first with the woman, then with the man and finally with both of them.

The student began to appreciate the effect of the absence of children on the couple's marriage and had the opportunity to participate in the debates. She tried to understand the delicate subject of adoption and the gentle way they have to handle painful feelings. Adoption is a major change in the lives of all those involved – child, biological family and adoptive family – and there is a great pressure on the social worker to consider what is the right decision.

A child aged 4 was abandoned by his parents. He was to be adopted by a young couple who had visited him many times while he was at a children's home. This child had never left the institution and had no idea what a family or even what an apartment was; he had never seen a cat. An attachment between the child and the prospective adopters seemed to be accomplished and the couple collected the child from the orphanage with the adoption file. The social worker, who had been the mediator in the case, accompanied the new family to their home, along with the student. However, when the child realized that the social worker was not going to stay with him in the adopter's home he started to scream and this startled his new parents. When they all finally went into the house, the family cat welcomed them. Once again, the little boy was scared and began to cry. It took some time for him to understand that the cat is a domestic animal and it would start to love him as well.

This was a useful learning situation for the student to realize how important it is to make adequate preparations with a child and the adopters for the placement of a child in a new family, especially dealing with separation anxieties.

A working knowledge of Romanian law in the specialist area of professional foster care and adoption is crucial (Parlamentul Romaniei 1998a, 1998b). This includes knowledge of these Acts:

- The Convention on the Rights of the Child adopted by the United Nations General Assembly on 20 November 1989 and ratified by Romania in September 1990. The Convention on the Rights of the Child has priority against Romanian laws and practices in a situation of conflict between national and international regulations regarding children's rights.

- The Hague Convention on Protection of Children and Cooperation in respect of Intercountry Adoption approved on 29 May 1993 and ratified by Romania in October 1994.

- The European Convention in respect of Children's Adoption signed in Strasbourg on 24 April 1967. Romania adhered to that treaty on 25 March 1993.

- The Constitution of Romania (Parlamentul Romaniei 1991) substantiates parents' rights and obligations to assure the development, education and instruction of their children, and the state's responsibilities to children, young people and disabled persons.

- A number of specific Romanian special laws and legal decisions and regulations for the protection of children in need of foster care or adoption.

The composition of the student's overall caseload encompasses a wide range; an age span from children, young people to adults, clients of both sexes with different ethnic origins (Romanians, Hungarians and Gypsies) with different cultures and lifestyles, poor and rich, from urban and rural areas of Cluj county.

The 'job description' model of practice learning

One specialist practice teacher is responsible for the group of students placed into the agency, along with a degree of team responsibility for each student. The teaching consists of individual and group supervision sessions with an open door policy for advice and consultation.

The practice teacher assesses the social work student's competencies in each year of study from the second to the fifth by using the following sources of information: direct observation of the student practice, feedback from colleagues employed at the same agency, other professionals, feedback from clients when appropriate, joint work with others, reports, recording, message-taking and discussions in supervision.

After the entire practice experience, the students must have demonstrated skills and competencies in direct services, advocacy at various levels, networking and evaluation skills. Some of them will choose to become specialists in the area of foster care and adoption and to achieve the Masters in Social Work.

We consider that using a clear job description for each year of study can create coherent practice learning. This is a transferable working tool for any social work placement, and the general competencies presented in this chapter are applicable to many public institutions that have a social work mission.

At the actual level of development of social work in Romania we believe that the 'job description' approach to training social workers is very useful because it eliminates and reduces a huge number of misunderstandings and anxieties for the students and practice teachers. The social worker's roles and functions are very vague and ambiguous even for the managers of the Romanian social work agencies and social workers lack a defined professional identity. This is understandable, if we remind ourselves that there was no social work education between 1969 and 1990. Only in the 1995 Romanian Catalogue of Professions has social work reappeared as a distinct profession, recognized by the Minister of Labour and Social Protection.

The job description approach is also a good organizing and planning tool for all parties in the practice teaching and learning encounter. In those countries where planning, organizing and time management are second nature for the majority of institutions and organizations, the need for student job descriptions is perhaps not seen as so important because there are frameworks, detailed guidelines and a set of performance indicators for most kinds of social work practice. However, this is not the situation in Romania and the job descriptions we propose are the result of negotiations between the faculty liaison person (fieldwork coordinator) and the practice teacher from the agency. The job descriptions serve as guidelines that will be adjusted to the specific learning needs of individual students, and it is the responsibility of the faculty liaison to write the final form of the students' job description. Similarly, the practice teaching is individualized in the educational supervision done by the practice teacher each week to help the student's growth as a professional.

Conclusion

From our perspective the social work practice syllabus, together with the placement job description, gives the students an appropriate map to navigate their practice-learning journey in an effective way.

The Romanian social worker needs to deal with very difficult social problems, not only at the individual and family level but also at organizational, community and societal level as well. The role of social change agent is an especially important one in Romania. It is a great challenge and, at the same time, a great opportunity to be a pioneer in the field of social work in a developing country like Romania.

Chapter Eight

Practice Teaching Using the Case Record

Lesley Cooper and Paul Searston

Introduction

Case records form an essential tool that enables practitioners to communicate with each other about their clients. Records contain important information about the agency, social problems, assessments, a chronology of the client situation, services provided, the nature of the clinical intervention and problems encountered. In many placements, one of the first orientation tasks given to students is reading case records. This may provide the basis for a general introduction to the clients of the agency or be the first part of the student's caseload. When students first encounter these records they may not appreciate the significance of this narrative, its structure, the professional and administrative language, and what it tells us about clients, practitioners and agency practice. On the other hand, practice teachers may appreciate neither the importance of the case record as a professional text nor how to use this record to improve students' cognitive socialization. The case record as a rich resource for practice teaching has largely been neglected. There is extensive discussion of case recording in social work. Ames (1999) in a recent review notes that historically literature on recording focused on the content, structure and style of records. More recent literature extends discussions to areas of accountability, use of technology, privacy and the value of records in safeguarding against malpractice.

This chapter describes a collaborative approach to practice teaching. Practice teachers and academic staff worked together to develop a practice teaching program enabling students to comprehend and understand agency records. This project initially formed part of an agency orientation to the client population, agency practices and social work concepts. The group nature of this orientation provided students within the agency with the cognitive skills to consciously monitor their own work and that of their peers in a supportive but challenging environment thus maximizing student learning. Academic staff contributed to this process by researching and devising the practice teaching initiative. Practice teachers provided agency case records selected according to client history, social problems and relevance to agency business. The most important contribution to student learning was made by practice teachers who modelled their particular practice expertise and skills. Beginning with a description of the changing practice environment and three foundation theories, this chapter describes the group application of cognitive strategies by practice teachers. It concludes with a case study, Abby, and student and field educator comments.

The changing practice environment

Prior to this initiative, practice teachers and academic staff had become increasingly concerned about pressures on agency staff, the quality and availability of student placements. It was apparent that many practice teachers were refusing to take first year students because of the work load associated with orienting new students to the agency and social work practice itself. Restructuring of agencies was, and remains an almost continuous exercise. Practitioner workloads were increasing, and practice especially in statutory agencies had become increasingly complex. The suitability of such complex work for students was doubtful. Although practitioners remained committed to student supervision, the amount of time available for students had decreased.

While agencies were feeling pressures of organizational and structural changes, academic staff were becoming concerned about variation in the quality of student learning during placement. Some students had rich and diverse experiences with intensive supervision while other students were less fortunate. This latter group of students experienced some or all of the following: excess of work, lack of work, inadequate and infrequent supervision, little support from agency staff or fellow students and no orientation to agency practice. Students, academic staff and agency supervisors in a formal review of the field education program expressed these concerns. Given this reality, university staff and practice teachers jointly made a decision to improve the readiness of students for practice using agency records and to work collaboratively on improving student preparation for agency work. Readiness for practice would be developed by exposing students to practice issues, practice methodologies and the full range and type of interventions used by the agency as outlined in agency records. Practice teachers and academic staff agreed on a group approach, as a way of accentuating the learning.

The new initiative

The intention in developing this new initiative was to minimize stress on practice teachers and to provide a more effective and collaborative learning environment for students. As one way of reducing the workload of agency practice teachers, academic and practice staff jointly discussed more effective ways of orienting students to the agency and its practice. Group approaches to student supervision and agency orientation were appealing.

Following Gardiner's (1989) assertion that concept drift from casework models to one-to-one supervision was evident, academic staff and practice teachers began making greater efforts to initiate collaborative educational activities for student practicum learning. Students as part of their practice orientation were placed in learning groups in large agencies. Students who met in these agencies were generally undertaking their placements in these or nearby agencies. Some of these students were also involved in group placements jointly supervised by the practice teacher and university staff. The learning groups' task was to prepare students for learning in the agency by using case records as a tool for developing the students' cognitive skills. In addition, groups provided opportunities for appreciating clients' strengths and weaknesses, services provided and the social work. The group provided the basis for learning and support.

Stimulating effective learning in placement

The practicum is an important place for student learning. In general, students on placement learn through immersion in routines and agency work practices. These work practices include working with clients, reading case files, attending staff meetings or case conferences, observing the work of others, writing case records and observing the work of supervisors and other staff.

Teaching students about case records has been characterized by debates and tensions between academic staff and field educators. Academic staff argue that recording does not have a high priority and is a skill best taught in the agency. Field educators argue that teaching case recording is a joint responsibility to be integrated at all levels of the learning process. It is not a necessary evil of agency practice and should not be left solely to the agency. Kagle (1984) notes that as a result of these deficiencies students are not learning about recording. In developing this collaborative venture, practice teachers and academic staff sought an authentic, planned approach derived from learning theories. Academic staff and field educators were determined not to divide teaching of content in the manner suggested by Kagle (1984, p.114) but to use learning strategies as the way to improve their understanding of practice issues.

This teaching initiative encouraged greater equity between students and a more predictable and explicit orientation to practice learning. Students would complete placements with a set of skills to be used in any later academic or practice setting. Given the increasing demands on agency staff, the aim of this new initiative was to engage students actively in a process of inquiry and discovery. The educational strategy combined cognitive skills, peer learning and group skills. There were three essential theoretical influences, which underpinned this collaborative initiative including group learning, constructivist approaches and reciprocal teaching.

Group approaches

According to Kaplan (1991) practice teachers have long experimented with group supervision as an approach to student learning. The influence of psychoanalytical theory encouraged one-to-one approaches during the 1930s and 1940s with the result that group approaches evolved from only the 1950s onwards. Despite the long history of group supervision, this practice was nevertheless viewed cautiously by practice teachers.

The aim of group supervision is student education and efficient client services. Such supervision has the added advantage of encouraging a more efficient use of staff resources for student education. A number of principles derived from Johnson, Johnson and Holobec (1993), Getzel and Salmon (1985) and Kaplan (1991) formed part group approaches:

- Work and learning are shared so that there is mutuality in learning and an expectation that students are expected to help each other.

- There is modified use of supervisory power and changes in distribution of that power from practice teacher to students.

- There is positive interdependence between the students who function as a group with shared learning goals, activities and shared rewards.

- There is both individual and group accountability. Each person is responsible for their performance but there is also a simultaneous responsibility to participate in group activities.

- There is development of collaborative skills which includes working as part of a team, social skills of sharing, taking turns, and giving and receiving help.

- There is development of and attention to group formation, group norms, sorting out group troubles and difficulties and then performing tasks and activities.

- The group members can take on diverse roles including facilitator, contributor, explainer, summarizer, initiator, observer and reporter.

One tacit educational assumption is that students learn best from experts. There is increasing evidence that students also learn from their peers. Skills of novice students are enhanced if client issues and case planning are discussed with other novices to the extent that novice counsellors learn more effectively from other novices than from experts (Hillerbrand 1989). Other writers have noted beneficial outcomes, such as the importance of increased cognitive analysis; problem-solving and team skills; improved students results; improved student outcomes; increased student retention and student satisfaction; promotion of positive attitudes and improved verbal and social skills (Kimber 1996). The clear conclusion is that group approaches are educationally effective while having added benefits of efficiency.

Constructivist views of learning

Constructivist views of learning mean that students construct their own meaning, understanding and views about social work practice through involvement in discovery, inquiry, debate and discussion (Hendry 1996). Teachers are therefore guides, not experts, who enable students to make their own meanings and think for themselves.

Piaget and Vygotsky have made a profound contribution to thinking about the way in which we learn with others. Piaget (1972) contributed to our understanding about cognitive development presenting learning as an active structuring and restructuring of thought rather than an increase in content. Each person will therefore construct knowledge based on their past and current experiences and their own mental mind maps and schema. This knowledge construction is assisted by cooperative efforts, provision of a variety of experiences and social interaction. Although some writers have argued that Piaget was more interested in individual cognition than in social interaction, Rogoff (1990) notes that Piaget emphasized the significance of interaction that promoted cognitive conflict. Cognitive conflict emerges in situations where inadequate reasoning is exposed, modified and reconceptualized. Group debates and discussions around controversial issues are important for development of new understandings.

Vygotsky (1978) assumed that knowledge construction is a significant social process with cognitive development occurring as a result of cooperative efforts to learn, understand and solve social problems. Vygotsky argued that individual intellectual development could not be understood without reference to the social context in which the person was embedded. Individual cognitive development is a product of social activity, guided by others who structure and model appropriate solutions to problems. Students are social beings who live and work in various cultural groups, organizations, communities and family situations. One of the central components of Vygotsky's theory is the zone of proximal development. Learning takes place when it can be extended beyond the current level of understanding with assistance from other more capable peers or teachers. In other words, the level of difficulty needs to be sufficient to challenge the students but not so difficult that they avoid it. The educator's role in this situation is to determine the appropriate level of difficulty that will enable student learning and then scaffold that learning by providing guidance to enable successful completion of the task. In making a translation to practice teaching, this theoretical framework suggests that effective learning requires the active involvement of the student. The supervisor as educator can guide the activities of the student but they cannot impose, lay down the law or force compliance to make learning occur. Learning occurs when there is mutuality and collaboration.

Reciprocal teaching

Constructivist views of learning and social interaction are merged in the work of Brown and Palinscar (1989). They developed a method of teaching comprehension strategies (summarizing, clarifying, questioning and predicting) which used peer group learning and modelling of thinking by peers and teachers. Teaching takes place in 'a cooperative learning group that features guided practice in applying simple, concrete strategies to the tasks of text comprehension' (Brown and Palinscar 1989, p.413). The teacher first models the steps in comprehending a text and then teaches students how they can use these steps in a group setting. With the teacher in the background, students using cognitive skills and various texts, teach each other.

This reciprocal model of learning provided the basis of practice teaching using the case record. Several aspects of the reciprocal teaching approach are worthy of elaboration in the context of placement learning. Although constructivist approaches assume that the student is self-directed, teachers can nevertheless assist self-directed approaches when they instruct students in particular skills and strategies to become effective learners.

One educational strategy used by practice teachers to enhance learning is modelling thinking and behaviour. Social learning theory as outlined by Bandura and Walters (1969) refers to the importance of modelling through a process of behavioural observation and imitation. This view of learning is sometimes referred to as the apprenticeship model in field education material. Practice teachers can easily model their behaviour. Skills in running and managing group behaviour are one example where students observe their supervisor's behaviour and follow this later with imitation and identification.

Another recent view is that of modelling *thinking* rather than *behaviour* (Idol, Jones and Mayer 1991). This is referred to as a cognitive apprenticeship. Within many agencies, practice teachers are those who have acquired a great deal of expertise in working with client groups. Such knowledge, skills and expertise are an important resource for students but this material needs to be accessible to them. Modelling thinking can be demonstrated by a process of *thinking aloud* about practice decisions, reasons for taking particular decisions or acting in a particular way and drawing attention to key concepts. This modelling of thinking captures all the stops, starts, attitudes and revisions that occur in reality as educators come to understand some aspect of practice or text. Students can also be encouraged to think aloud about their practice thus actively attending to their knowledge and processes of learning. The practice learning emerging from this strategy should not be underestimated.

Brown and Palinscar (1989) taught their students cognitive strategies using short expressive excerpts from the literature. The rationale for using the case record as a teaching text will be considered before explaining use of these cognitive strategies.

Selecting case records

In an outline of the history of social work case records, Kagle noted that 'case records are as diverse as the practice they document' (Kagle 1984, p.13). Although every agency determines their particular content and structure, common content features are also evident. The common content includes description of the client situation, assessment, services provided, implementation of work and termination. The structure of records does differ. Sometimes structure is left to the discretion of the worker but often structure (form and content) is predetermined by the agency.

In this initiative, practice teachers selected the case records for learning. Records were selected to illustrate agency mandate and practice. Over a six-month period, students were exposed to a range of records: narrative records, process recordings, social histories, court reports and problem-oriented records. Every effort was made to include material that covered social problems addressed in agencies: domestic violence, child abuse, racial issues, unemployment, palliative care, mental illness. Records were selected to cover diverse client groups so that clients varied in age, gender, marital status, ethnicity, economic status and sexual preference. In addition, every case included a variety of practice realities, methods of practice and service provision.

Practice teachers debated aspects of case record selection. One debate centred around the extent to which case records should represent excellent agency practice, a realistic representation of practice or contain examples of poor recording and weak practice. Case records were chosen which were neither uniformly excellent nor characterisations of practice's worst features. Selected records were rewritten to change names and identifying information to protect client and practitioner privacy. Case records selected were initially straightforward but during the course of the learning groups, increased in complexity.

Records selected were narratives rather than problem-based using abbreviated language. Records selected included the following information:

- legal and service function of the organization

- practitioner's role

- nature of the client/situation

- purpose of service

- practice modality and related theoretical constructs

- evolving process of service. (Kagle 1984, p.42)

These narrative records provide for learning about all aspects of social work practice. Each record has been selected to improve students' cognitive skills and to further their appreciation of the practice environment.

Strategies used by practice teachers

Practice teachers used case records to teach students the four cognitive strategies of summarizing, questioning, clarifying and predicting.

Summarizing

This is a description of key components in the overall case record and can encompass the key ideas, major themes, issues, or the client's story. The focus might be the whole record, a paragraph or 'chunk' such as the assessment. Summarizing provides the basis for student's self-monitoring of their understanding. If students find that they are not able to make a good summary then they should go back and reread the case record to determine the key issues. Particular case records permitted a variety of summary statements including the client situation, assessment, services provided and intervention strategies.

Questioning

This strategy involves formulating questions that arise from the text. This strategy is especially useful in understanding difficult texts where answers may not be deduced from the text itself. Students are encouraged to ask questions enabling them to check if the text as a whole makes sense. In this way they develop self-monitoring skills.

Clarifying

In using this strategy, the student explores aspects of words, phrases or practice concepts that are not familiar to the reader. As well as identifying words and phrases that require special clarification, students are encouraged to read further into the text to see if the meaning is apparent.

Predicting

This strategy involves formulating guesses, hunches and hypotheses about the success of the social worker in achieving the objectives or work with the client. Sometimes this extends to predicting the behaviour of clients and others involved in the case study. In addition to making these predictions, students can also propose alternative hypotheses.

Working with students

Group learning, constructivist approaches and reciprocal teaching methods formed the basis of student orientation and training of practice teachers. In the first learning group, practice teachers took the role of leader and facilitator to explain the group's purpose and the practice teacher's role. As the students developed skills at using the strategies, running the group and controlling the group, the practice teachers distanced themselves from the interaction. The students were enabled to control the group and the learning. The practice teacher intervened only when necessary to give support or direction to the student learning.

Students were allocated to groups of five to six participants. The practice teacher asked students to read the case record. Students were instructed to divide the text into convenient divisions to enable them to summarize. This division was usually a paragraph or a section of several paragraphs (e.g. case plan, assessment). Students were asked to identify any parts of the text that needed further clarification, list any questions that they would like to ask and make their predictions about the client based on their reading.

When this phase was complete, the practice teacher began a 'think aloud' about the text using the comprehension strategies described below. This 'think aloud' refers to modelling thinking. The practice teacher is expected to model her expert professional behaviour and thinking to students to ensure that students' efforts are directed to assisting each other. This modelling of practice teachers thinking is an important part of the process as students are exposed to the way in which experts think and reason about the content, structure and organization of case records.

Students were then encouraged to complete the tasks themselves. An initial leader was selected – with this leader role rotating several times within a group. Each student took turns summarizing the text, asking questions, making predictions and seeking clarification so that a range of responses was heard before the discussion began. Hence, students are able to self-monitor their performance. Students were encouraged to help their fellow students if they were stuck or having difficulty. If students faced difficulty with group processes, the practice teachers instructed students in the use of appropriate collaborative learning and group skills. At no time did the practice teacher take over the leadership of the group.

Strategies in action

The following summary is an incomplete extract from a narrative record written by a student in a community health centre and presented by the practice teacher for discussion. In this agency, the content and structure of records were determined by the student worker rather than agency procedure. The practice teacher selected this record because it represents work with victims of domestic violence, and differentiates between the statutory efforts of a state child protection agency and the long-term counselling orientation of a community health centre.

Abby was initially seen at the state child protection agency and then referred to a community health centre with a feminist orientation.

Abby

Abby is a single mother who has three children: Silas (4), Jo (2) and Beth (1). She is now pregnant with her fourth child. Abby became involved with the child protection agency when Silas was a baby. The child protection agency received notification of physical abuse after Silas was admitted to hospital and it was found that he had suffered fractures over a period of time and attempted strangulation. Silas was placed under a director general's order until the age of 6. Although the perpetrator of Silas's injuries was never confirmed, Abby and her defacto partner, Jay, admitted unintentionally harming Silas.

Silas remained in Abby's care but in accordance with the order, they spent several months in a mothering unit to enable Abby to develop her parenting skills. During that time Jay lived elsewhere and when Abby left the unit they moved into a housing trust home together with Silas. They have since had two children together, Jo and Beth. Abby is now 23 and Jay is 32.

Early this year, Abby left Jay due to a domestic violence episode in which he pulled some of her hair out. She took the children to a women's shelter but returned after a week. She told me later that 'she felt sorry for Jay' after hearing from her mother that 'he couldn't cope without her' and that he was 'very sorry for what he had done.' When she told me this, I was concerned about her lack of insight into the nature of domestic violence and the unlikelihood that Jay's behaviour would change. My belief was that although Abby presented as a confident, strong young woman, she had developed an emotional dependence on Jay.

My work with Abby focused on supporting Abby in parenting by reinforcing the knowledge and skill she had as a parent, her ability to protect her children and her strength as a person. I saw it as appropriate to build on what Abby would have learned about parenting in the mothering unit and I thought that if she saw herself as a strong mother, she would be less likely to accept the violence in her relationship with Jay.

By providing her with information about the nature of domestic violence, I attempted to enable her to reconceptualize her relationship with Jay. I was helping her to see the problem in a different way. If she knew enough about domestic violence, she might *know* she was being abused.

Through showing her that domestic violence follows patterns I hoped to demonstrate that the cycle of violence and power imbalance between them could be broken. I provided a visual representation of the cycle and patterns that relationships can follow.

The case description continues describing in detail the social work intervention.

›up discussion

Summarizing

Each student was required to summarize a paragraph of text. Initially students could not identify the logical divisions within narrative records such as the client problem, history of the problem, assessment, interventions and evaluations. This was surprising for practice teachers as they had always assumed that beginning students would have an appreciation of structure and content of case records.

Summarizing allowed students to become the producer of summary statements as well as evaluator and critic of their own and others' statements. Students found summarizing the most difficult skill of all to accomplish and a great deal of time was spent mastering this particular activity. The practice teacher initially modelled the use of summarizing and then encouraged use of the strategy giving encouragement until students could do this task alone.

The difficulty completing this task was surprising as the students were all graduates with prior work experience. Students initially had difficulty in differentiating between relevant information and peripheral information. They generally provided a summary as lengthy as the case study itself or provided brief responses capturing only one aspect of the case study. On one occasion, the practice teacher asked the students to summarize the intervention of the current social worker. Each student was able to provide a single statement although there was obvious confusion between interventions of the previous worker and current worker. Here are some of the individual answers provided.

The social worker:

- provided information about domestic violence
- educated the client
- raised client's level of awareness and insight
- supported client by reinforcing parenting skills
- informed client of community resources available to help her cope with the situation or to leave.

After these individual responses had been provided, the group again discussed and analysed their responses. The practice teacher again asked each student to summarize the specific interventions listed by the students. Towards the end of the groups, students actively assisted their peers especially if they were having difficulty in expressing their ideas or capturing the essence of the text. The result was a more concise summary and group interdependence and responsibility for one's peers.

Questioning

Students enjoyed the questioning most of all. Students were able to generate a wide range of questions resulting in lively debates about clients, social problems and agency practices. Many students drew on their prior working experiences in health and welfare agencies. The questions generated insights into a wide range of issues going far beyond the scope of the case record. Students began by asking questions of the case study, but then expanded this to question each other and propose answers. The different views of students in the group allowed the students to go beyond their present level of understanding and engage with other possibilities. Through use of these questioning strategies, students engaged in cognitive conflict. They constructed and then reconstructed the case material for themselves so that it was meaningful to other students in the group. Again, the peer nature of their learning was evident.

Some of the questions raised and discussed included:

- Who is Silas's father and does Abby still have contact with him?
- Was Jay the perpetrator of violence against Silas?
- Was the fact that Jay is not Silas's father a factor in the abuse?
- How does Abby keep the children safe and protect them against Jay?

Clarifying

Clarification also enabled a deep student-to-student discussion about a range of issues (including an outrage at the practices of the child protection agency). Many terms in social work, such as 'support', have common-sense meanings in everyday language: but these same terms have more specific meanings in the context of social work practice. Students were therefore encouraged to approach the task of clarification by using a veil of ignorance so that clarification of words and text stimulated inquiry, curiosity and learning. Students found that discussion of meanings of words and text stimulated debate and allowed them to construct meanings and then build on those meanings. It stimulated a curiosity in the issue of domestic violence and encouraged discussion of links between child protection and domestic violence. Some terms students raised for clarification included:

- notification of physical abuse
- placed under a director general's order
- unintentionally harming Silas
- domestic violence episode

- 'felt sorry for Jay'
- 'very sorry for what he had done'.

Predicting

Finally, students were asked to predict case outcomes. Students were divided. Some thought that Abby would leave as a result of the agency intervention while others thought that she would continue with her current behaviour. As a way of resolving this issue, students devised a list of factors that would support these different positions.

Practice teachers' comments

This peer learning approach to agency practice using case records was appreciated by practice teachers as it provided a more efficient and effective approach to student orientation. By examining case records, students were introduced to a variety of formats, client issues and problems, a range of intervention strategies, the nature of the service delivery system and legal factors underpinning practice. This orientation assisted preparation and readiness of students for actual practice.

Practice teachers regarded summarizing skills as most important. Many participants indicated the major skill needed for supervision, communication with other staff, making referrals and writing case records was being able to summarize the key issues. At completion of the program, practice teachers indicated that students could differentiate various types of records and understand the importance of records especially the use of clear and concise language. One outcome that was sometimes difficult to manage was an increase in student questioning during supervision. Students were comfortable debating issues and not taking anything for granted. Practice teachers found that their work and that of the agency was questioned by students. Overall, practice teachers found students were more confident in their agency practice.

Students' comments

Students differed from their practice teachers in their appreciation of cognitive skills. They found that the most important skills were questioning and predicting rather than summarizing which they found to be least helpful. The value of questioning was useful not only on placement but also in the classroom and to their learning generally. The students indicated questioning:

- Made me look more deeply at the work. I was able to see questioning as a non-judgemental way of looking at issues.

- Made me think about what I was reading in the case records.

- Was important because we need to be accurate at gathering accurate information and critiquing ourselves and others.

Questioning contributes to a deep approach to learning practice.

Students noted specific improvement in their approaches to learning social work practice.

- I can now look at some texts and critically evaluate.

- I am becoming conscious of the cognitive strategies to understand social work records. These strategies have also helped with client assessment.

- This program taught me that I can positively and critically evaluate what I read.

- It helped me to discover that I am a 'troubleshooter' sort of person.

- These sessions taught me to go slower when I read new case material.

- I was helped in understanding the assumptions of social work texts and practice.

- I can identify and hone in on the essential issues or information that I have overlooked before.

- I now will look for different things.

- This program helped me to look for things that I might have skipped over previously.

Students found that they were better able to evaluate critically, review and analyse case material. Consequently they did not take information at face value, but began to question assumptions, concepts, and clients. It also changed their way of using and writing case notes and many appreciated the house rules and agency conventions for recording client information.

- Although the program was about the use of cognitive skills, it also taught me how I might write case notes especially separating facts from observations and feelings, summarizing the client's story effectively and including the relevant facts.

- There is a lot more to case records that meets the eye. I will not take all the info as facts and at face value. Case notes are very subjective and make a lot of assumptions. Unpacking those assumptions can be difficult for new workers.

- I was able to see how case notes could be misread or vague. It clarified how to write case notes so they can be understood by colleagues.

Students also felt that the groups allowed greater opportunity to link theory with agency practice. Discussion of domestic violence and child protection in Abby illustrates this issue.

Students were positive in terms of the peer learning approach. They valued new ideas and found that their peers' perspective was useful to practice. Peers made a valuable contribution to deepening their understanding about people and problems. Many indicated that if their peers had not raised specific issues, they would not have thought of these issues themselves. Students also valued information about agency resources. Students found the process of learning non-competitive and non-threatening. They were able to both support other members of the group and extend the ideas and thus learning of the group.

- It gave me the opportunity to learn from other students.

- I learnt by listening to the very different ideas of other students. They made me stop and think about a broader range of issues.

- I did not realize the diversity of backgrounds among other students. We made use of the knowledge and expertise of other students and found that this contributed enormously to discussions.

- It helped for all students to take the role of facilitator, adviser, leader and supporter.

- I appreciated the support provided by other students if I ran out of ideas.

- All students were expected to contribute equally and they did.

Conclusion

This conclusion outlines some of the critical features of this program and offers suggestions for others wishing to implement this initiative. Social work records are a rich source of learning. In the selection of records for this program, the quality of practice is of less importance than the record's coherence. Begin with simple records and progress to those containing more complex information. Learning groups were organized at the beginning of the first placement and continued throughout the first placements. Some students and staff thought that group learning was too long. Based on our experience, a program of six to eight, two-hour sessions would be sufficient to achieve the program goals.

Group processes are important. The leader is required to model their cognitive thinking and group skills. Our group leaders experienced difficulty in modelling all cognitive strategies (summarizing was particularly difficult for students and educators) and in being the group facilitator rather than the leader or expert. Staff development and trial runs using experienced practitioners was an important aspect of this process. This enabled us to identify glitches before working with students and address our own limitations in using cognitive strategies. Groups worked best when leaders handed responsibility over to the students but were available to guide and redirect the process when students became stuck.

In summary this chapter describes a practice innovation in which academic staff and practice teachers worked together to orient students to their first placements using agency records. In developing this program, practice teachers drew on several educational theories including group learning, constructivist approaches, and reciprocal teaching. Outcomes from this initiative were improved student thinking. Students acquired many cognitive skills, a deep appreciation of client problems, an understanding of therapeutic approaches and importantly the agency case records. Above all students developed the capacity to question themselves, written material and their practice teachers.

Acknowledgement

The teaching initiative described in this chapter was funded by the Australian Government's Committee for University Teaching and Staff Development.

PART III
SOCIAL WORK LEARNING IN DIFFERENT SETTINGS

Chapter Nine

Practice Learning
in Hospital-based Settings

Nigel Hall and Revai Senzere

Introduction

Social work and social development training are undertaken at a variety of institutions throughout sub-Saharan Africa, more than half of which are located in South Africa. Most of these institutions offer fieldwork as part of their curriculum, which is seen as an integral part of training.[1] However, severe constraints do limit the scope of fieldwork, generally to urban areas – although the Zimbabwe School of Social Work for many years (until financial constraints limited the variety of placements) extended fieldwork to include a wide range of developmental agencies throughout the country. The core agencies providing placements usually comprise departments of social welfare, local and international NGOs, municipal or local authority agencies, 'para-statal' organizations (such as the post and telecommunications corporation employee welfare services) and hospital settings. This chapter focuses in particular on the fieldwork setting of the general hospital within Zimbabwe.

Social work within general hospitals

Social work within general hospitals in Zimbabwe has gradually gained momentum after the hospital administrators and other professionals in the medical field realized its contribution in the treatment of the patient from diagnosis to after-care. However, social work retains a complementary function in this secondary setting compared to other agencies like the Department of Social Welfare, whose main function is the direct provision of welfare services to clients.

Following a demand for social workers in hospitals and requests made by medical social workers for students, the Zimbabwe School of Social Work, some years ago, placed students on fieldwork placements in this setting.

While social work within the medical setting is now widely accepted in Zimbabwe and is gaining momentum, very little has been written about the practice of social work in this context from a Zimbabwean perspective. This has created some problems as students on fieldwork largely depend on the personal experience of their supervisor and the few sources of literature available. This chapter highlights some of the areas that students cover during their fieldwork practice in the medical field; four areas have been chosen, which represent major areas covered by social work field training in hospitals:

- work with psychiatric outpatients

- work with children in the Rehabilitation Department

- work with people affected by HIV/AIDS

- teamwork with other medical professionals.

Work with psychiatric outpatients

A variety of agencies offer services to psychiatric outpatients – and these include such governmental agencies as the Ministry of Health, clinics run by the urban municipalities, voluntary organizations such as the Zimbabwe National Association for Mental Health (ZIMNAMH), the Zimbabwe National Traditional Healers Association (ZINATHA) and other private self-help groups dealing with specific illnesses, such as schizophrenia. Various professionals work with mentally ill people – from medical doctors and nursing staff, to psychologists, social workers and volunteers. One case of a client to be known as 'Misheck' has been chosen to illustrate social work learning in the context of working with psychiatric outpatients.

Misheck

Misheck was employed as a general labourer in a food manufacturing company. He was a father of five, but his family stayed in the rural areas, while he occupied a one-roomed rented accommodation in town. Misheck's wife would come to town once every month-end to collect money for groceries and other needs and it was during one such visit that his wife discovered that her husband had a problem, but could not detect the source. He had sleepless and restless nights, was refusing to go to work and had developed a rather arrogant manner. However, despite his protests, Misheck's wife had managed to bring him to hospital where he was seen in the outpatient department and later referred to the psychiatric clinic to see a psychiatrist. There the diagnosis was given as depression.

The student social worker, with her supervisor, attended the clinics as part of her learning and this was when the student met Misheck. The case was allocated to her as a case study. As this was her first experience with psychiatric patients, the student initially had to rely on her own imagination and developing practice wisdom regarding his condition. In Zimbabwe, mental illness is culturally associated with negative spiritual causation due to failure to appease ancestral spirits, through bewitchment, or as punishment for the 'bad' things a person may have done in the past. Confronted with such a situation, but with some theoretical knowledge gained at the School of Social Work, the student had to choose her point of intervention, which initially involved interviewing both the patient and his immediate family.

As stated by Wintersteen, Mupedziswa and Wintersteen (1995), it is clear that families continue to bear a heavy responsibility for providing assistance to family members with mental illness. Families provide for mentally ill people partially from choice, but more so, because there is no alternative, as there is minimal support from the mental health system. As Wintersteen and colleagues comment:

> Those social workers, nurses and other psychiatric personnel who come into contact with families should make it a point to be available to answer questions, provide advice and helpful suggestions, and generally treat them as colleagues in the business of rehabilitation and treatment. (Wintersteen *et al.* 1995, p.95)

Assessment and intervention

The supervisor directed the student to discuss the problem fully with the patient and his family and respect their beliefs and views in working with them. Hence, she had to get to know what the client (i.e. Misheck's wife) thought was the source of Misheck's problem. The student had to establish what her feelings were regarding her husband's illness (and his own views on this) and what the two thought would be solutions to their difficulties. The student was required to look into the problems that could have contributed to the illness and those that had been brought about by the illness. It was only after probing into these different areas that she and the family, plus the medical personnel, would be able to assist in the treatment process.

At interview, the student was able to find out that Misheck had gone through difficult times over the past months due to bereavement and financial constraints. He had lost his mother six months before and had borrowed money to arrange for the funeral from his employer. Due to the number of his problems, Misheck had started drinking heavily, sometimes on account. This obviously made the situation worse as finances became more strained.

Taking account of this scenario, the student had to decide on the mode of intervention. Misheck and his wife were both of the idea that he had been bewitched. For the student to explain the illness in terms of stress or other 'western' factors was a daunting task. This made the whole job difficult as she felt that if she could not break through at this point, then she had not done enough. As part of the learning process, the supervisor had to remind her of the importance of learning the beliefs and customs of one's clients as these could otherwise serve as an obstacle in the treatment process. She had to accept their beliefs to allow progress, but keep within herself the theoretical knowledge on stress and depression she had obtained at the school.

Misheck was given some treatment and had to come back for review within a week. On his return, the social worker was faced with a new problem. Misheck had developed a sexual dysfunction as a side-effect of the drug the doctor had prescribed; despite explanations offered by the student social worker the wife insisted that the drug was not acceptable. It was finally agreed between the doctor and social worker that the drug would be substituted with another one not as strong.

The student had still another task – dealing with the practical concerns that were affecting the family. First, she had to talk to the employer to secure Misheck's job and also arrange deduction of a reasonable amount from Misheck's salary towards repayment of the loan, but at the same time to leave sufficient to ensure the survival of the family. The three worked together to work out Misheck's monthly budget so that he could learn to live within his means. As time went on significant change was noticed in Misheck and his disturbed behaviour lessened. Eventually he improved sufficiently to warrant an ending of the social work intervention.

The case illustrates that although the explanation was originally cast in terms of 'bewitchment', by maintaining respect and consideration for the patient and his family and carefully examining their circumstances, together with use of social work skills including counselling, the student was able to assist the patient in reducing his level of stress and helping in his recovery.

Work with children in the Rehabilitation Department

The Rehabilitation Department in the general hospital is a place where children with disabilities are taught to cope with their disabilities with relevance to their own environment. The department was set up to assist children in coping with their individual problems, which vary from serious physical disabilities to other serious congenital disorders. With the most severely disabled, most of the work is done with parents, whereas children are more involved where the disability is less severe.

Role of social work in rehabilitation

Since the students have to be trained within the goals and functions of the agency, it would be initially beneficial to define the role of the social worker in the Rehabilitation Department. The social worker identifies individual and group problems and mobilizes resources from other agencies in order to intervene appropriately and enable the rehabilitation process to take place. It is the social worker's role to help in the transformation of the home environment to make it suitable for the child. This makes home visits a real necessity. According to Hall (1990), the students are expected to help individuals and families with social problems, develop an ability to diagnose and remedy these situations and help clients to find adequate solutions based on the methodology and techniques learned during theoretical training.

Work in the Rehabilitation Department can be challenging and emotionally upsetting for the students due to the sensitive nature of some of the children's disabilities. The students need to be able to avoid overly sympathizing with the children and instead deal with them in an empathic and caring way. The students have to learn to act professionally and learn about the physical and mental conditions and how to cope with them. Certain disabilities create social problems that are difficult to overcome; hence, the students can be faced with some very difficult situations. This can result in their feeling a failure due to the lack of achievement of set goals. Consequently, the support and advice of the supervisor is essential to help the students overcome these feelings.

Expectations of the student in rehabilitation work

However, it may be useful to look at what is expected of students on placement in the children's Rehabilitation Department. This can be seen in the context of the needs presented by the children. One child, for example, might require certain aids to enhance the rehabilitation process, so the students should develop interest in the functions of other helping agencies so that they can make use of them when the need arises. Students who use their initiative to mobilize resources will be seen as more impressive to the supervisor than those who act on instructions only.

Another child might need a change of environment as a result of having to use a wheelchair. This might even mean the renovation of a house, which could require thousands of dollars that the family might not be able to afford. Moreover, the student's services may be needed in developing a proposal for funding and influencing donors to assist financially.

A situation could arise whereby certain members of the family might not want to accept a child born with disability – a vivid example being that of a child who was born with a hole in the spine. This weakened her lower limbs. Instead of accepting the disability, both the husband and the mother-in-law attributed the disability as (spiritual) punishment for infidelity on the part of the mother. She was divorced instantly. Being unemployed the mother was left with the sole responsibility of looking after the child. Despite counselling the respective relatives, they would not change their minds. They had a conviction that it was taboo and unheard of to bear a disabled child within the family and the student was given the responsibility of dealing with the mother's feelings of rejection. She was able to do this through counselling and with the help of the supervisor was able to secure maintenance deducted from the husband's earnings every month.

Intensive intervention

Certain situations might require intensive intervention on the part of the medical social worker: for example, a situation whereby there are several children with disabilities within the family, which can create severe impoverishment and hardships.

One such case is that of a woman who had six children, all disabled, with five microcephalic children and one child with cerebral palsy. All these children required special education and care. The parents needed intensive counselling so as to enlighten them on the dangers of continuously bearing children in the hope of producing a normal child, which was very unlikely. The student had to identify areas of intervention, which were financial assistance (a resource not available to her agency), and in-depth counselling that she tried to provide within her capabilities. Although she offered as much help as she could, in the end she also had to refer the case to the Department of Social Welfare, which has responsibility for the provision of financial aid to the destitute.

Group approach

Certain problems demand a group approach as opposed to family casework. Here the students have to employ their knowledge of group dynamics gained during theoretical learning. This helps them in grouping clients and using the appropriate techniques in problem-solving as well as assessing the effectiveness of the methods used. Children with similar disabilities and perhaps similar social backgrounds may be grouped together and groupwork carried out in helping them cope with their disabilities and the emotional problems that extend from these difficulties. With the assistance of the occupational therapist and physiotherapist, physical aids can be made from locally available materials and assistance can be sought to buy those aids that cannot be made in the Rehabilitation Department. Work with disabled children not only provides useful experience to students on fieldwork practice, but also demands a lot of determination and patience on the part of the students and guidance and support from the supervisor.

Work with people affected by HIV/AIDS

Sub-Saharan Africa has 70 per cent of the world's total of HIV/AIDS infected people, with 23.3 million estimated cases of HIV or AIDS. AIDS is a very serious problem in Zimbabwe, with overall adult prevalence rates of 25.8 per cent and antenatal care surveillance data indicating a rate as high as 46.7 per cent outside major urban areas (UNAIDS/WHO 1998, 1999). Consequently, a majority of hospital beds in Zimbabwe are taken up by people with AIDS, or suffering from the various opportunistic infections, such as TB and diarrhoea. Although HIV/AIDS has become a very common problem, it is still stigmatized and difficult to acknowledge directly.

Sensitivity to the needs of patients with HIV/AIDS

Dealing with patients who have contracted HIV/AIDS requires careful and tactful handling and there is need to guide the students in their practice from the beginning. First and foremost, it is vital for the students to work with these patients in an accepting and non-judgemental way, maintaining confidentiality and sensitivity to their emotional and physical needs. The students will need to assess the patient's situation, including

- the attitude of the patient with regards to the illness

- the duration of the illness

- the patient's prognosis

- attitudes of other family members to the illness and also society at large

- the social and financial status of the patient.

How then do these notions relate to how the students should deal with the patient? If the patient denies the diagnosis and does not understand the implications of the illness, this determines one's entry point. Instead of trying to help the patient cope with the condition, one is faced with the often enormous task of trying to make them understand and accept the situation, i.e. getting over the denial stage.

Traditional views on chronic illness

The time the individual has lived with HIV/AIDS is another factor requiring consideration, since it determines the stage of adjustment of the patient. Where prognosis is poor and the disease is either very advanced or progressing very quickly, the areas requiring social work intervention might require urgent attention. Different family members adopt different attitudes to chronic illness, especially concerning AIDS – and similarly regarding cancer. Within the cultural context among most Zimbabweans, cancer is a disease brought about through bewitchment. If the right traditional healer is found, the ailment can be treated. AIDS is viewed by many as having the same origin, while with others who now understand its mode of transmission, it is a disease that carries with it a stigma. As such, diagnosis is usually not made public knowledge on the part of relatives as this might lead to rejection of the patient, and negative consequences for the family as a whole. Members of society at large also share the same feelings and this tends to reinforce feelings of isolation and stigmatization. As anti-retroviral treatment is completely out of the question due to its extremely high cost, and stigma is high, there is little motivation to admit to the condition. However, it is important that patients accept their condition, as positive living, physical care and the support of others are likely to prolong the patient's life and ease suffering.

The financial and social status of the patients also determines how the social worker will deal with them. An individual who is financially sound might only require assistance in getting paid care givers, whereas the poor will require volunteers and need considerable material help. One's social status also affects how people with HIV/AIDS react to their diagnosis, with those of high social status finding it more difficult to admit to the condition.

Student knowledge and skills in working with HIV/AIDS

This situation can be quite demanding and stressful for students, who will need to be equipped with knowledge of the disease and coping skills. Because of the devastating implications that HIV/AIDS – or any terminal illness – has for both the patient and the family, the provision of comprehensive, physical, material, psychological, social and spiritual care and support becomes essential. However, the success of the students largely depends on the support of other professionals and agencies, particularly that of their own supervisor. The students' success is also determined by the family's attitude and cooperation. As students work with the family and patient, they have a number of questions to answer. Family members worry about who will take over their relative's responsibilities and in particular the expenses involved in treatment and care. The family and patient require continuous counselling as a coping mechanism.

The student might be faced with the task of making arrangements and decisions about impending death and bereavement ahead of time, although traditionally the idea is not easily welcome as it is taboo to discuss these matters. The student has also to work with the patient in a bid to have them accept the impending death and later work through specific tasks to ease both their own and their family's situation. Arrangements have to be made concerning the care of children or dependants of the patient during illness and after death. Family members have to be encouraged to support each other – sharing their feelings, fears and hopes – as well as dealing with any unresolved conflict, anger, frustration and the feelings of guilt before the patient dies. The students have to know that individuals and families have different coping mechanisms and therefore need different types of support. This is a difficult but challenging area for social work practice and one that students on field practice should experience as they will be dealing in one way or another with HIV/AIDS once they start work.

Teamwork with other medical professionals

It is important for students to develop familiarity with a team approach in social work practice, particularly in the hospital setting. However, working with a variety of professionals can be a daunting and challenging experience for the student. Teamwork is not always 'smooth sailing', as it carries with it problems emanating either from the individual personalities involved, or from different professional perspectives and views about the same problem – which can be functional if dealt with in a collaborative and collegial way.

A student on fieldwork practice will not be spared this experience. It would be interesting to examine how students can cope with such situations and the benefits to be accrued from such experience.

Familiarity with departments in the hospital

On arrival at the institution, the students are introduced to all departments within the hospital so as to be acquainted with the environment in which they will work. There are several departments within the general hospital, which can be related to learning about social work practice in different ways.

First, there is the *Records Office* where patients' records, either as in- or outpatients, are kept. This office is also responsible for keeping records on births and deaths. Everyone with problems not viewed as medical in nature is referred to the medical social worker, and these records are also maintained here. It becomes necessary to know how this department operates, when and how the records are kept, if the medical social worker is to be effective in the delivery of these services. The *Stores Department* is an area that has to be known by the students on placement, as it is responsible for material requirements for use by the students and other departments, i.e. stationery, mobility and other aids used in the rehabilitation process.

The *Mortuary* is another department that works closely with the medical social worker. One would wonder how such a dreadful area relates to social work! It is worth mentioning that the cost of burial has gone up in Zimbabwe; furthermore, due to the economic history of the country, there are several hundreds of thousands of aliens that came to Zimbabwe to work on the farms and mines as general labourers. Most of them never settled down and have no families. When these people die, they automatically become a state problem and have to receive a pauper's funeral. It is the social worker's duty to investigate and if found that there is no immediate or contactable family, to recommend for the deceased that kind of assistance. Failure to do so speedily might have serious repercussions on the whole institution, as the mortuary is very often full to capacity. The experience of students has been that this area was the least desirable during placement.

Having said that, it is worth mentioning that the concept of team approach starts from the 'general hand' up to the superintendent who is the head of the institution. In this regard, it is vital for the student to be introduced to other staff before the onset of fieldwork practice. This is particularly important to students on practice in a psychiatric wing or institution of the hospital, where their security heavily depends on other staff members. An example of such a situation is of a student nurse who always looked down upon general hands but was saved possible death by the same personnel after she had been unexpectedly throttled by a psychiatric patient while giving him medication.

A general observation is that most students on fieldwork enjoy teamworking with other professionals. This conclusion has come about after observing their input, self-initiative and achievement during ward rounds with doctors, nurses, physiotherapists, psychiatrists, psychologists and occupational therapists from admission to discharge. The reason for this is probably due to the clearly stipulated goals when working with other professionals, compared to the ambiguity in other areas.

Admission and discharge of patients

On admission of the patient, and depending on the presenting problems, the student is requested to intervene from the very beginning. Using interviewing skills, the student has to assist in the diagnostic process. Once the problem is identified, the student through ward rounds is able to participate in the treatment of the patient. The hospital administrator, who is in charge of the transport department, may authorize the use of a vehicle and driver to enable students to pursue their goals. It is in this light, therefore, that teamworking and interdependence is inevitable.

While patients are in hospital, the students have to prepare for their discharge. The students are charged with the responsibility of working outside the hospital to ensure that the environment is conducive for the patient. They also have to assist the family in case of any social problems arising after discharge, which may in some cases demand a change in occupation, or preparation of the home to make it more suitable for the patient, particularly in the case of physical disability. The student will need to work with the occupational therapist and perhaps the employer to secure something suitable for the condition of the patient. The student has to ensure that communication remains an ongoing process that should be kept open to allow each member of the working team to be informed of progress and keep up-to-date with the patient's situation.

Tapiwa

The case of Tapiwa, a man aged 23 years who was injured in a serious train accident, is an example of the good fruits of teamworking. He had been in and out of the general hospital for the previous three years before the case was handled by the social worker. Tapiwa had a son aged 4 years and his wife was unemployed. Due to the prolonged stay in hospital and the use of a wheelchair for mobility, Tapiwa had lost hope of ever walking again, let alone being able to enjoy a conjugal relationship with his wife. Out of frustration at the persistence of his medical condition, he had instructed his wife to go back to her relatives.

When this came to the attention of the student social worker, she thought she could be of help. She managed to convince the patient that although he had been labelled as a paraplegic, his condition could change one day. She was also allowed to speak to Tapiwa's wife, who was now feeling despondent and after being told of the sad news of returning to her parents she needed support to pull her through this crisis period. The student also started attending physiotherapy sessions with the patient and giving him moral support.

In the mean time the orthopedic surgeon, physiotherapist, occupational therapist and the medical social worker had together managed to convince the employer to change the work environment by putting up a ramp so that Tapiwa could access his workplace in a wheelchair. His job was also changed from general hand in a Veterinary Department to that of a telephonist. The Railway Company had given him an articulated wheelchair and money which allowed him to purchase a house in one of the suburbs near his workplace.

He was discharged and went back to work, but the hospital team, including the student, kept on giving him professional support. The family expressed satisfaction with this increased level of care, which in no small part was due to the interest and commitment demonstrated by the student.

Conclusion

Social work in medical settings is a challenging area of social work practice, which requires careful handling and cooperation with the family and the patient. Success is difficult to measure since the behaviour of the patient might come from other sources, e.g. physical and mental deterioration or improvement, medication and other factors, rather than necessarily one's own input, and these are things to be imparted to the student engaged in practical field training. The multi-disciplinary working arrangement of the general hospital provides opportunities for students to develop their professional skills and growth as practitioners. The variety of cases and the many demands made of social workers in the general hospital is a fruitful area for training and confidence building of social work students.

Note

1   The connotation of the term 'fieldwork' is here the notion of work outside of class setting – the term should not be taken to imply any particular form of social work practice.

Chapter Ten

Practice Learning in the Voluntary Sector

Elaine King, Rob Mackay and Joyce Lishman

Introduction

In this chapter we examine the richness and range of learning opportunities available in the voluntary sector in Scotland for social work students undertaking courses leading to the UK professional qualification, the Diploma in Social Work (CCETSW 1995). We use two contrasting settings which provide services for people with mental health problems in the North of Scotland to examine how voluntary sector placements enable students to meet the values, knowledge, understanding and skills requirements for the award of the DipSW.

The chapter begins with a brief introduction to the context both of the voluntary sector in social service provision and of social work education and training in the UK. We then examine the role of specific settings in the voluntary sector in developing students' values, knowledge and skills. First, we examine the role of an advocacy service in developing both students' knowledge and understanding of the legal, policy and organizational context of practice and their values and skills in empowerment and advocacy. Second, we examine the role of residential projects in developing students' understanding of the impact of life history, of institutions and of transitions on the current situation of service users and how this understanding may be used to promote user choice and access to improved quality of life (Seed and Lloyd 1997).

Voluntary sector service provision in the UK

The Report of the Commission on the Future of the Voluntary Sector defined voluntary organizations as 'The voluntary coming together of individuals to engage in mutual undertakings for the common good' (National Council for Voluntary Organization (NCVO) 1996, p.15).

However, defining the voluntary sector in the UK is problematic generally because:

> voluntary organizations perform a large number of functions in society, contain a huge variety of organizational forms and are active across a wide range of industries. (Kendall and Knapp 1995, p.85)

The main functions can be summarized as including education and training, community development, housing and environmental issues as well as social service provision. According to Brenton (1985) the functions of voluntary organizations may be classified broadly as follows:

- service providing function: providing a direct service, such as information, advice or support
- mutual aid function: developing self-help or mutual exchange and support
- pressure group function: influencing policy through campaigning, direct action and lobbying
- individual advocacy: presenting a case on behalf of an individual e.g. in mental health, or developing self-advocacy
- coordination and development function: liaising with, coordinating and promoting the voluntary sector.

There is no central registry of voluntary organizations. They include political parties, trade unions, sports clubs, trades associations, churches and universities (an estimate of 500,000 voluntary organizations: Fieldgrass and Fieldgrass 1992). However, to overcome some of the problems associated with lack of clarity about the size of the sector, the International Classification of Non-Profit Organizations (ICNPO) was devised which has been

> specifically developed to capture and categorise areas of voluntary sector involvement and at the same time be compatible with classification systems used within other sectors or across all sectors. (Kendall and Knapp 1995, p.75)

The profile of the sector is perhaps most associated with the delivery of social services (ICPNO, group 4), which is also the area most thoroughly researched.

Services provided include those for people with physical or sensory disabilities, with mental health problems and with learning disabilities, for children and families, for older people, for carers and for people from ethnic minorities. As Kendall and Knapp point out, the larger organizations, such as Barnado's and Age Concern, 'have incomes in the millions or tens of millions of pounds brackets, and employ several thousand full-time and part-time staff alongside volunteers nationally and locally in the provision of both mainstream and pioneering services' (Kendall and Knapp 1995, p.75).

In social services provision, voluntary organizations can be defined as

> independent bodies operating outside the statutory services but receiving financial government funding. Voluntary organizations are themselves diverse ... and range from small scale community groups to organizations with national and international branches and affiliations. (Lishman and Wardell 1998, p.3)

Alcock (1996) suggests voluntary sector organizations are best defined negatively. For example, they are not part of state provision, they are not directly accountable to elected representatives and they are distinct from independent or private organizations because they do not operate for profit. More positively, Alcock (1996, p.67) is clear that the voluntary sector 'plays an important role in the development and delivery of welfare services but it is a complex and diverse role'. The traditional distinctions between the private, statutory and voluntary sectors have become increasingly blurred as voluntary organizations increasingly use business practices and engage in purchase provider relationships with the statutory sector (Kendall and Knapp 1995). Care in the community policies promote a mixed economy of care, enabling consumer choice to be fully exploited and a balance between more effective use of statutory provision and stimulation of voluntary, private and independent organizations (Orme and Glastonbury 1993).

Voluntary organizations in the social service sector vary in size, affiliation (local, national or international), funding, service delivery and organization (including use of paid workers and/or volunteers), management infrastructure and training. They also vary in terms of purpose; for example, policy development or service delivery.

- In terms of size we can contrast large UK national organizations such as Barnardo's and NCH (National Children's Homes), providing children's services throughout the UK, and Scottish national organizations, such as the Church of Scotland (providing a range of services for older people, children and people with drug problems) with locally based services such as the projects described in this chapter.

- In terms of funding, the implementation of the National Health Service (NHS) and Community Act 1990 (with its emphasis on local authorities as enabling purchasers rather than providers and a mixed economy of services in social welfare and social care) has led to a growth in both the private sector (in particular in relation to older people) and the voluntary sector in providing services on behalf of the local authority via contractual and quasi-contractual agreements. In terms of organization, voluntary organizations range from formal to informal structures with an increasing emphasis on formality of organization (Lishman and Wardell 1998).

- In terms of purpose, national organizations are more likely to combine policy development with service delivery although Save the Children in Scotland has recently refocused on policy development rather than service delivery.

The role of assessed practice learning and practice teaching, in qualifying social work education and training

The 1990s witnessed a major shift towards a competence-based approach to educating and assessing social work students in the UK. This was heralded by the Central Council for Education and Training in Social Work publishing its Paper 30 document in 1989. This set out the rules and requirements of the DipSW and was subsequently revised in 1995. CCETSW (1995) sets out requirements for students to demonstrate values, knowledge and competencies (see below for more details).

Criticisms of this predominately competence-led approach to social work education and training in Scotland included a perceived denigration of a knowledge and research base for social work and potentially simplistic definitions of competence based on functional analysis. In the North of Scotland, voluntary organizations have demonstrated a sustained interest and commitment to providing practice learning opportunities for students, partly because of their recognition of the contribution students make to practice and policy by the fact that they question, they bring 'new' knowledge and they have an impartiality or neutrality. In addition, there are financial rewards (voluntary organizations in Scotland are paid a daily rate of £17 by higher education institutions for student placements, whereas local authorities are not, although they do receive central government funding specifically for students they take on placements).

The model most frequently used for practice teaching in the voluntary sector is that of 'long-arm' or off-site supervision (Lawson 1998, p.237) where 'an identified supervisor based in the same location as the student has responsibility for the student's day to day practice but another, qualified practice teacher links with both the student and supervisor and has a wider managerial teaching and assessment role'.

Here, we identify the potential generic roles of the long-arm practice teacher and the 'link supervisor'. Inevitably, these will need to be contextualized when we examine the contrasting settings we use as case studies.

The practice teacher

It is the role of the practice teacher to offer regular weekly supervision to each student and to help the students to

- examine and develop their interpersonal skills
- increase their understanding of the user/client, their history and their current situation
- integrate theory, and apply social work values, to their practice
- analyse and reflect upon their practice
- reflect upon, and evaluate current practice
- make the transition from student to practitioner, and take responsibility for their professional development.

The practice teacher is required to observe students' practice, to provide feedback to students on their ability to meet CCETSW requirements and to provide a final assessment of the placement and a report.

The link supervisor

The person given this role is sometimes the manager, or an experienced member of staff in the establishment. The link supervisor provides day-to-day line management of the placement and in addition

- introduces the student to the agency
- teaches the student about agency policies and procedures
- introduces them to the written documentation

- assesses the student by obtaining the views of staff and residents for the final report.

They, too, supervise the student and they have a central role to ensure the quality of service provided by the student for clients.

Hence, we have identified briefly the roles and responsibilities of key actors in the 'long-arm' model of practice learning. Lawson (1998, p.238) further clarifies the advantages in terms of 'dual sources of experience and knowledge' from which students can draw. Potential concerns, she argues, arise from the triangular nature of this method of practice teaching, with the potential for alliances, coalitions and inclusion/exclusion. An understanding of the complexity of three way relationships and a clarity of roles and responsibilities best ensures that the advantages of the model outstrength the disadvantages.

Practice learning in the voluntary sector

Policy and practice in mental health services

The development of mental health policy, services and practice in the 1990s in the UK mirrors wider changes identified earlier in the role of the voluntary sector, but also includes issues and tensions specific to the field of mental health. Specifically, in relation to mental health services, the following issues have emerged (Ulas and Connor 1999):

- the focus on 'mental health' rather than 'mental illness' and the recognition of a diversity of needs and situations including people with short-term mental health problems, and people with long-term problems who may have spent substantial periods in hospital

- the challenge to medical models of illness and treatment and the way in which these may have affected access to services, on the basis of race, gender or age

- the growth of the user movement including self-help groups, user-led services and (more rarely) user-led research

- the impact of care in the community policies, described earlier, in relation to mental health services has led to the discharge from hospital of people who have spent considerable time in large-scale institutions, divorced from the community

- subsequent concern and media publicity has focused on the lack of resources to ensure that the transition from institution to community is successfully undertaken

- at the extreme, public concern has arisen about 'patients with severe and enduring mental health problems' who do not continue to take medication after leaving hospital, become ill, cause distress to others, or become a danger to others (including complete strangers) (Ulas, Myers and Whyte 1994).

The voluntary sector provides a range of services which include residential and group care for people leaving long-term hospital care, supported accommodation, supported employment, day care, and drop in centres. Inevitably this means dealing with the tensions embedded in mental health services between the promotion of user rights and the protection of the public, and between user needs and the availiability of resources.

Learning about organizations

Advocacy Services Aberdeen (known as ASA) is a small local voluntary organization providing free and confidential advocacy services to users of social work and health services. Since its inception, ASA has devoted considerable energy to developing policies, procedures and structures (ASA 1997). Currently, the staff consists of one manager, four advocacy coordinators, one mental health advocacy worker and one administrative worker. One part of ASA is a mental health project (with a coordinator and an advocacy worker who has an outreach remit and a number of volunteer advocates). The agency has had four students on placement with one student is current on placement at the time of writing. A 'long-arm' model of supervision has been adopted because the manager, who acts as link supervisor, does not have a social work qualification or time to undertake the role of practice teacher.

Social work students in the UK have to demonstrate that they are competent in 'Working in Organizations' (CCETSW 1995), which is one of the six core competencies required of social work students.[1] Hence, students are expected to have knowledge about how organizations work, including policy development and implementation. In addition, students are expected to have organizational skills and show their competence to

- demonstrate capacity to work as an accountable and effective member of the organization in which placed

- contribute to the planning, monitoring and control of resources

- contribute to the evaluation of the effectiveness, efficiency and economy of services.

In the context of one voluntary organization, ASA, it is possible to illustrate how these quite general and rather bland expectations can be realized through using strategies that enable students to learn through being active within the agency.

How, then, does ASA enable students to learn about organizational skills? It is not sufficient simply to place the student into a corner with a pile of agency documents and expect them to read these without further discussion. Effective learning requires an approach that is designed to provide the student with experience of the various facets of the agency and then provide an opportunity within supervision for reflection and thinking about relevant issues. This praxis helps students to understand the totality of the organization and their part as a worker within it (Freire 1972).

Let us examine some of the learning opportunities for students at ASA. Students are always expected to take part in the weekly team meetings (used for planning future work and events, such as the organization of the next volunteer training programme), as they are regarded as part of the team. This helps students to feel included as part of the team, and also provides them with essential information about current work undertaken by team members, highlighting current issues and problems. This allows students to gain an overall sense of different projects operated by the agency, as well as to develop a feeling for personalities and relationships.

A second way in which students can learn about the organization, its structure, processes and dynamics is to observe regular committee meetings (such as the board of directors' meeting, the finance subcommittee, the mental health subcommittee, and so on). At the annual general meeting, the students can observe the process of accountability directly, through the reporting of activities and achievements, as well as the authority vested in a new board of directors for another year. This gives students access to all the significant people within the organization. These meetings also expose students to real situations and problems, in which sometimes the powerlessness of staff and board director may be all too apparent. As, for example, when ASA experienced a chronic lack of room space but lacked funding to lease commercially available office space. Students quickly appreciate the reality of such situations and become drawn into discussions about strategies the agency might adopt, and may even provide fresh perspectives on problems. For example, one student influenced developmental planning by writing a short piece about equal opportunities policies, to provide evidence of her understanding of anti-discriminatory practice in relation to barriers (such as language) that people may experience in accessing advocacy services. She was asked to present this policy proposal to the team meeting for discussion and the proposal was subsequently pursued at a board meeting. There was a consensus that the student had identified a real issue that needed further development.

To facilitate students' learning through such experiences, ASA has found it useful to develop a practice curriculum (Doel *et al.* 1996) as a way of making explicit and systematic those aspects of knowledge, values and skills that a student must address. This encourages students to reflect analytically on their experiences, to make links with teaching from university and generate their own understandings from the specific experiences from which they may then be able to generalize and transfer to other experiences and settings.

One student was able to build on her perceptive observations of the processes of the annual general meeting and relate this to organizational teaching she had had at university. She saw ASA as an open and democratic type of organization that may have to adopt more bureaucratic features as it expands. She commented:

> During supervision sessions I was helped to link the theory and knowledge which I had learned at university, such as organizational psychology and symbolic communication, to these real events. In a way, this placement enabled me to develop the skill of active reflection while working, which meant that supervision could be more in-depth, and as a result the learning was greater.

Other learning devices include a reflective 'learning log' (detailing reflections on the experiences of the placement), or well-researched commentaries on some aspects of the organization. The precise nature of these tasks would vary both according to the student's learning style (Kolb 1984) and to negotiation that takes place between practice teacher and student. Such written accounts can then be used as evidence to show the student has appropriate knowledge in relation to working in organizations.

Learning about the legal and social policy context

The acquisition of legal knowledge by social work students is vital, as all social work practice within the UK is grounded in a legal context. While on placement, students are expected to demonstrate that they are able to 'work in accordance with statutory and legal requirements' (CCETSW 1995, p.27).

What are the issues for students on placements in voluntary agencies that provide services to people with mental health problems? First, usually the contact between service user and worker takes place on a voluntary basis and is not required by statute. Hence, in some voluntary mental health placements students must look beyond the individual domain to the broader legal authority legitimizing the voluntary organizations' actions and services, for example, the Social Work (Scotland) Act 1968 or the NHS and Community Care Act 1990. ASA is able to provide a rich source of learning opportunities for students about legal knowledge and its application to practice. This is clearly related to ASA's function as a rights-based organization, whose clients approach ASA with a wide range of concerns or problems about other agencies and professionals. These clients approach ASA mainly because they want accurate information on their rights and how to secure these in practice from those agencies and professionals.

Some students may initially be anxious that a placement in a voluntary organization will not provide necessary learning about the law. As practice teachers we can demonstrate confidently that applying knowledge about the law is an essential feature of ASA's work. In the field of mental health, typically, clients will come to ASA with concerns about medication, about restrictions of movement under a mental health order and about standards of care from professionals. University teaching provides a sound legal knowledge; students are able to develop their understanding of law by drawing upon the expertise of experienced colleagues within the agency and by researching aspects of the law in relation to specific requests made by clients for information. This cognitive skill of searching for relevant legal information and evaluating its applicability to a situation provides excellent learning for students, as one student commented:

> Most of my learning in this area came from my statutory placement. However, within the advocacy project I was able to move beyond merely applying relevant statutory orders to being able to assist clients to understand the implications of the law in their situations.

This comment emphasizes that students have to use excellent communication skills in order to explain legislation through a dialogue to enable the client to understand the significance of the law for his/her situation. This can be quite a complex process and not so 'dry' or technical as it may at first appear. It includes the ability to listen to the client's story, to be supportive, to offer respect and unconditional positive regard. The case study concerning 'Eleonor' (see below) provides a more detailed example of the skills and processes involved in such sensitive communication. Some experiences such as these occur naturally in response to situations brought by students to supervision. In addition, it is useful formally to include within the practice curriculum (Doel *et al.* 1996) broader consideration of the function of law within social work practice. So, for example, a student may be asked to examine a paper about law in social work in order to evaluate critically the value of a rights-based approach to practice and more widely the value orientations associated with different pieces of legislation. Assessment tasks may also reinforce this requirement to analyse critically the relationship of the law to social work values and practice.

Closely associated with the need for students to understand legal aspects of social work is the requirement that they understand the social policy context of practice. Again, placement opportunities in the voluntary sector provide opportunities for students to understand the impact of social policy on individuals and the links between personal situations and political, policy and structural agendas.

One example of a natural opportunity to learn about social policy occurred at ASA when one student was asked to work with a group of long-term patients at a local psychiatric hospital, whose ward was being closed. The local health trust was proposing that their future care be provided by a private organization. Here, the student was able to make the connection between this proposal and the impact of governmental policy on community care, one of the objectives for the delivery of community care services being 'the development of a flourishing independent sector' (Department of Health 1989).

The student, as an advocate, was then required to work with each patient and their carers to make an informed decision about this proposal as an option. As an example of a proactive approach, this involved the mapping of a social policy theme at different levels, national, local, agency and individual. In the mental health field, this illustrates recent policy initiatives in Scotland, the development of the 'mental health framework'. It is, therefore, possible to ask a student to research such an area and produce a map or a flow diagram that highlights connections between a service issue, such as advocacy to the work of policy-makers, at different levels. Taking the example of advocacy, it can be understood at these different levels:

- National level
  In relation to Mental Health Framework for Scotland – 'Advocacy is a means of enabling people to have their views represented individually and collectively' (Scottish Office 1997).

- Regional level
  'An improved Grampian advocacy service for people with mental health problems should be available by April 2000' (Grampian Health Board 1998).

- Aberdeen city level
  Included in the plan for 1999:
  'To investigate ways of developing advocacy services including funding' (Aberdeen Framework Group 1998).

- Agency level
  The constitution of Advocacy Services Aberdeen has as its main objects: 'to provide an advocacy service for the residents of Aberdeen' and 'to assist such persons to obtain their full rights and privileges in relation to health, social work and housing issues'.

Thus, by developing such a conceptual map the student is able to understand that individual work with clients relates directly to mental health policy agreements and statements at city, regional and national level. This helps to render processes of strategic planning much more accessible and meaningful to the student.

A key element of social policy in relation to mental health continues to be the development of community care, illustrated by the shift of emphasis from hospital services to community based services, the decline in hospital beds, and an increase in the numbers of people with mental health problems living in the community. The impact of such transitions for individuals leaving long-stay hospitals, or currently being admitted to psychiatric hospital because of the 'severity' of their 'illness' cannot be overestimated. Students in mental health voluntary settings such as ASA learn directly of the impact of community care policy on individuals. They are able to learn through careful listening as to the experiences of people undergoing transitions of one kind or another.

Learning about user rights and empowerment

We have set the work of ASA's students within an organizational, legal and social policy context. We now examine how their learning experiences and opportunities to meet the DipSW competency requirements of assess and plan and intervene and provide services may be underpinned by a rights-based approach. The approach has two dimensions: one part relates to developing an understanding about how the student (on behalf of ASA) works with the client and provides advocacy services, while the other involves the student becoming aware of how a service user has been or is being treated by another agency.

Students at ASA are given the role of an advocacy worker, not that of a social worker, although through this experience they are expected to demonstrate social work competencies. As preparation for this role, students are inducted into ASA's policies and procedures including principles of advocacy and introduced to relevant literature on advocacy and empowerment (Braye and Preston Shoot 1998).

What pieces of work do students get involved in at ASA and how do these relate to rights and empowerment? The work is similar to that of a caseworker, in that it is office based and involves meetings with a client either in an office or in the person's home. Documents have to be produced, including a 'reasons for contact sheet' and a record sheet, just as in any other agency. Students regularly draft letters which clients wish to send to a service providing agency. Also, they provide balanced information about choices that a client may request and they may accompany clients to formal meetings organized by a statutory agency. Importantly, students spend a lot of time listening to clients telling their story – how they feel they have been treated including expressions of fears, frustrations and problems. Clients may speak of not being listened to by professionals. Developing a person-centred way of working is essential for students, as they learn how to attend to a person's thoughts and feelings arising out of a particular situation (see the case study about Eleonor). There is great value in students' listening carefully to words and phrases used by individuals and reflecting on the meaning for the person. It is by showing respect for an individual person that a student can initiate a process that may be empowering for the clients.

From this experience students derive some essential learning about the nature of professional power. Fortunately, students do witness good practice from some professionals, but sadly not all. Given the function of ASA as an advocacy project this is hardly surprising. Hence, students may witness incompetence such as the conference chairperson who does not follow basic guidelines in running an effective meeting or who demonstrates negative attitudes towards clients at meetings, such as a refusal to take seriously what a client has said. This is important learning for the student, to be drawn out and reinforced during supervision. The student should be able to articulate the difference between poor and competent practice. One device to facilitate this ability is the Critical Incident Review (Butler and Elliott 1985), in which students are asked to review, in writing, an incident that caused them concern and to include their thoughts as to how this situation could have been better handled. This encourages positive, strategic thinking, not merely the ability to highlight deficiencies.

In supervision, students are also encouraged to apply this learning to their own practice, role and relationships. They are required to examine what power they have as an advocate, what type of power this is and how they use it. The objective of this exploration is to encourage a student to develop awareness of power as a general issue and to make specific links with their own practice with service users. Such an understanding includes recognizing standards of interpersonal communication, sharing of oral and written information and the need to make explicit the role of the advocate. The practice teacher has a significant role here to act as a bridge for the student between the worlds of advocacy and social work, while recognizing their boundaries.

An exciting aspect of the student experience is how a rights-based approach can achieve results and secure services or amendment to services that the person has requested. Dalrymple and Burke (1995) have written about how the law can be used to empower clients, for example through the use of legal rights to obtain much needed services. Examples from students' work include the case of a service user who, with the assistance of a student, wrote to a psychiatrist requesting a change of medication, which was quickly granted. Another example concerned a parent of a teenager, diagnosed with a serious mental illness, who felt 'stupid' listening to a psychiatrist talking about her son's 'condition' and his drug regime. The ASA student embarked on an empowering process of listening to her, providing relevant information, affirming her rights as the son's main carer and discussing with her various approaches she could make to her son's psychiatrist. While this intervention continues, the client has indicated that the student's approach has given her confidence to approach the psychiatrist in her own right. Such a positive response to advocacy is confirmed by Sim and Mackay (1997), who found that it was empowering for clients to have their experiences validated and valued by another, especially where this leads to a positive result.

In witnessing such results, ASA students receive instant feedback about the efficacy of their actions. This is rewarding for the students and helps considerably to develop their confidence. This increased confidence is not restricted solely to their capabilities as an advocate, but transfers to their competence as a social worker and helps to crystallize, in the student's mind, a personal and professional identity – based on personal style, with clearly specified strategies to adopt as a qualified social worker.

Learning about the impact of life history

The setting here is less specific than in the ASA and is based on a range of residential establishments for people with mental health problems. The emphasis is on group and individual care, the creation of a non-invasive and therapeutic atmosphere, and the promotion of self-esteem.

The experience and expectations of students

Students are expected to undertake sensitive, gentle and patient interpersonal work with residents, building trusting relationships, improving residents' self-esteem, promoting their rights and enhancing their quality of life, in order to help them leave behind some of the 'baggage' of their past and make positive decisions and choices about their future. Hence, students are expected to demonstrate a value base which mirrors the central tenets of social work: questioning previous assumptions, recognizing and challenging discrimination, promoting dignity and choice, and building on the strengths of individuals (CCETSW 1995). Students learn the necessity of working as a member of a team, rather than acting completely autonomously, in order to ensure that the resident experiences a continuity of care. They are required to work as part of a wider team with professionals in a range of other agencies including health, housing and employment. In their university course, students will have begun to examine relevant theoretical frameworks to develop an understanding of

- the impact of individuals' life experience and emotional development on their current psychological functioning

- structural, contextual, societal and legal factors affecting individuals and their lives

- how to make relationships, formulate assessments and plan interventions, and the necessary skills involved.

Connecting theory to practice

The practice teacher has a key role in helping the student to locate their practice in a theoretical context. For example, knowledge, theory, and research about residential social work, keyworking and life space interviews are central to this placement. Theories, knowledge and research about task-centred intervention, groupwork, crisis intervention and psychosocial methods are also relevant. The use of life storybooks, life histories and reminiscence work are also of crucial relevance to these settings. The student will have been introduced to the concept of discrimination, and this will be their opportunity to gain an understanding of, and work to combat, the particular stigma attached to the label of being 'mentally ill'. This may be only one of several negative stereotypes which affect the resident's life and view of themselves.

The students will also bring knowledge and understanding about early development, attachment, the life cycle, loss and change and the impact of transitions. This will help them to begin to think sensitively about the residents and their experiences. From records and case histories, however fragmented some of these are, the students will also learn that the residents have often been separated for some years from the community, and distanced from managing their own affairs. Frequently, relationships with family and friends have broken down, and they are now expected to live with strangers, in an unfamiliar environment. Clients too, will be aware of being assessed and trying to prove themselves competent, not unlike the students.

In the case description that follows every care has been taken to protect anonymity. It is an amalgam of different settings and students. It does not therefore reflect specific practice in any one setting, the practice of any one student, nor is it the history and situation of one service user. All the knowledge and research theory mentioned in the case study was discussed in detail within supervision using appropriate textbooks. Reflection was encouraged by the use of written process recordings, and detailed verbal accounts of client contact. Regular direct observations of student practice were a rich additional source of information on their work and their relationships with service users.

Eleonor

Eleonor was a young woman, who, as a result of a stroke during an unplanned pregnancy, had a residual weakness in her right side and difficulty walking unaided. She wore special thick-soled orthopaedic boots, loose clothes with velcro fastening, and asked to be taken in a wheelchair. She had a miscarriage in the wake of her illness, and there followed a long year of inpatient psychiatric treatment for depression. Her mental health gradually improved, enabling discharge to a residential facility in the community. By then, her family no longer visited, distanced by her stay in hospital and their own fear of her possible mental instability.

Eleonor wanted to leave the large faceless ward, with its reduced staff levels and low levels of individual attention. However, when leaving became a reality, she was unsettled by how much she wanted to stay in the safe and predictable world where little was expected of her and her routines were prescribed. The assessment of her needs, made shortly after her arrival in the small residential community based home, resulted in a care plan. This included, with her full agreement, an expectation that she make regular efforts to walk. Care staff felt positive about this, because she would have greater independence, and mobility is valued as a goal in many residential settings. Despite the plan, Eleonor seemed to avoid walking exercises and staff became disappointed at her unwillingness and felt worn down by her demand for help. For Eleonor, the initial excitement and buoyancy created by the move had been replaced with misgivings, unexpected, renewed sadness about the baby she had lost and a sense of missing her family. It was a crisis, and recognized as such by staff.

Her keyworker understood that Eleonor needed increased individual attention, and the student, as co-keyworker, was given a role in befriending her. Eleonor formed a real attachment to the student, and thought her wonderful – perhaps reflecting responses suggested by crisis theory. She became quite dependent on the student's company, which involved pushing Eleonor in her wheelchair on request, at times to local shops and at other times around the building itself, from bedroom to dining room and back. This seemed to contravene the original plan of encouraging her to walk.

Throughout, the student was encouraged by her practice teacher to listen carefully to what Eleonor had to say, and continue to offer warmth and companionship, a non-judgemental and non-directive relationship. The relationship the student had offered had, as a central feature, 'unconditional positive regard'. Clough (1981) writes how self-esteem is undermined for a resident when others continuously expect more than that person can achieve at the time. The student also had a role in helping to empower Eleonor, as an advocate for the nature and level of care she wanted at that time.

Eleonor's mood was growing brighter, and this seemed to reflect her growing trust in her new 'home', the security it offered, and the positive experience of the new relationship with the student social worker. Life cycle theory (Gibson 1991) suggested to the student that this change in mood could provide a basis for increased autonomy. Certainly, safety and belonging underpins further development in Maslow's hierarchy of needs (Maslow 1970).

The student was encouraged by her practice teacher to think carefully about what Eleonor might be experiencing. They discussed the transition from hospital, the loss and change involved and the potential to evoke remembered losses from the past. They considered the severed attachments she had experienced and the emotional regression that was now a feature of her interactions. The student read appropriate bereavement theory including Marris's (1974) analysis of the need for predictability in our lives, a fear of new situations and a desire for 'homeostasis'. In supervision, they considered the applicability of crisis intervention, and the short-term but intensive nature of the support recommended. Uncomfortable with Eleonor's devotion to her, the student's understanding was increased by reference to object relations theory, which describes the strength, but short-term nature of such a 'needs-led relationship' within a wider psychodynamic perspective (Brearley 1991).

In these early days of the placement, theory led and informed the student's practice. As the student was encouraged to build a trusting relationship with Eleonor on the basis of active listening and empathic responding, she began 'where the client was', and not where she would have liked her to be. She arranged occasional outings for them both, and concentrated on making small improvements in Eleonor's quality of life on a day-to-day basis. Some opportunities had to be arranged: shopping trips to choose some new clothes required special transport, others came naturally in the course of the day's routines, like baking some scones for tea.

In supervision, the student and practice teacher discussed aspects of residential care, such as the importance of liaising with other staff and the role of the keyworker. The student attended and participated in unit staff meetings, and when shifts changed she helped explain Eleonor's feelings in order to promote wider understanding. She read records and continuation sheets, and she contributed to them. She was encouraged to read relevant literature on residential care, such as Clough (1981) and Mallinson (1995).

Clough (1981) highlights the importance of staff not linking their own self-esteem to residents' progress. In addition, he stresses the need for staff to have regular support and supervision in order to carry out their difficult and sometimes apparently unrewarding daily care tasks. He further describes how residents can try to please staff, and can be dutiful, thankful and accepting, expressing gratitude born out of dependency rather than choice. This may mean residents agree to care plans, which they do not fully endorse. Therefore, there might be some positive aspects to Eleonor's refusal to practise walking – as she was holding on to what she wanted to do.

The student continued to use supervision to explore theoretical frameworks and their application to the setting, including the concept of life space interviewing and the importance of using every opportunity for purposeful and therapeutic intervention. Applying her theoretical understanding, the student made some of the 'chores' pleasurable, shared activities. She also encouraged Eleonor's choices over what to wear, what she might eat, and how she would like to spend her day. In this way she increased Eleonor's self-esteem, promoted her identity as an individual and restored some of the 'boundaries of self' which institutional care had blurred. It was 'task-centred practice' (Doel and Marsh 1992) with a shared agenda and achievable goals, which would act as positive reinforcement and was a vehicle of user empowerment.

Gradually, over several weeks, Eleonor shared more with the student. She described her childhood, as an only child, as 'very special'. She talked of her parents' dismay at her pregnancy, the imagined retribution of her stroke and the overwhelming anger and grief at the miscarriage. The student understood the importance of hearing and accepting all of her pain and of validating her experiences. The separation from family and their decision to reduce contact had confirmed Eleonor's view that she was indeed worthless. Psychosocial work offered the opportunity for Eleonor to reflect upon her past, and in so doing she gained some insight into why she had angrily rejected out of hand her parents' more recent attempt to contact her. The student considered these reflections and wondered if Eleonor could begin now to move forward. One day, when they were in town, Eleonor asked to stop as they passed a shoe shop. Looking over her shoulder and gazing into the window along with her, the student heard her say softly:

'If I had shoes like that I would dance.'

At first, she failed to register the significance of her words. Caught off guard, and in her personal rather than her professional self, she agreed enviously that the smart, black, high-heeled shoe on its revolving platform in the window was a thing of beauty. Then she checked herself recalling Eleonor's exact words, thinking of her existing footwear, so lacking in femininity and symbolic of disability, the orthopaedic boots!

'Would you like proper shoes, Eleonor, especially made for you?'

There are few miracles in social work. More often there are keys to progress, if we stop to listen.

Conclusion

In this chapter we have tried to demonstrate the range of learning opportunities the voluntary sector in the UK can provide for qualifying students in social work. We have briefly outlined characteristics of the sector, in particular in relation to mental health services, and tried to convey the particular characteristics of practice teaching and student assessment requirements in the UK. More broadly, we have illustrated the range of learning and assessment opportunities for the DipSW offered by the voluntary sector.

In particular, we hope to have demonstrated what we believe to be a fundamental integration of learning in social work (and therefore of learning needs, opportunities and outcomes), in terms of personal, individual histories, life stories and experience of change, disruption and transition; structural influences on individuals of class, gender, race, disability and age; and social and legal policy requirements.

We have demonstrated the range of relevant social work interventions including advocacy, rights promotion, life story work, and life space work. In the case of Eleonor, the significance of the shoes will include understanding of the impact of her life history, life story work, life space work, empowerment and task-centred work. The voluntary sector provides a real opportunity to ensure students learn about a range of theories in relation to individual development, structural influences and intervention, and that they are able to evaluate these critically.

Our experience leads us to believe that service users in the voluntary sector are empowered to be confident in expressing their views, concerns and requirements of service provision. Similarly, students are empowered to gain confidence in their personal and professional skills and social work role. The practice teacher witnesses a growth of confidence and individual talent, as service users and students are confronted with addressing the challenge and opportunity of transitions in their lives.

In Scotland, the voluntary sector provides for social work students a holistic learning opportunity where attention to and understanding of users' life histories is combined with a promotion of users' rights and choices. Such a rich combination, we believe, is more likely to be offered in the voluntary sector than in the statutory sector, where assessment tends to focus on current need and is constrained by available resources and less on life history or empowerment.

We began this chapter by alluding to the complexity of the voluntary sector and the problematic nature of defining it. We end by suggesting that such definitional 'problems' are, in fact, a strength. The voluntary sector in social service provision is diverse and multipurpose, but it therefore encompasses policy development and innovation, practice innovation, practice and service delivery, which can be person-centred and holistic, specialized in relation to particular user groups and influential in promoting service user rights and empowerment. For social work students in Scotland, where the voluntary sector is committed to the continuum of education and training, voluntary sector placements provide highly skilled practice teaching by practice teachers and link workers, a clearly defined practice curriculum and the opportunity to integrate diverse but necessary strands of social work. This includes the legal, structural and social policy context, the personal impact of individuals' life histories on their current life course and stage, the range of relevant assessment models, the range of intervention strategies, the underpinning generic skills and an emphasis on user rights and empowerment.

We believe the complexity and diversity of the voluntary sector leads to the richness available for student learning opportunities.

Note

1   The six core competencies are communicate and engage; promote and engage; assess and plan; intervene and provide services; work in organizations; develop professional competence (CCETSW 1995).

Chapter Eleven

Culturally Competent Mental Health Services for Latinos
An Examination of Three Practice Settings

Kurt C. Organista, Peter G. Manoleas and Rafael Herrera

Introduction

The purpose of this chapter is to discuss and illustrate models and methods of culturally competent mental health practice with Latinos in the United States in three major practice settings: hospital-based outpatient clinic, outpatient private practice, and urban mobile crisis team. The chapter will proceed by providing brief socio-demographic and mental health profiles of US Latinos, followed by a framework of culturally competent social work and mental healthcare. The content of this chapter is designed to inform clinical social workers who now provide the bulk of mental health services in North America. Estimated at nearly 200,000, clinically trained social workers now exceed the combined number of psychiatrists, psychologists, and psychiatric nurses in the USA (O'Neill 1999).

Socio-demographic profile

The US Bureau of the Census (1994) projected that the Latino population would reach 31 million or 10 per cent of the US population by the year 2000. By the middle of the twenty-first century, it is estimated that one in four Americans will be Latino, as is already the case in major states such as California and Texas. Understanding the mental health and general social welfare needs of Latinos will require continued research to illuminate the considerable heterogeneity within this population with regard to acculturation histories, socio-economic status, risk and protective factors, etc.

For example, according to the US Bureau of the Census (1994), Latinos are composed of the following major national origin groups: Mexican (64.3 per cent); Puerto Rican (10.6 per cent); Cuban (4.7 per cent); Central and South American (13.4 per cent); and Other (7 per cent). These Latino groups vary with regard to socio-economic status and consequently in their risk for health, mental health, and social problems. For example, 7.3 per cent of non-Latino whites live in poverty as compared to 15.4 per cent of Cubans, 26.4 per cent of Mexican Americans, and 32.5 per cent of Puerto Ricans.

Latino mental health profile

During the 1980s and 1990s, a small but growing number of population-based, mental health surveys have been conducted on large, representative samples of US Latinos. These studies can be used to convey a profile of Latino mental health. For example, in the Mexican American Prevalence and Services Survey (MAPSS), Vega et al. (1998) assessed mental disorders in 3012 adults of Mexican background in California. This survey also examined the relation between acculturation and risk for mental disorders by comparing US born Mexican Americans, short-term Mexican immigrants (less than 13 years in the USA), and long-term Mexican immigrants (13 years or more in the USA).

Results of the MAPSS revealed a dramatic increase in mental disorders the longer that Mexican Americans have lived in California. That is, for nearly all of the major mental disorders assessed, there was a positive association between acculturation and risk for lifetime prevalence of diagnosable mental disorders (e.g., any affective, anxiety, or substance use disorder). For example, nearly 50 per cent of US born Mexican Americans met criteria for a diagnosable mental disorder as compared to 32.3 per cent of long-term Mexican immigrants, and 18.4 per cent of short-term Mexican immigrants. These findings led Vega et al. (1998) to conclude that acculturation has deleterious effects on Mexicans who migrate to the USA. Thus, culturally competent mental health services are needed to address the declining mental health of Mexican Americans and other Latinos in the USA.

Framing culturally competent practice with Latinos

Manoleas (1994) articulated a preliminary social work cultural competency model consisting of three key components that students can use to approach their varied practice settings:

- the knowledge base needed to understand sensitively the cultural and social experience of diverse ethnic groups

- the skill base needed to assess sensitively and intervene with problems affecting different ethnic groups

- the value base necessary for social work professionals to pursue cultural competence (e.g. understanding the cultural relativism of problem definitions and solutions, commitment to social justice).

In his latest articulation of culturally competent social work practice, Lum (1999) similarly includes skill and knowledge bases but begins his model with cultural awareness to refer to a social worker's personal and professional experience with diverse groups in society. The last dimension in Lum's model is inductive learning which refers to a lifelong process of continuous, open-minded (i.e. less deductive) learning about cultural diversity on the part of the social work students and professionals. Social workers are encouraged constantly to gather new information about diverse clients, both formally and informally, in order to remain culturally competent and relevant. Finally, Lum discusses the four dimensions of his model across both generalist and advanced levels of practice. The result is a four (dimensions) by two (levels of practice) model.

However, because the distinction between general and advanced levels of practice is frequently arbitrary, perhaps a more useful way to recast Lum's model is to consider his four dimensions across generalist and domain-specific social work practice. For example, culturally competent mental health work with Latinos requires both generalist skills, across different mental health settings, and specific skills within each different mental health setting.

Generalist Latino mental health practice

Because Latinos continue to underuse mental health service, while overusing health and religious services for emotional and interpersonal problems, outreach to where Latinos live, work, and seek help is essential. Hospitals, churches, and natural support systems within the Latino community are logical places in which to make Latinos aware of needed mental health services. To maximize success, mental health services need to be easy to access (both physically and financially) and must be culturally and socially acceptable.

With regard to assessment, it is important to consider presenting complaints within the cultural and social reality of Latino clients who are often likely to be immigrants, poorer than average, and occasionally confronted by acculturation related conflicts. Based on an ecological framework, Lum (1996) recommends assessment of psycho-individual reactions at the micro level and socio-economic impacts at meso and macro levels.

Interventions need to be congruent with the cultural and social reality of the Latino client. For example, the central role of the family in most Latino lives (Sabogal *et al.* 1987) makes family therapy a viable way of addressing a variety of problems, especially conflicts between couples or between parents and children (Falicov 1998). Short-term, problem-focused therapies also represent practical ways of responding to the pressing, low-income circumstances of many Latino clients as well as to their expectations of an active, educating, and prescriptive therapist. Given the western European and mainstream American values embedded in most forms of contemporary psychotherapy, intervention approaches often need to be modified to fit the Latino experience. At the same time, it is also necessary to work outside Latino culture by teaching clients new cultural skills that help them to function more fully in their essentially bicultural reality.

Practice setting I: hospital-based outpatient clinic

Psychosocial medicine and the treatment of depression

The Cognitive-Behavioral Depression Clinic at the San Francisco General Hospital provides outpatient mental health services to low income and ethnic minority medical patients. Because the clinic is located in the predominantly Latino Mission District, services have been designed to respond to the special needs of Latino patients who comprise about half of the caseload.

Latino patients are predominantly Spanish speaking immigrant and refugees with multiple medical, mental health, and economic needs. For this reason, mental health services have been blended with case management services which have been described in more detail elsewhere (Organista and Valdes Dwyer 1996). Social work students frequently co-lead depression groups in addition to providing case management to a caseload of group participants. This combination of training provides an excellent opportunity to assess and intervene with Latino client problems at both the psycho-individual (i.e. symptoms of depression) and socio-economic levels (e.g. addressing economic, vocational, and educational needs) as recommended by Lum (1996).

Outreach efforts

Obstacles to mental health services typically encountered by Latinos are decreased at the Depression Clinic by providing free (subsidized by research grants), hospital-based (available, accessible) services by linguistically and ethnically matched therapists (acceptability). In terms of outreach, primary care physicians and medical staff have been trained to recognize and refer patients suspected of depression. Clinic staff telephone patients to offer them a psychological evaluation for depression based on their physician's recommendation. Therapy is offered to patients that meet criteria for major depression. Persons with active substance abuse, cognitive or psychotic disorders, are referred out for appropriate services.

Psychosocial assessment

Psychological evaluations consist of a Spanish language clinical diagnostic interview. Not only do patients have the opportunity to describe their symptoms and their contexts, but also the conversational tone of the interview resonates with the manner in which Latino patients typically prefer to personalize even professional relationships and interactions. Social work interns conduct standard psychosocial evaluation of patients' general social welfare needs with special attention to common issues and problem themes observed in the local Latino population: level of acculturation and language needs; conditions of migration to the USA (e.g. fleeing civil war in Central America); socio-economic needs; lack of documentation in the USA, family stress and conflicts, etc.

Intervention issues

Patients are offered 16 weeks' group cognitive behavioral therapy and six months of concurrent case management by Spanish speaking, bicultural Latino clinicians. Because case managers serve as group co-facilitators, they can reinforce the lessons of therapy while simultaneously working on outside issues. Trainees working with Latino clients are usually Spanish speaking Latinos themselves. However, non-Latino trainees that speak Spanish can also learn to work effectively with Latino clients with more intensive supervision (e.g. co-leading groups with supervisor, reading background literature on the Latino mental health).

Cognitive behavioral therapy (CBT)

During group therapy, student therapists address three areas: cognitive-restructuring, activity schedules, and assertiveness training to improve mood. A treatment manual developed at the clinic is used to guide therapy. Patients are given their own copy of the treatment manual that contains outlines of each session and forms for doing homework which is assigned and reviewed each week.

Behavioral interventions to improve mood include increasing pleasant activities, especially those that cost little or no money (such as walks in the park or beach, having a cup of coffee in a charming café, etc.). Trainees are taught that modifying mainstream interventions to fit Latino culture requires being aware of values embedded within them. For example, implicit in behavioral activity schedules is the mainstream American value of needing to 'take time out for one's self'. This message is de-emphasized in group because it can run contrary to the traditional Latina gender role that places family needs first. For this reason, patients are initially encouraged to increase pleasant activities with family members. Eventually they are encouraged to do some solitary activities with the culture-based rationale that they will be able to return to family responsibilities with more energy, better mood, less resentment, and so on.

Pleasant activity schedules overlap with assertiveness training in which female clients are often taught how to set limits with demanding family members or to negotiate greater sharing of household and child-rearing responsibilities with husbands. As with activity schedules, it is imperative to recognize that traditional Latino culture may be at variance with assertiveness as a modern, western, and particularly North American concept and technology.

Traditional Latino culture emphasizes communication that is polite, personable, non-confrontational, and deferential (especially to people of higher status based on age, gender, social position); this is especially true for women who are taught to be submissive to men and to subordinate their needs to those of the family (Comas-Diaz and Duncan 1985). For these reasons, assertiveness training must be modified to fit Latino culture.

Trainees are taught that treatment goal is to 'biculturate' patients by introducing assertiveness as an American skill that is effective in areas like work, school, agency settings, and interpersonal relationships. The value of familism is invoked by encouraging patients to model assertiveness for their Latino American children. Student therapists are taught to stress culturally compatible aspects of assertiveness such as the emphasis on communication that is not only direct but also honest and respectful. Assertiveness is introduced as a way of improving family relationships and not just advancing individual independence and accomplishments as is typically stressed in the literature.

Based on recommendations by Comas-Diaz and Duncan (1985), cultural factors that interfere with assertiveness are discussed including strategies for responding to negative reactions from spouses and other family members. For example, patients are taught to preface assertive expressions with phrases like 'With all due respect' (which acknowledge status differences) and to respond to negative reactions with explanations like 'Expressing my feelings makes me feel less resentful and closer to you.'

Cognitive restructuring begins by teaching patients the difference between helpful thinking that improves mood and adaptive behaviors and unhelpful thinking that does the opposite. Next, cognitive restructuring is streamlined by teaching a 'Yes, but ...' technique in which patients are taught that much of their depressed thinking amounts to half-truths about problems in need of elaboration and completion. That is, rather than label thinking as distorted or irrational, students are taught to support and challenge patients simultaneously by encouraging them to seek the full truth in their problems. The following vignette illustrates the applications of CBT techniques to common problem themes in the Latino clinic population.

Esperanza

Esperanza was a middle-aged Mexican immigrant who spoke only Spanish and had lived in the USA for the past 15 years with her husband and 3 children, the latter now married with children of their own. Esperanza was referred to the Depression Clinic by her primary care physician whom she visited regularly for health problems which included arthritis and beginning stages of diabetes. Esperanza met full criteria for major depression disorder which she attributed to stressors at home such as being expected to take care of her grandchildren frequently (without pay), and difficulty getting her husband to share in household chores, even though she also worked outside of the home at a local restaurant. She was also becoming increasingly afraid of becoming diabetic.

Participation in group therapy helped Esperanza to realize that her problems were not unique. Another woman with diabetes shared how she had adjusted her Mexican diet and how insulin kept her illness under control. When Esperanza expressed that she was afraid of such a serious disease that could result in amputations and death, cognitive restructuring was used both to empathize with and challenge Esperanza by telling her that she was partly

– but not totally – correct. We then asked her to complete the following sentence which we wrote on the chalk board:

Yes, diabetes is a serious illness that can result in amputations and death *but...,* to which Esperanza and other group members responded: ...but not for everyone and...but not if you control it with diet and medication. The clinical case manager assigned to Esperanza arranged and attended a meeting with her and her doctor to clarify diet and medication issues.

With regard to taking care of the grandchildren, we used assertiveness training to help Esperanza express to her married children that she did not feel appreciated and that if they were saving money on babysitters, that they should pass on some of that savings to her. After role-playing, Esperanza was still unable to carry out the goal outside of therapy because deep down inside, she believed that it was her duty as a grandmother not only to babysit, but also to enjoy it! Group members reminded Esperanza that she worked outside the home too and that she had less extended family in the USA to help her shoulder this responsibility. She was eventually able to talk to her children, who were forthcoming with compensation and finding alternative childcare a couple of times each month.

Asking Esperanza's husband to help more with household chores was another matter. The group discussed how things were different in the USA, how both wives and husbands need to work outside the home as well as inside the home. We then role-played with Esperanza ways of being assertive and respectful by prefacing assertive communications with 'With all due respect', and 'Would you permit me to express a concern to you?' We also prepared Esperanza for ways of dealing with predictable negative reactions by having her role-play her husband and then responding to negative reactions with statements like 'If you do not permit me to express my concerns, I am going to keep them inside and feel distant from you when I would rather feel close to you.'

Behavioral contracts were used to encourage Esperanza to resume reinforcing activities in which she used to engage before feeling so depressed (such as going out to lunch with friends, English classes, etc.). Each week we checked the activity schedules of group members along with their daily self-ratings of mood. Group members were taught to be aware of the relation between mood and reinforcing activities, assertive communications, improved relationships, and countering depressed thinking with cognitive restructuring. By the end of 16 weeks of group, Esperanza's depression was mild and manageable.

Evaluation

With regard to evaluation, our clinical/research team has just completed an auspicious report on a randomized trial comparing group CBT with and without clinical case management (CCM) (Miranda *et al.* 2000). Participants in this study were 199 clients (77 Spanish-speaking Latino, and 122 English-speaking, predominantly non-Latino white and African American clients). Results revealed less dropout from the group CBT plus CCM condition versus group CBT alone. Group CBT plus CCM was also more effective in decreasing depression and improving functioning *but only for Spanish-speaking Latino clients*. This latter finding is consistent with past research by Sue *et al.* (1991) demonstrating that ethnic and/or linguistic matching in therapy improved retention and outcome for Latino and Asian clients low in acculturation, but not for Anglo or African American clients. Miranda *et al.* (2000) concluded that Latino clients were the most responsive to group CBT plus CCM because of their special linguistic and other acculturation related needs.

Practice setting II: outpatient private practice

This section examines culturally competent private outpatient psychotherapy services for Latinos. It builds upon the framework offered earlier in this chapter by introducing the concept of clinical algorithms. A clinical vignette, broken up into snapshots taken at different times in the development of the therapeutic process, will be used to illustrate possible uses of algorithms in clinical practice.

The concept of clinical algorithms

The term 'algorithm' comes from mathematics where it refers to any method of solving a problem by repeatedly using a simpler computational method. This sequence is often displayed in the form of a flowchart in order to make it easier to follow. Clinical algorithms have been used in medicine for some time to guide physicians in the clinical decision-making process by employing decision tree formats. At each branch of the decision tree, the clinician is confronted with either a yes-no question, or a question that defines parameters such as laboratory values. The algorithm model described here is new and is intended as a conceptual guideline for providing culturally competent psychotherapy to Latino clients.

The case study below is intended for social workers in outpatient settings. The case is that of a 40-year-old woman seen over a period of time of about one year. The setting is a private practice outpatient office, the majority of referrals being from public (Medicaid) sources.

Latino culture versus service delivery imperatives

Effective assessment and psychotherapy with Latino clients flow from the successful engagement and subsequent relationship between the therapist and the client (*personalismo*). For example, trainees are taught to address clients with formal forms of address until a greater level of familiarity warrants less formality. Similarly, one is taught not to presume to ask intrusive questions of Latino clients until a comfortable level of familiarity and trust has been reached. While bicultural Latino trainees are usually adept at enacting such a relationship protocol, Anglo trainees usually need to be made aware of their own culture-based tendency to more quickly enact a task-oriented relationship protocol in therapy (e.g. beginning treatment with 'What problem brings you here?').

There have been a few attempts to study the ways that Latino clinicians work with Latino clients or patients. For example, Manoleas *et al.* (2000) surveyed 65 Latino mental health clinicians working in outpatient agency settings specifically geared to serving Latino clients. It was generally found that the techniques of such clinicians were based upon a mixture of standard clinical techniques and Latino cultural traits. The general focus on family context and functioning as well as a strong advocacy role were significant findings, along with a widespread notion of contextual assessment of all problems or pathologies.

Hayes-Bautista and Chiprut (1998), in an ethnographic study of the ways in which Latino physicians dealt with their Latino patients, concluded that doctor interactions with the patients were guided by specific cultural adaptations of clinical algorithms (e.g. personal, informal manner while taking medical histories). This paradigm also appears to be useful in helping social work students conceptualize culturally competent outpatient psychotherapy with Latino clients.

Engagement algorithm

The first clinical algorithm we will call the engagement algorithm (see Appendix A for a flowchart illustration). It can be used to teach social workers in training how to assess their ability to engage and develop a positive clinical relationship with the Latino client. The initial issue involves an assessment of the client's language dominance, or the best language for the first clinical encounter. In the case of monolingual Spanish or Spanish dominant clients, clinicians must decide whether or not they are linguistically competent enough to conduct the assessment and therapy. If yes, they continue; if no, they refer the client.

Amparo

Amparo was referred for treatment by the local county mental health program. In the initial session, it was immediately clear to the therapist that Amparo was very fluent in English. As the session proceeded, it became apparent that much of Amparo's intense and unresolved feeling had to do with the constant belittling and insulting she received from her mother. The things the mother said to Amparo were all in (Mexican) Spanish and the client relayed these comments with the same intonation, intensity, and language used by her mother. The therapist decided that his facility with Mexican Spanish was good enough not to lose any of this significant clinical data.

The second issue in the engagement algorithm is an assessment of the client's comfort level in counseling/psychotherapy. If the client appears to have been socialized or acculturated to this mode of help seeking, the clinician may proceed. If not, some psycho-education about what therapy is and how it works is in order.

The third part of the engagement algorithm involves an assessment of the client's degree of acculturation, or, more properly stated, transculturation, which refers here to the ease and comfort with which the client can alternatively function and be in both Latino and Euro-American cultural situations. This involves learning about the client's country of origin, dates and circumstances of immigration if applicable, and which generation the client represents in the USA. Having done this, clinicians must ask themselves if they feel culturally competent to deal with the many issues presented by the client's background such as social class, colorism (discriminatory treatment by other Latinos based on skin shade), national background, racism, immigration turmoil, or intergenerational conflict (Falicov 1996). If the answer is yes, the clinician proceeds to decide upon an initial modality for treatment. This decision involves whether the client is the 'identified patient', and should be treated as such, or if couple or family therapy is indicated from the outset. If clinicians feel they are not culturally competent to deal with the issues presented by the client, they can consult with a colleague or supervisor who is or refer the client to another clinician.

Amparo was born and raised in south Texas. Her early years had been spent being raised by a variety of extended family members from both sides of the US/Mexico border. She reported memories of early abuse of both a physical and psychological nature, as well as a very difficult childhood which involved being sent to harvest onions in the fields at a very early age. She had been raised in a fairly strict Catholic way, but upon becoming a young adult, embraced elements of Chicano Nationalism, clearly identifying herself as Chicana rather than Mexican American. She also came to believe in such traditional things as elements of *santeria* and *espiritismo*, which refer to different spiritual beliefs embracing elements of the supernatural, communication with the dead, and other ways of explaining her current realities. The therapist felt sufficiently knowledgeable about these issues to have a feel for the complex roles they played in the client's life, the development of her identity, and the conflicts they presented.

The fourth part of the engagement algorithm involves an assessment of the client's stated request. First of all, Latino clients may present with stories of severe environmental threats such as violence, or possible violence, children in gangs, threats of deportation, discrimination, or serious acculturation problems. They may present with serious physical and or psychological problems. They may also present seeking support, guidance, or help negotiating the dominant culture. Clinicians must also consider whether or not the client is mandated to attend therapy. If clinicians feel equipped to deal with the stated requests, they must then select appropriate interventions such as a supportive approach, a problem-solving approach, a cognitive-behavioral approach, case management, etc., and decide which 'ancillaries' to involve including teachers, clergy, etc., or agencies such as child protective services, probation, or other treatment agencies.

When the clinician eventually asked Amparo what he could do for her, she responded with, 'Help me accept my diagnosis'. When he asked her what this was, she said 'Bipolar' . After questioning her further, the clinician suspected that what she might be saying was 'Help me understand and fully accept the complexities of who I am'. In this case, culturally competent psychotherapy required that the clinician respond to a variation of the client's stated request, and to sufficiently explore its basis (e.g. psychiatric history).

The fifth part of the engagement algorithm has to do with gender and/or sexual preference. Supervisors and trainees must confront the question of whether or not they are able to deal with the culturally conceptualized gender or sexual preference issues. This could mean a Latino clinician attempting to deal with the issues of a sexually abused Latina client, an Anglo clinician with a client whose issues stem from their psychosexual development in a Latino family, or any clinician's attitudes towards gay or bisexual issues. If unsure, the clinician should pursue consultation or supervision as needed.

Finally, in the development of the clinical relationship, clinicians must ask whether or not there are shared cultural metaphors for communicating. If yes, they can seek common terms and metaphors for communicating. If the answer is no, clinicians may seek strategic personal self-disclosure in order to foster *personalismo* and discover shared idioms for communicating.

> Amparo would frequently find herself confronted with vivid memories of past abusive situations. At these times she was overcome with an almost uncontrollable anger, and felt like she could find relief only by drinking alcohol to the point of almost passing out. She sometimes referred to these as episodes of *coraje* [rage] which in the moment seems to consume the entire being and spirit. The therapist subsequently referred to this whole cognitive chain of events as *coraje*, and they both knew precisely what was meant. Social workers in training can learn to cue into such culture-based forms of expression and to use them to join with clients.

Assessment algorithm

The assessment algorithm specifies a hierarchical order in which problems can be assessed. It suggests data that should be gathered and how it can be ordered as well as which, if any, interventions may come first. An initial question trainees can be taught to pursue in the assessment algorithm is, 'Is the client and/or the client's family currently stabilized?' Latino clients and their families confront enormous pressures in US society that may result in personal and/or familial instability. The second part of the assessment algorithm involves identification of problems and symptoms using standard intake and assessment guidelines (psychiatric history, current stressors, etc.). After a standard mental status assessment is completed, the clinician decides whether in fact symptoms are present which constitute a formal psychiatric diagnosis, a culture-bound syndrome, problems in living, or whether no pathology is present.

> Amparo initially came to the therapist with the diagnosis of bipolar affective disorder given to her by the Euro-American psychiatrist she was seeing for medications. The therapist's culturally sensitive diagnosis ran more along the lines of post traumatic stress disorder with depressed features and recurrent *coraje*. She had been given an antidepressant, an anti-manic agent, and some benzodiazepines to be taken as needed for her strong emotional episodes. The *standard* stance of the therapist would have been to work with the client on

medication compliance and immediate abstinence from alcohol as primary treatment goals. Instead he chose to work actively with the psychiatrist on the diagnostic formulation and medications. The anti-manic agent made Amparo feel groggy and crazy. The therapist was concerned that Amparo was incorporating chronically crazy into her self-image in such a way that it was causing her to feel desperate and like giving up. The psychiatrist agreed to reconsider his diagnosis and discontinued the anti-manic agent with good results. The therapist was also concerned about habituation to benzodiazepines and the psychiatrist agreed instead to give her Navane which she had successfully used in the past during emotional outbursts. She continued to take her anti-depressants but the need for *any* medication decreased, and her self-medication with alcohol decreased to zero as therapy proceeded.

Treatment algorithm

A basic consideration in the selection of treatment methodology is addressing whether the main problems and/or symptoms the client is experiencing are attributed to proximal or distal causes. Proximal causes are those which exist currently, or in the recent past. Distal causes can be recurrent, intrusive memories, or cognitions of distant past events that result in currently serious symptoms. If the clinician decides that proximal causes are primary, then the indicated interventions may be crisis management of recent or current events, or a present oriented problem-solving approach. If the clinician decides that distal events are most causative, then a more dynamic approach to addressing the current or intrusive memories, cognitions, or patterns can be used. Trainees are taught that the process of culturally competent therapy with Latino clients will inevitably involve the flexibility on the part of the clinician to switch back and forth between standard psychological interventions, utilization of culturally based strengths, and the employment of advocacy, problem-solving, and psycho-educational approaches.

With each issue confronted, the clinician must decide if culture, in this case, the Latino experience in the USA is contributory or not. This involves an ongoing interpretation of issues within the cultural context. For example, the clinician may need to decide if a particular client's reaction to an environmental situation is within the limits of expectation given the discrimination the client has experienced, or if it is out of proportion and therefore symptomatic. Residual anger, if present, may be understandable, yet so crippling as to render the client socially impaired. Work with Amparo involved managing her outbursts in the short term with the objective of her not engaging in self- or other destructive behavior while in one of her episodes of *coraje* (proximal causes managed). At the same time, ongoing work was also oriented towards decreasing the frequency and intensity of the outbursts in a permanent way (distal causes addressed).

Basic cognitive restructuring techniques were employed with Amparo. The cognitive chains of intrusive memories leading to strong emotional flooding and alcohol binges were reduced in both frequency and intensity. There was, however, another major issue which needed to be worked through. The therapist was apparently one of the first men in Amparo's life to treat her with consistent *respeto* (respect) and demand nothing in return. Late night drunken calls to the therapist's voice mail professing her love for him decreased in frequency, and eventually she was able to discuss these issues in the session while sober. The therapist had shared very little of a personal nature with Amparo up to this point. He decided to tell her simply that he was involved with someone. This brought an enormous sense of relief to Amparo, who was able to abandon fantasies of a personal relationship with him and accept the limits of the clinical relationship. Flexibility in the therapist's clinical orientation was thus required as he momentarily shifted from his basic cognitive approach to address the transference issues more characteristic of a psychodynamic approach, but with culture-based self-disclosure.

Final comment on algorithms

The division of the outpatient therapeutic process into the three algorithms outlined above is for conceptual convenience. There is no question that each of the algorithms is present in the other two to some degree. For example, the engagement process and the relationship development processes continue throughout the duration of the therapy. Similarly, ongoing assessment and refinement of problem definition continues throughout the course of therapy.

While a new idea, clinical algorithms may provide trainees with a convenient conceptual method of thinking about culturally competent outpatient psychotherapy services for Latino clients. Algorithms have the advantage of being able to integrate clinical, cultural, and environmental factors into a unified method of planning and implementing treatment. While not intended to be a cookbook approach to providing services, they provide a systematic way of making clinical decisions. At the same time algorithms offer us a way of determining which elements of culturally competent services may not be available, and therefore warrant referral to another clinician.

Practice setting III: urban mobile crisis team

This section briefly describes the operation of a county operated mobile crisis team headquartered in Oakland, California, and its affiliations to the rest of the mental health system, and other public and private agencies and law enforcement. A crisis intervention practice model is presented followed by a case vignette from the mobile team's files to illustrate how the model can be utilized in a culturally sensitive manner to the benefit of Latino clients.

Development of Alameda County's crisis response team

In California, and as part of the Behavioral Healthcare system, the county of Alameda operates a community crisis response team (CCRT) that began service in 1987 as part of an effort to reduce the number of unnecessary visits to the county's psychiatric emergency room, decrease unnecessary hospitalizations, and as a means of providing non-emergency mental health services to a growing homeless population. Another objective of the program was to bring mental health services to others in the community that, for a variety of reasons, do not seek mental health services. Because few services are available after 5:00 p.m., police typically receive numerous calls that are not law enforcement related.

One of the primary responsibilities of the crisis team is to assist patrol officers with the evaluation of situations that seem to be mental health related. The broad scope of what can be construed as 'mental health' gives the crisis team the opportunity to intervene in situations that would otherwise go unnoticed. Such opportunities, unfortunately, present themselves quite often in the Latino neighborhoods, where poverty, discrimination, substance abuse, domestic violence, unemployment, language barriers, and other high stress indicators, increase the risk of the development of mental health problems.

Practice setting and operation of CCRT

The CCRT operates out of a county crisis clinic between 3:00 p.m. and 11:00 p.m. and is staffed with two clinicians, one of them an experienced and licensed social worker. The other team member is usually a junior clinician or social work intern. Interns of various backgrounds have trained in this practice setting, each with distinct advantages depending on their demographic profile (e.g. Spanish or Chinese speaking, female gender, African American, etc.).

The team begins the day by reviewing any calls for services for the day, as well as outstanding calls from the previous day. This is followed by a trip to the police department to check out radios and attend a police 'line up' which is essentially a brief meeting of all officers starting their duty shift to inform them of anything not routine that may be occurring in the city.

The crisis team operates from a vehicle and the evaluations and interventions may be done in a wide range of settings such as (literally) on the streets and back alleys, hotel rooms and lobbies, stores, bars, hospitals, gas stations, private homes, apartments, and back yards, to name a few. It is not unusual for the team to perform an evaluation through the partially opened window of a police car while the client sits handcuffed in the back seat.

The police radio gives clinicians on the team rapid access to police, fire, and county sheriff departments, as well as paramedics, ambulances and other emergency agencies. The mobile crisis team also makes full use of cellular phones to communicate with clients and their families, case managers, child and adult protective services and other agencies. The team can also refer clients to contracted outpatient clinics and can arrange for medication evaluations, ongoing mental health or substance abuse services, and maintains affiliations with other human service agencies.

Affiliation with other agencies

Alameda County's mobile team has formal and informal agreements, for the mutual referral of clients, with several agencies including some that are Latino focused with names like Clinica de La Raza (the People's Clinic) and Casa del Sol (House of the Sun), located in predominantly Latino neighborhoods. The crisis team also responds to requests for evaluation and mental health intervention of the residents of local homeless shelters and can also access shelter beds for individuals or families in need of lodging. In addition, the mobile crisis team has also developed affiliations with local universities as a training site for graduate students specializing in mental health.

Although Latinos underutilize mental health services, they frequently come to the attention of the mobile crisis team because of its inherent outreach orientation. Many of the clients seen by the mobile team are individuals with no current or prior psychiatric history but who find themselves in a crisis situation because of psychological, psychosocial or economic stressors. While the interventions are flavored with the background and orientation of the team members, trainees are taught that the overreaching approach is an eclectic one.

Crisis intervention model

Student trainees are taught that the mobile crisis team's approach to intervention follows a flexible six-step model outlined by Gilliland (1982):

1. defining the problem

2. ensuring client safety

3. providing support

4. examining alternatives

5. making plans

6. obtaining client commitment.

These steps are encompassed in the assessment of the situation and include an estimate of the severity of the crisis, and the client's current emotional well-being and ability to cope after the team has gone. Next, students are asked to consider how working with Latinos may require modifications of the above steps to account for significant cultural deviation from the norm. For example, the definition of the problem in the case of a 22-year-old Latina college student (still living at home) needs to take into account, not only her opinion but also the opinion, wishes and expectations of her parents. Steps to establish support should consider the extended family to which many Latinos belong, but should not assume that every Latino has one or that it is available. Exploring alternatives and obtaining commitment for a given plan of action may need modification to ensure that it is not incompatible with the client's usual help seeking pattern including the use of such natural support systems as the church, natural healers, and other helpers. A Latino man once made a memorable remark that illustrates how different tools can be put to work toward the same goal. Initially reluctant to see a psychiatrist for insomnia because he was already consulting a *curandero* (Mexican folk healer), he said, 'OK, I once had to use a burro and an ox to get my car out of the mud.'

The monitoring of police radio calls, while on duty, enables the crisis team to respond to calls that would otherwise not come to its attention (e.g. traffic accidents, fires, assaults and robberies). Training students to listen with a 'culturally sensitive ear' makes possible interventions such as the one described in the vignette.

Consuelo

While walking home from the bus stop Consuelo is robbed with a gun pointed to her face. She is pushed into the ground and kicked by her attacker. The call goes out on the police radio as a routine 'take a report' on a robbery call. The officer assigned radios back with a request for a 'Spanish speaking officer' and mentions that the victim, calling from home, is 'very tearful and upset'. Her tears and the crying of young children can be heard over the radio. Even though there was no request for the mobile crisis team to assist, the team announces, via police radio, that it will respond to the call and that it will be able to assist with the translation for the report.

Consuelo is a 28-year-old woman from El Salvador who came to the USA in 1990. She is separated from her unemployed husband and is the mother of a toddler and two elementary school age children. While she works, the children are taken care of by her mother-in-law. The children are restricted to the small apartment in a neighborhood that is not very safe due to a great deal of drug dealing. Consuelo had just been robbed of $600 from a paycheck she had just cashed to pay her overdue rent. While she only suffered minor bruises, she was very tearful, hyperventilating and trembling. She is hardly able to speak as she tries to comfort her frightened children.

In addition to the four living in the apartment, there are now three police officers and two members of the crisis team at the door. While the police are there by request and in their official capacity, the civilian crisis team is not. The student observes the supervisor who politely explains to Consuelo and her mother-in-law (before entering their apartment) that the crisis team members are not police, that they work for Alameda County, and are there to help translating. Next, the student is introduced as the other Spanish speaking team member. Consuelo appears relieved at being able to speak in Spanish and, apologizing for the lack of seating space for everyone, invites the team in. Once invited, the team informs the officer in charge that the team can stay as long as it takes, and recommends Consuelo be given the opportunity to tell what happened first and answer specific questions needed for the report later.

While Consuelo tells her story to the student in the kitchen, the supervisor comforts the children by playing with them in another room, occasionally checking in to observe the interview. This allows Consuelo to tell what happened with less concern that her words and tears will further upset the children. The student is taught to use her recollection of events as an on-site emotional debriefing and indicator of her coping capacity. Consuelo, as it turns out, is not unfamiliar with guns and violence. As a child in El Salvador she was once forced out of her home at gunpoint with her family and witnessed the beating of an older brother with a rifle butt. Based on her story and symptoms, a tentative diagnosis of Acute Stress Disorder is made by team members.

In addition to the intervention provided that day, which included a call to the landlord by the team to explain what happened and lend credibility to the story (the landlord granted an extension), the following was initiated: Consuelo was to be seen the next morning by a Spanish speaking clinician at the crisis clinic, a referral was made for the mother-in-law for a variety of medical complaints, and efforts were started to look into the possibility of alternative childcare for the children.

Training issues

Many factors, perhaps not so evident in the vignette, that were necessary for the events to have unfolded as well as they did can be used in the training of culturally responsive mobile crisis clinicians:

- The crisis team leader knew that it was unlikely that a Spanish speaking officer would respond to the call given the shortages of Latino officers in the local police force. This points to the importance of training interns to be aware of services available to Latinos in the practice setting and in general.

- Assuring the client that crisis team clinicians are 'not police' reassured the woman in the vignette that her immigration status was of no concern to them and facilitated cooperation.

- The crisis team could also count on the fact that, because of the language capability, both the police and the client would welcome their participation.

- Knowledge of what many immigrant and refugees from Central America and Mexico have experienced and witnessed was also helpful in establishing contact with the client and in formulating a possible diagnosis and treatment plan.

- Trainees are taught to create the opportunity for clients to tell their story at their own pace, in their native language, and out of earshot of others (e.g. children) in order to maximize fuller expression.

Potential and limitations of this practice model

Because there are no empirical data to suggest a 'best practice model' for Latinos, crisis team students are taught that crisis intervention and other short-term, problem-focused interventions should be the foundation of mental health services in general, and particularly to Latinos and other ethnic minorities (Herrera 1996).

Even though popular and available in many communities, no systematic studies regarding the effectiveness of mobile crisis service have been done. One survey found that service systems collect insufficient data on the effectiveness of mobile crisis services making evaluation difficult (Geller, Fisher and McDermeit 1995). How effective mobile crisis services are depends on how 'effectiveness' is defined. There are countless situations in Latino communities where mobile crisis services can bring relief, comfort, and hope by providing skillful and culturally sensitive crisis intervention services to individuals and families. The reduction in the number of unnecessary emergency room visits or hospital day stays are all worthwhile outcomes that can be included in formulas to measure program effectiveness. However, students are also made aware that the outreach focus of mobile crisis services can uncover tremendous unmet needs resulting in an increase in demand for services.

Conclusion

This chapter discussed and illustrated culturally competent mental health services to US Latinos in three different practice settings: hospital-based outpatient clinic, outpatient private practice, and urban mobile crisis team. While these three different domain-specific practice areas require different specialized skills (e.g. cognitive-behavioral therapy for depression, crisis intervention, etc.) they are similar in employing general practice approaches that are sensitive to Latino culture and experience in the USA. That is, each practice setting employed outreach efforts, bilingual and bicultural clinicians, and a flexible blend of mainstream intervention strategies and culture-based values, communication and relationship protocols.

For the sake of student training, the first practice setting emphasized how standard cognitive behavioral techniques can be modified to fit Latino culture and experience by making students more aware of the mainstream values underlying them. The second practice setting emphasized a flowchart-like, algorithmic approach to mapping engagement, assessment and treatment strategies in outpatient therapy. The third practice setting illustrated how Latino sensitive mobile crisis services could work with other city-wide public services (e.g. police, mental health) to meet Latino mental health and other social service needs. Together, these three practice areas provide valuable learning opportunities for students and represent viable variations on the theme of culturally competent mental health practice with Latinos in the USA.

APPENDIX A

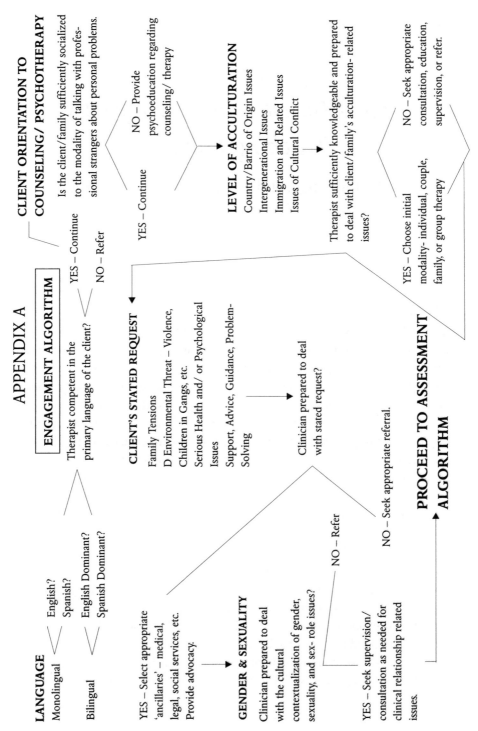

CLIENT ORIENTATION TO COUNSELING/ PSYCHOTHERAPY

Is the client/family sufficiently socialized to the modality of talking with professional strangers about personal problems.

YES – Continue

NO – Provide psychoeducation regarding counseling/ therapy

LEVEL OF ACCULTURATION

Country/Barrio of Origin Issues
Intergenerational Issues
Immigration and Related Issues
Issues of Cultural Conflict

Therapist sufficiently knowledgeable and prepared to deal with client/family's acculturation- related issues?

YES – Choose initial modality- individual, couple, family, or group therapy

NO – Seek appropriate consultation, education, supervision, or refer.

ENGAGEMENT ALGORITHM

Therapist competent in the primary language of the client?

YES – Continue

NO – Refer

CLIENT'S STATED REQUEST

Family Tensions
D Environmental Threat – Violence, Children in Gangs, etc.
Serious Health and/ or Psychological Issues
Support, Advice, Guidance, Problem-Solving

Clinician prepared to deal with stated request?

NO – Seek appropriate referral.

PROCEED TO ASSESSMENT ALGORITHM

LANGUAGE

Monolingual — English? Spanish?

Bilingual — English Dominant? Spanish Dominant?

YES – Select appropriate 'ancillaries' – medical, legal, social services, etc. Provide advocacy.

GENDER & SEXUALITY

Clinician prepared to deal with the cultural contextualization of gender, sexuality, and sex- role issues?

NO – Refer

YES – Seek supervision/ consultation as needed for clinical relationship related issues.

Chapter Twelve

Field Instruction in University Teaching Hospitals

Marion Bogo, Judith Globerman and Lorie Shekter-Wolfson

Introduction

University teaching hospitals in Canada have employed social workers since early in the twentieth century. While primarily committed to the education and professional preparation of physicians and nurses, hospitals affiliated with universities have, since the 1980s, become more receptive to the education of allied health professionals, including social work. Social work departments became an expected part of these hospitals and developed innovative quality field education programs. A range of varied and complex inter-organizational activities between the social work departments in the hospitals and schools of social work emerged. More recently, economic and social conditions have led to dramatic changes in the Canadian healthcare delivery system and in the structure of these hospitals. This in turn has had a significant impact on social work practice and field education.

A conceptual framework was developed to study the inter-organizational factors in university–field partnerships that affect field education (Bogo and Globerman 1995). We use this framework in this chapter to describe and analyse several models of social work field education that have been used in university teaching hospitals over time. A university teaching hospital model, the Teaching Centre, developed in traditional hospital organizations. As hospitals restructured from functional to programmatic organizations, the Teaching Centre model of education was adapted. As social workers gain more experience in these programmatic organizations new models for field education are emerging. The analysis of these models reveals that field education is both enhanced and constrained by the organizational mission, structure and ways of operating. As the hospital changes, the field education model must change. An understanding of restructuring and the new organizational form is critical for social work educators in the university and in the field who remain committed to offering quality field education programs in teaching hospitals.

History of social work in Canadian hospitals

The Canadian healthcare system is a publicly funded and administered universal system that is designed to provide accessible healthcare services to the Canadian population. University teaching hospitals are designated by the government to provide medical education for physicians-in-training. Social work in these hospitals typically began with the employment of a few social workers to assist in managing destitute patients. As the appreciation for the impact of psychosocial factors in health, illness, recovery, and coping grew, more social workers were attached to various hospital units, and a social work department was formed with a director. These departments hired individual social workers and had responsibility for establishing and maintaining professional practice standards through supervision and continuing education. Social work field education was primarily offered by individual social workers who chose, for their own personal and professional reasons, to offer a practicum to a student. Since each social worker was accountable to the director of social work, this decision was not made in isolation. While directors saw the social workers' primary role as service provision they were generally supportive of field instruction and of offering practicum to a modest number of students, rarely greater than four.

Since the mid-1970s university affiliated teaching hospitals have expanded their educational mission from medicine and nursing to include allied health professions such as social work, physiotherapy, occupational therapy and speech pathology. Recognizing the mission of university affiliated hospitals to contribute not only to patient care, but also to teaching and research, university and hospital administrators began to expect that all professions be fully engaged in education and to some extent, in research. At the University of Toronto this new institutional culture in the university and in the hospital created a favorable context for the matched university and hospital educators, including social work, to consider a systematic approach to the education of social work students in hospitals. There was a need to expand field education beyond the ad hoc individual 'apprentice' field instructor initiated model. In consultation with faculty members, the social work department in each university teaching hospital organized a coherent field education program and each institution's program became known as a Teaching Centre.

The analytic framework

In an attempt to study the key components of the relationships between schools of social work and field agencies that contribute to quality field education, a conceptual framework was developed, pilot tested, and continues to be used in current research (Bogo and Globerman 1995, 1999). We shall use this framework to describe and analyse the conditions under which the Teaching Centre model, as well as the other models discussed here, work best. The four key components of inter-organizational relationships are

- commitment to education
- organizational resources and supports
- effective interpersonal relationships between the organization and the university
- collaboration and reciprocity.

The Teaching Centre model

The Teaching Centre originated in traditional health organizations under the auspices of social work departments. The model functioned effectively in 16 teaching hospitals for 15 years between 1978 and 1993. The director of social work or a senior social worker was jointly appointed by the setting and the school of social work as an educational coordinator and given institutional authority to coordinate a field education program for social work students. The program was reflective of both generic social work and the hospital's specialized knowledge and practice. Currently only four of these teaching hospitals have this model in place. The analytic framework will be used to describe and analyse the original Teaching Centre model.

Commitment to education

The social work Teaching Centre functioned in university affiliated teaching hospitals with strong ties to the university and an appreciation for the importance of education for all health professions. With this institutional sanction from the hospital board of directors and senior hospital administration, the social work department committed itself to a continuing long-term partnership for the purpose of furthering both social work education and practice. While the initial focus was on field education, as will be discussed later, this partnership expanded to include continuing education and development and testing of social work practice knowledge through research activities. This commitment was formalized as part of the mission statement of the social work department.

Under the leadership of the educational coordinator, a field education program was developed to reflect the generic competency expectations of the university and the specialized competencies of hospital social work, especially in the particular organization (Bogo and Taylor 1990). Initially this involved the articulation of theoretical and clinical knowledge for social work practice in the specific hospital. The field education program aimed to prepare graduates for direct practice with individuals, families, and groups, interprofessional team work, and practice on behalf of clients and consumers (which includes advocacy, coordination, resource development, program and policy change).

Furthermore, this process of identifying the theoretical, empirical and ethical foundations of practice assisted in preparing social workers to become field educators as they helped students understand the integration and application of knowledge and values in their practice (Bogo and Vayda 1998). A conceptual model provided a general framework from which specific elements of an educational program were derived. It guided the selection and development of a rich and diverse set of learning opportunities. For example, a general knowledge competency for all social workers in health is knowledge of the bio-psychosocial aspects of health and illness. The field instructor must determine where and how the student will learn this knowledge regarding the population on their specific unit. In addition to direct clinical and community practice, the field instructor identified learning resources and opportunities such as bibliographies, research projects, and community and voluntary associations. Typically, all Teaching Centres offered seminars for social work students to teach specific substantive knowledge and skills relevant to the populations, problems, policies and context affecting that setting. Seminars also used students' and workers' cases and projects to demonstrate a range of practice approaches used in the hospital. Peer consultation and interprofessional learning experiences about organizational issues were offered to develop attitudes and behaviors conducive to team practice. Students were also assigned to social workers and other professionals for specific practice learning, to supplement assignment to the primary social work field instructor. Students were welcomed at department meetings and staff development events and often had access to interdisciplinary teaching programs so that the entire range of teaching and practice activities of the hospital were framed as resources to promote student field education.

Organizational resources and supports

The educational coordinator helped select, train and support new field instructors. Student learning contracts and evaluations were reviewed and the educational coordinator consulted with students, field instructors and the faculty field liaison (tutor). Priority was given for the educational coordinator to participate actively with the school of social work in the development of curriculum policy and field practicum programs, for example in the design of continuing education for field instructors. Finally, the most supportive hospitals provided financial support and encouragement for educational coordinators and field instructors to attend and present their teaching practice at conferences about field education.

The Teaching Centre flourishes when there is congruence between the espoused mission and the kinds of resources allocated to education. Our research found that in the traditional hospital with a functional department and director of social work, the educational coordinator is given the mandate to provide an educational program. Success depends on the educational coordinator having authority, autonomy and resources, such as time, space and budget, and the department expecting and supporting social workers to be involved as field instructors (Bogo and Globerman 1999). When field instruction is valued and supported it is included in the social worker's job description and performance evaluation, with the time allocated for student educational instruction taken into account. As well, a high priority is attached to university and hospital activities for training new and continuing field instructors. The educational coordinator role is supported so that the incumbent has the resources to develop the program and has opportunities for self-development as an educator.

Interpersonal relationships

In the Teaching Centre model the educational coordinator was the major link between the hospital and the university's faculty field liaison and over time assumed the major educational and administrative functions of that role. In the initial phase of developing the Teaching Centre there was frequent and intensive interaction between the educational coordinator, the field instructors, and the faculty field liaison as they experimented with the program and processes of field instruction. As the hospital social workers gained more experience in field education, they gained confidence in their program and their ability to respond effectively to issues of teaching and learning in the field. The major role which educational coordinators and field instructors played in ensuring the success of the field program was appropriately recognized and institutionalized by the hospital and the university.

The educational coordinators formed a Teaching Centre committee with teaching faculty responsible for the field practicum. This committee functioned as a steering committee, identifying issues of concern for Teaching Centres and field education in general, and providing leadership for recommendations for curriculum in class and field and for continuing education for field instructors. Working relationships between the hospital social workers and the faculty field liaison are deepened with familiarity and knowledge of each others' respective expertise. A division of roles and authority develops that empowers the educational coordinator and the field instructors to function as colleagues with teaching faculty in social work education.

Collaboration and reciprocity

One aim of the Teaching Centre model was to use strong inter-organizational relationships to contribute to the development and testing of social work practice knowledge. University-based staff interested in the health field could collaborate with social work departments in hospitals to promote and develop practice research in areas of mutual interest. A number of innovative projects were developed. Ten health settings and four teaching faculty members formed a health research consortium to conduct research on high risk screening (Bergman *et al.* 1993; Bogo *et al.* 1992). As well, two hospital-based social work research units were developed to promote practice-based research, research education, and the dissemination of new knowledge.

These collaborations further strengthened working relationships and joint activities in education were planned such as joint sponsorship of visiting lecturers, a social work study group from Japan, and a retreat on the future of social work in the health field. Hospital social workers were invited to lecture in university courses and teaching faculty were invited to present their research at the hospitals. A special post-masters practice research course was developed for social workers at the Teaching Centre hospitals. Finally, audio-visual library collections of the hospitals and the school of social work were made available for use by both organizations.

In conclusion, the Teaching Centre model thrives in the context of a strong, central department in university teaching hospitals that are committed to an academic mission of patient care, teaching and research for all professions. The structured model recognizes and promotes the expertise of the social workers as practitioners and teachers of that practice. The university faculty facilitates their development as field educators and collaborates with them in practice development and research. Students benefit from the rich range of educational experiences in organizations committed to high standards of care, continuous learning, and inquiry.

The changing context for social work in Canadian hospitals

During the 1990s, the Canadian healthcare system experienced dramatic changes, with reduced funding from the federal government to the provinces for health and social services. As a result, to combat the fiscal crisis in healthcare, new models of hospitals have emerged. The Canadian healthcare system continues to be primarily a publicly funded healthcare system organized according to the principles of the Canada Health Act 1984, ensuring universality of healthcare (Government of Canada 1984). However, hospitals have been granted the ability to generate their own income to make up for reduced federal and provincial transfers. They are also granted incentives from the government for reducing costs and increasing community participation.

Hospital restructuring has included re-engineering, downsizing, mergers, shifts to managed care, product-line management, program management, patient-focused care and learning organizations. The common characteristic is change – change from something, it is argued, that was inefficient and ineffective, to something that is cost effective and efficacious (Tidikis and Strasen 1994).

The particular models used mainly in teaching hospital reorganization in Canada have been shifts from conventional, bureaucratic hospital organizations to facilities that place the patient as the central focus. The continuum of hospital organization put forward by Charns and Tewksbury (1993) has been, for the most part, a useful summary of the organizational shifts in Canada. At one end of their continuum is the bureaucratic, traditional hospital with a hierarchical organizational model in which services are centralized and organized by functions. It is usually depicted as a pyramid with the decisions coming from the top down. Canadian social work departments in teaching hospitals have traditionally been organized in this way, with a director of social work and social work supervisors or team leaders responsible for the standards of practice and supervision of front-line social workers. These bureaucratic organizations with functional departments are virtually disappearing in Canada.

At the other end of the continuum are programmatic hospital models, characterized by a flatter hierarchy. They are organized in a number of ways. In fully program management models discipline-specific departments such as social work are eliminated with the rationale that if the departments do not exist, a layer of organization will be eliminated resulting in a decrease in bureaucratic hyperbole, cost reductions, and a greater focus on the patient (Globerman and Bogo 1995; Globerman, Davies and Walsh 1996; Lathrop 1993). Departmental functions (for example, discharge planning, psycho-education, family and patient support) are no longer 'held' by a social work department and are instead managed by the programs as they see fit (Browne *et al.* 1996; Herbert and Levin 1996).

In the new models one sees a new language, which includes concepts such as patient-focused hospitals, shared governance, and multiskilled professionals. The operating principles of these organizations are collaboration, coordination, interconnection, shared resources, synergy and integration (Lathrop 1993; Leatt *et al.* 1997; Peters 1992). One also sees new types of structures which include professional standards councils. The object of these transformations is to reorganize care to focus on the patient so the care is more directly linked to the mission of the teaching hospital, and is more cost effective. The implication is change from something that placed focus on the functional departments themselves, (and their concern with their own disciplines such as 'social work'), to a focus on the patient, seen now as the consumer or the customer. The logic underlying these shifts is that hospital organizations have lost sight of their purpose and must regain this by turning the focus away from internal processes towards their consumers (Beatty and Ulrich 1991; Flower 1992; Moore and Kelly 1996).

In these new teaching hospital organizations, the programs are usually organized by patient disease such as 'cancer' or by some patient characteristic, such as 'ageing'. The social workers are hired, evaluated and fired by the program director who is usually a physician but can be a representative of any of the health disciplines. There are no functional departments responsible for performance appraisals, continuing education, discipline standards, supervision, staffing or discipline accountability. In relation to social work student education, the Teaching Centre no longer exists under the auspices of a social work department and has virtually become obsolete in most programmatic organizations. The continuation of the educational components of the Teaching Centre depends, in most cases, on individual social workers' opportunities and personal commitment.

The program management model

The transformations in hospitals have had dramatic effects on discipline-specific or functional departments such as social work and consequently on social work field education. By the year 2000, 12 of the 16 hospitals had moved to programmatic organizations and a number of these hospitals had merged. The program management model for field education evolved as a response to restructuring. Where field education was organized centrally in teaching hospitals through the Teaching Centre model, field education in many teaching hospitals in program management has shifted back to the earlier practice of being dependent on individual social workers' motivation to provide field education without the formal support or sanction of a department of social work. The overarching result has been fewer field practicum offerings, isolated students in large teaching hospital settings, fewer trained social workers to provide student education, and reductions both in student seminar programs and in connections between the university to the field. Some settings have attempted to develop creative responses to the changing teaching hospital organizations, such as one field instructor supervising multiple students who are then linked to other staff in the organization for cases and projects. Although this model is practised in many settings, the difference in restructured programmatic organizations from the traditional model is the lack of social work 'overseers' resulting from the absence of a departmental structure.

Reorganization of teaching hospitals has also had an effect on social workers' decisions to educate social work students, in that medical student education retains primacy in teaching hospitals. The result is that interdisciplinary programs in university teaching hospitals perceive social workers' contributions to medical student education as more valuable than student education of social work students. The university's response has been to emphasize the importance of education of allied health disciplines (of which social work is one) but the value to the program directors (who are usually physicians) of multidisciplinary education has yet to filter down from the senior administrative levels.

Commitment to education

In teaching hospitals organized by program, the provision of field education is now entirely at the initiative of the individual social workers who must also gain the support of their team by presenting a rationale for the use of their time to the program director or other program staff. Without a discipline head to advocate on behalf of the discipline, the commitment to education has, in many instances, become reduced. With competing demands on social workers in programs, some of which include educating other multidisciplinary team members, individual social workers' motivation to provide field education may not be enough to entitle them to offer a practicum.

Our current research with programmatic teaching hospitals has determined that after several years of these discipline-specific structures social workers tend to stop attending them and identify more strongly with their teams than with their professional disciplines (Globerman 1999; Globerman *et al.* 1996), though in a number of programmatic organizations social workers have organized themselves into peer consultation groups and developed standards councils, continuing education committees, and student education groups. Social workers have also joined together across institutions to provide shared social work student seminar programs. This has addressed issues related to time away from programs and shrinking resources.

Organizational resources and support

Organizational support for student education in programmatic models varies. As we have noted, in these organizations interested social work field educators must form some sort of collective voice and compete with other allied health disciplines for office space, computer and office telephones, and financial support for field education activities. Where programmatic organizations have maintained educational coordinators these individuals rarely have authority over other social work staff and program directors and do not have education budgets. The programs determine if resources are allocated for field education of social work students.

The change in commitment to education and lack of resources allocated to education for allied health disciplines demonstrates a shift in authority from senior hospital and university administrators to the program level. Interestingly, this shift has not occurred with the education of medical students where senior administrators continue to enhance and provide leadership for innovative and quality medical education. The perceived reduction in the importance of education for all health professionals coincided with reductions in government funding of hospitals and hospital restructuring. In the face of diminishing resources choices are made about what to support and what to eliminate or neglect, exposing underlying organizational priorities.

Interpersonal relationships

Communication between the hospital social workers and the university is compromised in programmatic organizations. With reduced authority to organize functionally, disciplines such as social work rely on individual social workers to connect with the university. In many situations when the Teaching Centre educational coordinators are maintained, they are appointed solely by the hospital rather than dually with the university. In some cases the educational coordinators rotate at the setting.

These models have resulted because the hospitals have redefined the educational coordinators from providers of educational leadership to recruiters of social workers as field instructors. In many cases these individuals are not senior social workers as previously defined in the Teaching Centre model, and are instead line workers with no authority in respect of their social work peers who self-select to offer a social work student practicum. The resulting communication with the university is frequently an information exchange and not a collaboration between the school and the educational coordinator to develop and champion a quality field education program. Where previously the university field liaison was closely involved in working with the educational coordinator to provide a quality field educational experience for a group of students, the current educational coordinators most frequently find themselves functioning as conduits of information.

Collaboration and reciprocity

Reciprocity with the university is reduced in programmatic organizations because it is no longer about cooperation with a collective of social work educators with a strong voice sharing concerns, ideas, programs and research with university colleagues. More frequently, the university field coordinators are familiar with one or two individuals and weakly linked with the full complement of social workers at the hospital who could provide field education. The reciprocal relationships are, therefore, likely to be more restricted and joint programs and projects are rare.

The emerging context for social work in Canadian hospitals

With the advent of more conservative governments in Canadian provinces, and thus reductions in funding to health and social services, social workers have found themselves under increasing pressure to practice social work 'reactively'. Attending professional councils has been seen as a low priority while caseloads and program expectations have soared. With no encouragement and no rewards for professional development and with increased expectations to discharge patients more quickly and to provide services not traditionally seen as social work, student education and professional development are occurring less frequently. New models of practice are emerging which emphasize cross-training and in some cases have social workers carrying occupational therapy and nursing roles (such as transferring patients, portering patients, admission paperwork). Social workers have to learn the business of social work such as workload and quality indicators, and resource allocation that historically were the responsibility of the social work directors. With reductions in social work positions and development of product-line management, social workers find themselves practising in unfamiliar ways. Allegiances to programs have strengthened while to the profession they are weakening. It is likely that this may be a transition state, since social workers are keen to survive and provide the best practices.

Although the shifts to program management have been pervasive, the consequences for student education of the allied health disciplines were not initially evident. In many cases, the social workers experienced increased autonomy, self-direction, growth, and empowerment when freed from departmental supervision and authority (Globerman 1999). However, in the current climate in Canada, social work in hospitals and social work student education reflects competing demands and split allegiances. Our current research indicates that a combination of the complexity of the cases with which social workers are involved, the new models of practice and the lack of priority to provide student education, have all conspired to lessen the numbers of student practicum offered when compared to the Teaching Centres.

Meeting the challenge: the evolving model

Let us consider the four key components of inter-organizational relationships between universities and field settings to review how might we meet the challenges that we have described in this chapter (Bogo and Globerman 1995).

Commitment to education

In the past, commitment to educating social work students was sustained by the convergence of individual and institutional factors. Individual social workers' altruistic desire to give back to the profession (Bogo and Power 1992) was supported by the social work department's commitment to professional development. Without social work directors and educational coordinators the social workers in hospitals are looking to the university to have a greater presence and provide more consultation on practice first, and field education, second.

Organizational resources and support

Sharing of university resources, in the form of library and computer resources, practice expertise and research support, is likely to help to ground the university's presence in the teaching hospitals. Through developing interorganization relationships that begin with the social workers' practice needs and not primarily the university's needs for practicum sites, the social workers will be more inclined to experience a stronger desire to participate in field education. In the Teaching Centre model institutional commitment to social work student education was part of the hospital's mission, and resources and support were allocated to achieve institutional goals. In program managed settings, while education of all professions remains part of the stated institutional mission, resources are not necessarily allocated accordingly and the university and the hospital need to exchange resources to meet their mutual needs (Bogo and Globerman 1999). The university can develop a range of resources that enhance social work practice in the hospital. From this base it is hoped that new relationships will develop and strengthen and social workers may more readily participate in offering field education.

Interpersonal relationships

Success in the future for social work education in teaching hospitals will depend on the ability of the university to develop interpersonal relationships at two levels of the hospitals: with senior hospital counterparts and with individual social workers. The more the university initiates activities and advocates for all health professions, the more the hospital administration will promote, from the senior levels, education of allied health disciplines. Moreover, the more the university gives to individual field instructors, the more social workers will free up time and resources to provide field education. University-led involvement will enhance interpersonal relationships which, in turn, will feed social workers' commitment to education.

Collaboration and reciprocity

In the current context, the hospitals' involvement with the university is no longer institutionally governed and driven. The organizations' values have shifted from a clear, evident focus on education and research for allied health disciplines to reflect an increased value and focus on practice outcomes and output. As a result, social workers no longer look to the university as a place to be supported in field education, but instead are looking for an exchange of resources to help them do their jobs and to practise well. In these circumstances, student education is more likely to occur when social workers experience inputs from the university that support the social work enterprise. In programmatic hospitals this has been reflected in the request for continuing education from the university regarding new models of practice that reflect the current hospital reality. Head of the list of requests from workers to the university is for short-term, evidence-based practice models that sustain them in the new teaching hospitals.

Universities in Canada are also experiencing budget cuts and have fewer staff to provide consultation and liaison to the field. However, what is clear from our research is that the university must take a more active role in initiating relationships at senior levels in the hospitals as well as with individual social workers. A useful initiative at the University of Toronto is the formation of a Council of Deans and Directors of a range of health science professions who have developed greater influence within the university and with the hospitals by speaking with one voice. The council was able to identify common issues and advocate for solutions regarding professional education in university teaching hospitals. One successful innovation is the creation of positions for senior health professionals, paid for by the university, to develop and coordinate professional education in six designated university teaching hospitals.

An interesting dilemma has emerged with respect to social workers in program managed hospitals where there are no social work supervisors. Social work has traditionally placed great value on 'supervision' and the monitoring of practice. At the same time social workers see themselves as 'systems thinkers', best placed to understand and work in teams, and to empower others to help themselves. However, as strong team players, social workers can struggle to champion themselves and, instead, join with the interdisciplinary teams where their 'work' happens (Globerman 1999). The university has a role in initiating interorganization relationships and collaborations to raise the profile and credibility of the profession in the hospital. In the traditional hospitals, all disciplines struggle with allegiances; however, if disciplines in university teaching hospitals are to maintain their professional standards, develop new practice knowledge, engage in continuous quality improvement, and evaluate practice then discipline-specific bodies need to exist with power and authority of office.

Conclusion

Social work education in Canadian university teaching hospitals has been transformed over the past half century. An analysis of factors that contribute to quality field education and enriched inter-organizational relationships and activities reveals that the organizational contexts of these hospitals is critical to understanding successes, reversals, and future challenges.

The Teaching Centre was developed in a resource-rich climate where social work in hospitals was valued, had high profile and was expanding. Social work educators and their hospital counterparts initiated the development of the Teaching Centre model as an ideal type. With the advent of program management and the dismantling of social work departments, social workers in hospitals and the university found themselves reacting to organizational changes as they tried to maintain the Teaching Centre model.

In order to meet the challenge of providing quality field education in the evolving teaching hospitals without central social work departments, university social work educators must devote considerable time to building relationships with key personnel at various levels of the hospitals. Academic leaders in university social work programs must be visible and active with hospital administrators. They must champion social workers and advocate for resources for social work education within the hospital. Joining with other allied health professions in the university has proven to be an effective way of obtaining resources for education. The challenge for the university and the field is to find ways for the university's educational and research resources to support the practice needs of hospital social workers. Field instruction might then be viewed as an exchange for continuing professional development.

Organizational values, priorities, and administrative models either support or constrain the possibilities for social work practice and education. Furthermore, the hospital's organizational context is itself a reflection of the broader societal, economic, and political climate. Social work educators need to use a broad contextual analysis of the relationship between the universities and the hospitals to anticipate and relate to continuing change in the health sector.

Keywords

Class setting

academic setting; alumni; classroom; college; educational establishment/ institution; laboratory setting; polytechnic; school of social work; training institute; university

The class setting refers to the *educational establishment* or *institution* where students pursue their learning of social work. The learning in the class setting is associated with the *academic* content of the programme. This might take place in a *university, polytechnic, training institute* or *college,* and at postgraduate or undergraduate level. The word *college* is often used as a general term for the higher education setting. Graduates from any higher education course are sometimes referred to as *alumni.*

Colleges sometimes run classes which attempt to simulate the conditions found in practice in the agencies by creating a *laboratory setting,* often using skills training and video feedback.

Competencies

accreditation; assessment; core competencies; evaluation; learning goals or objectives; outcomes; performance criteria; portfolio; practice assignment; practice competence

Social work students are *assessed* to see if they are competent to practise as social workers. The most important, generic competencies are often referred to as core. The practice teacher/field instructor usually makes a recommendation of 'pass', 'fail' or 'refer' for further work, or 'satisfactory'/'unsatisfactory'. In the UK the notion of 'ready to practise' or 'not yet ready to practise' is developing.

Methods of assessment on placements vary. The most common has been a report written by the practice teacher/field instructor, which includes material and *practice assignments* by the student, such as case notes. There is an increasing move towards *competency-based assessment,* in which the *learning objectives* are carefully detailed, and the student is expected to provide evidence of achieving these objectives, using agreed *performance criteria*. In the UK, practice teachers also face an assessment if they wish to gain the Practice Teaching Award; they are assessed by means of a *portfolio*, which is a collection of evidence of ability collected over time. This system of *accreditation* is designed to guarantee the quality of practice learning available to the students.

The word *evaluation* has slightly different meanings; sometimes it may imply a formal measurement of a student's abilities at the end of placement, which is its most frequent use in North America. Alternatively, it may refer to the quality of the placement (and the whole programme), in terms of helping students to achieve their *learning goals*. This is its most frequent usage in the UK.

Consultant

> mentor

A consultant or *mentor* usually refers to a person with considerable experience and expertise who is able to provide consultation and teaching. On training programmes for practice teachers/field instructors, a consultant or mentor helps the trainee to develop skills in practice teaching/field instruction.

Field liaison staff

> academic staff; class (-based) teachers; college staff; course teacher; director of fieldwork; educators; faculty; joint appointments; lecturer; placement team; tutor; university staff/teacher

The members of the *academic staff* at the educational establishment (university, college, etc.) who are responsible for communication with practice teachers/field instructors are called field liaison staff. This responsibility might fall to one or two people, or be shared by a team of academic staff (*placement team*). The person with primary responsibility is sometimes designated the director of fieldwork. The term *tutor* is used in the UK for the members of the *university staff* who are responsible for providing college support to the student while on placement.

There are other *class-based teachers*, members of the academic *faculty*, who are not involved in the student's learning outside the educational establishment. In the UK and Australasia the general term for all college-based teachers, whether involved in liaison or not, is *lecturer*.

Some educational establishments have set up *joint appointments* with social work agencies, so that one person (or sometimes a pair) works partly as a member of faculty at the university and partly as a practitioner in the agency.

Pedagogue

In the Anglo-Saxon world there is no professional group known as pedagogues. In much of the European mainland this is a distinctive profession, working with people in ways that are analogous to social work, but with a greater emphasis on the educative functions.

Placement

> block placement; concurrent placement; curriculum; educational contract; field education; field instruction; field practice; field practicum manual; field programme; fieldwork; learning contract; long-arm supervision; placement of particular practice; practice curriculum; practice learning; practice teaching; practicum; student supervision

A placement is the period of learning that occurs when a student is located in a social work agency. What the practice teacher/field instructor does is referred to as *practice teaching, student supervision* or *field instruction;* what the student does is referred to as *practice learning.* Although these terms refer to the same activity, there are subtle differences between 'supervision', 'instruction' and 'teaching'.

Practicum is a North American term which brings together the notion of the placement and also what is to be learned on placement – the *practice curriculum.* The practice curriculum might be designed for general learning about social work, or for a *particular area of practice* (such as child protection or mental health).

Most programmes provide a placement handbook or *field practicum manual* to guide the placement, with information about the *educational contract* or *placement agreement* which spells out expectations for the placement and the areas of practice to be learned (the curriculum), the regulations for assessing the level of a student's practice competence, and the placement arrangements, such as the required number of meetings between university staff, practice teachers/field instructors and students during a placement.

Arrangements for placements differ; for example, the overall length and whether they are *block* (five days a week) or *concurrent* (some part of the week on placement and some part in the class setting). Some students receive teaching from *long-arm* (off-site) *supervision* from a practitioner who is not their day-to-day supervisor.

Note: the term 'placement' is also used by practitioners to refer to children placed in foster care, residential care, etc.

Practice

This word is used in an alarming number of different ways in social work. At its most general it refers to what social workers do (social work practice), and therefore what students need to learn to do. As a result, 'practice setting' (see below) refers to the learning on placements in social work agencies. However, some social work programmes have 'practice classes' which are based in the educational setting; these are designed to prepare the student for the practical work on the placement.

As a verb, 'to practise' can mean either to be engaged in social work practice, or to be rehearsing something – as in 'practice makes perfect'. Practice is also often put in apposition to theory, with a notion that theory takes place in the educational setting and practice in the work setting. This division is being increasingly challenged.

Practice setting

agency; client; employer; enterprise; establishment; field; institution; organization; practitioner; public welfare department; service organization; service setting; service user; social department; social office; social welfare agency; statutory agency; voluntary (non-profit) agency; welfare agency; workload

The practice setting refers to the *agency, enterprise* or *organization* where students pursue their learning about social work practice (in other words, where the student is placed). The agency's principal responsibilities are to its *clients* and *service users,* not the student. The professional staff in the agency are often called *practitioners,* and it is some of these practitioners who have students placed with them, as well as continuing to work with their *workload* of clients or service users.

Examples of types of practice setting are residential care, group care, community work, children and family settings, hospitals, probation and correctional work. Generic terms for these kinds of agencies include *public welfare departments, social (services) departments* and *welfare agencies;* those with specific legal responsibilities, such as child protection, are called *statutory agencies. Voluntary agencies* are those which are non-governmental and do not make a profit. Agencies are sometimes characterized as urban or rural, and described along ethnic lines (for example, a Maori agency).

The practice setting is often summarized as the *field* – a location for social work students to learn about social work practice. The field is most frequently used to distinguish from the *class* as a setting for learning.

Practice teacher / field instructor

field educator; field supervisor; field teacher; long-arm supervisor; specialist or semi-specialist practice teacher; student supervisor; student unit organizer

These terms all refer to the person in a social work agency who has the responsibility for teaching a student who is placed there. The term *field instructor* is usually found in North America; in the UK and New Zealand the term has changed from *student supervisor* to *practice teacher*. Just to confuse matters, in the North American context the term 'practice teacher' is used to refer to persons in the educational setting who teach classes in social work practice. In this book the term is used as it would be in the UK – except where stated otherwise.

Some students receive teaching from a person not in direct day-to-day supervision of their work, and this person is referred to as a *long-arm supervisor* or *teacher*. Some practitioners specialize in practice teaching / field instruction, so that – although they are employed in a social work agency – they spend a proportion of their time (*semi-specialist*) or all their time (*specialist*) teaching students. Sometimes this might be organized around a *student unit* within the agency.

Programme

course; education programme; in-service training; programme provider; training course

Together, the class-based learning (in the educational establishment) and agency-based learning (in the social work organization) make up the *training programme*; the balance of learning in the educational setting and the work setting varies, but can often be half and half. *Programme providers* is a collective term for all those who are responsible for the training programme.

In North America, the term *course* is used as a precise term to refer to specific elements in the programme; in the UK and Australasia it is used to mean the whole programme (though it often implicitly excludes the placement components, as in 'we haven't done that on the course yet', meaning the classroom).

There can be a tension between the training components of a programme (to produce competent agency workers) and the educative elements (to develop critical professionals). Some agencies provide *in-service training*, where their employees receive training while retaining a salary or stipend from the agency, and often the training is delivered by the agency itself.

About the Authors

Rashida A. Atthar is a B.A. (1985) with Psychology and Sociology as major subjects from St. Xavier's college, Mumbai and M.S.W. (1987) from the College of Social Work (NN), Mumbai. Ms Atthar has worked with NGOs and private companies in the field of health, development, gender and communication acquiring both research projects, field work and management experience. She has also been invited as guest lecturer for the M.S.W course at NN. Ms Atthar has written papers on development theories and their implication for the status of women, health policy, participatory development and communication, NGOs and international development and has completed her pre-doctoral from TISS. Ms Atthar has made paper presentations at international conferences amongst which her paper on 'Sustainable Development– Its Relevance for Developed and Developing Countries' received the best paper award at the 1997 Madrid conference. At present Ms Atthar is involved with research and teaching in the area of communication and sustainable development with NGOs.

Claire Betteridge recently qualified as a social worker in England and took up a post in a children and families team. The placement within the asylum project described in Chapter 4 contributed much to her development as a practitioner. She looks back on her time within the asylum project as a positive experience and something that will remain with her for some time to come.

Marion Bogo is Professor and Sandra Rotman Chair in Social Work at the Faculty of Social Work, University of Toronto, Canada. She is the former Acting Dean, Associate Dean, and Practicum Coordinator. Professor Bogo's academic, practice, and consultative activities focus on social work education and social work practice. She led two Canadian research projects as co-principal investigator, which led to the development of a model of field practice education. She has published extensively on field education including numerous articles in international journals and The Practice of Field Instruction in Social Work (1998, 2nd edn, co-author with E. Vayda). Professor

Bogo has been invited as guest lecturer and consultant to schools of social work in Canada, United States and Asia. Currently she is Principal Investigator on a Social Sciences and Humanities Research Council project that investigates the impact of organizational restructuring on field education.

Silvia Cioaza is a social worker at the Romanian Foundation for Child, Family and Community in Cluj-Napoca, Romania. She holds a Bachelor of Social Work degree. Silvia is part of the second cohort of graduates from Romania and one of the more experienced practitioners in childcare and family support in Romania. She was trained as a supervisor and practice teacher by British specialists and had the opportunity to experience an overview of a functional system of social services (in France as a TEMPUS scholar in 1994): this has contributed to her decision to remain in the social work field. Silvia's main professional interests are in foster care and adoption, social marketing and community organization.

Lesley Cooper is Associate Professor in the School of Social Administration and Social Work at Flinders University of South Australia and the Director of Field Education.

Therese J. Dent is Assistant Dean for Field Education, George Warren Brown School of Social Work, Washington University, Missouri, St. Louis, USA. Responsible for field education program at a US News and World Report top ranked school of social work in the USA. She is coordinator for social service component for the five-year $2.4 million Joint Community Development grant obtained by the Washington University Medical Center Redevelopment Corporation from the US Department of Housing and Urban Development.

Mark Doel is Professor of Social Work at the University of Central England (UCE) in Birmingham, England. He graduated from Oxford University, qualified in social work at Hull University and worked for many years as a social worker and practice teacher in the UK and the USA. For ten years, Mark held a joint appointment as a social worker with Sheffield Social Services Department and a lecturer in social work at the University of Sheffield. He has worked as a researcher in Portland, Oregon, and as an independent training consultant in the UK. In 1996, he became Head of School of Social Work and RNIB Rehabilitation Studies at UCE. Mark has written and researched extensively in the area of practice teaching. Recent books include *The Essential Groupworker* (with Sawdon) and *The New Social Work Practice* (with Shardlow).

Judith Globerman is Associate Professor, Faculty of Social Work, University of Toronto, Canada and former Academic Coordinator of the Practicum. Her research and practice focus on family care of the elderly, social work as a health profession, adaptation to health and illness, and social work field education. Dr Globerman's research and practice has included a longitudinal study examining families' experiences with a relative with Alzheimer's Disease funded by Health Canada, a study with Marion Bogo on inter-organization relationships between field agencies and the university funded by Social Sciences and Humanities Research Council of Canada, the coordinating of a hospital-based social work research unit, and Principal Investigator on a Social Science and Humanities Research Council project on adaptation of children and families to chronic illness.

Nigel Hall is Senior Programme Officer/Editor at the Southern Africa AIDS Information Dissemination Service (SAfAIDS), a regional organisation concerned with the HIV/AIDS epidemic. He previously worked for the School of Social Work in Zimbabwe as Senior Lecturer and Director of Fieldwork programmes. Nigel is also on a voluntary level the Vice-President (Africa) of the International Federation of Social Workers, a global organisation representing the social work profession (based in Bern, Switzerland) and is editor of a new journal *Social Work in Africa*. He is a Zimbabwe citizen, but completed his social work training and worked for ten years as a social worker in the UK.

Ben Harvey has recently qualified as a social worker in England. He spent a few months on a sessional contract with Cambridgeshire Social Services, assisting the Asylum Team. Ben then joined the Refugee Council as an Asylum Advice and Support Worker at the Immigration Reception Centre in Oakington, Cambridgeshire.

Rafael Herrera graduated from the School of Social Welfare, University of California, Berkeley, USA in 1973. He holds Board Certified Diplomat status with the American Board of Examiners in Clinical Social Work and the National Association of Social Workers. He has been on the faculty at the School of Social Welfare since 1990 and, in addition to teaching MSW students, serves as the Director of Admissions. His experience since the mid-1970s in mental health includes service as Program Director of Highland Hospital's Department of Psychiatry in Oakland, and Director of Alameda County's Community Crisis Response Program.

Steinunn Hrafnsdóttir graduated in 1988 and completed an MA in Management from the Faculty of Social Sciences, University of Kent at Canterbury in 1991. She worked as a part-time teacher and departmental manager at the Department of Social Work, University of Iceland 1992–99. Since 1999 she has been working on her PhD at the School of Social Policy, Sociology and Social Research, University of Kent at Canterbury, besides being an independent scholar at Reykjavíkur Academy and a part-time teacher at the Department of Social Work, University of Iceland. She has conducted courses in human service management at the University Institute of Continuing Education. Her research area is on human service management, field practice and social policy. She has published articles in Icelandic and in English.

Heidi S. K. Hui received her social work training at the University of Hong Kong and joined the Department of Social Work, University of Hong Kong as field instructor in 1988. She has practice and field instruction experience in a wide range of fields including youth work, family and individual counselling, rehabilitation and elderly services. Her research interest is in the area of rehabilitation studies.

Frances Y. S. Ip was educated in Hong Kong and Canada, and has extensive experience in working with handicapped and elderly people in both regions. She joined the Department of Social Work, University of Hong Kong as a field instructor in 1990. Her research interest is in the areas of rehabilitation and elderly services.

Sigrún Júliusdóttir, PhD, is a professor and Chief of Social Work Education at the University of Iceland. She got her MSW from University of Michigan, Ann Arbor (USA) and PhD from Gothenburg, Sweden. She is a licensed psychotherapist, trained in supervision and consultation. Until 1991, Sigrún was a Chief Social Worker at the University Psychiatric Clinic in Reykjavik. She also conducts courses for professionals at the Institute of Continuing Education. She runs a small private practice in couples and family therapy. Her research area is on family matters, supervision and the development of social work as a profession and an academic discipline. She has written books and articles in Icelandic, Swedish and English.

Elaine King is a Senior Practice Teacher with Voluntary Service Aberdeen, in a post funded by CCETSW. Her previous experience includes medical social work, and generic fieldwork. Her special interests are mental health, and homelessness. She is also a lecturer/tutor at the Robert Gordon University, Aberdeen, Scotland where she teaches social work methods and human growth and behaviour.

Bjarney Kristjánsdóttir is a clinical social worker and family therapist at the Department of Child and Adolescent Psychiatry at the University Hospital of Iceland. She graduated from the University of Iceland in psychology 1974 and in social work from the same school in 1982. She has further training in family therapy and systemic psychotherapy at Kensington Consultation Centre, London. She has a long experience in clinical social work at the University Hospital of Iceland and in 1994–97, she was a department chief in the social services in Reykjavik. She was a part-time teacher in the Nursing School of Iceland 1974–78 and is a practice teacher at the Department of Social Work, University of Iceland. She runs a small private practice in Reykjavik, working with systemic psychotherapy for families, couples and individuals and supervision.

Anna Y. L. Leung received her social work training at the University of Hong Kong and joined the Department of Social Work, University of Hong Kong in 1978 as a field instructor. She was appointed Co-ordinator of Field Instruction in 1989. Her practice and field instruction expertise is in the areas of family and individual counselling, and working with handicapped children. Besides field instruction and social work education, she has also published on social work with the families of children with special needs.

Joyce Lishman is Professor of Social Work and Head of the School of Applied Social Services, Robert Gordon University, Aberdeen, Scotland. She was editor of the *Handbook of Theory for Practice Teachers* and is general editor of the Research Highlights in Social Work series.

Rob Mackay is Lecturer in Social Work at the Robert Gordon University, Aberdeen, Scotland and course leader for the postgraduate diploma/MSc in community care. His teaching interests include social work theory and practice, inter-professional work, anti-discriminatory practice, community care, user involvement and advocacy. He previously was a CCETSW funded practice teacher at Voluntary Service Aberdeen and has a long serving commitment to the North of Scotland Practice Teaching Panel. He is also involved with Pillar, Aberdeen a voluntary organization of mental health service users and Advocacy Services Aberdeen.

Jane Maidment is currently lecturing in field education at Deakin University, Australia. She practised for eight years as a social worker in the field of psychiatric services for elderly people before joining the University of Canterbury in New Zealand in 1994. Jane has just been awarded her PhD on teaching and learning social work in the field education in New Zealand.

Peter G. Manoleas has been a full-time clinical faculty member at the School of Social Welfare, University of California, Berkeley, USA, since 1984 while maintaining a part-time, Oakland-based, independent practice. He has published numerous articles in the areas of substance abuse, mental health, and cross-cultural practice and is the editor of *The Cross-cultural Practice of Clinical Case Management in Mental Health* (1996). He currently serves on the editorial board of the *Journal of Social Work Practice in the Addictions* and is a regular reviewer for *Psychiatric Services*, and serves on the steering committee for the Alcohol and Drug Section of the National Association of Social Workers (USA).

Kalindi S. Muzumdar graduated from the University of Bombay, where she qualified in social work. Soon after securing the MSW degree, Professor Muzumdar was employed as a faculty member by the College of Social Work, Nirmala Niketan (NN), Bombay, India. She taught both the undergraduate and postgraduate students and supervised students placed in municipal schools, municipal hospitals, children's and women's institutions, police stations and the Juvenile Aid Police Unit. She initiated the project to place students in police stations and the residential quarters of the police personnel and an organization for women in distress under the auspices of the College of Social Work (NN) and the state government. She worked as a faculty member of the NN until 1992 and retired as Vice-Principal. She is currently a visiting professor. In her retirement, she has been working as a family counsellor after college hours.

Nicoleta Neamtu is a Lecturer at Babes-Bolyai University, Cluj-Napoca, Romania. Nicoleta is at the forefront of the reinvention of the social work profession in Romania, as a lecturer, practice coordinator and manager of the first qualified team of social workers. She has compensated for a lack of mentor in Romania by studying abroad, as a Visiting Researcher (Junior Fulbright Grantee) in the USA. Nicoleta also won Unicef and European Union scholarships in England (1997) and Scotland (1994). Her work is diverse, publishing in the fields of non-profit management, child welfare and social inequalities. Nicoleta is a doctoral student in sociology and senior law student at Babes-Bolyai University.

Kurt C. Organista is an Associate Professor of Social Welfare at the University of California, Berkeley, USA. He teaches courses on psychopathology, stress and coping, and diversity competent social work practice, including social work with Latino populations. Dr Organista is interested in Latino health and mental health and conducts research in the areas of HIV/AIDS prevention with Mexican migrant laborers, and the treatment of depression in Latinos. He currently serves on the editorial boards of *Ethnic and Cultural Diversity in Social Work, Hispanic Journal of the Behavioral Sciences* and the *American Journal of Community Psychology*.

Karen Patient completed her social work qualification and gained employment in a full-time position with Cambridgeshire Asylum Team. Seeking a position closer to her home, she is presently enjoying her work as a social worker with a team working with older people in Essex Social Services Department, England.

Paul Searston is a social work graduate from Flinders University, Australia and participated in this teaching initiative. He is currently working as a social worker in the Department of Human Services, Mt Gambier in the area of child welfare.

Revai Senzere is a practising social worker with the Department of Social Welfare in Zimbabwe. She completed her Diploma in Social Work in 1981. From 1982 to 1990, she worked as a medical social worker in four different central hospitals in Zimbabwe – Mpilo, Ingutsheni, Bulawayo and Harare (psychiatric wing). During her service as a medical social worker, Revai supervised about ten students. She did her degree in social work in 1989, joining her present employer in 1990.

Steven M. Shardlow is Professor of Social Work at the University of Salford, England, and editor-in-chief of the *Journal of Social Work*. Previously he has worked as a social work practitioner and manager. He has been involved in international social work, particularly in Europe through research, consultancy and development work. Current research interests are in the following areas: professional ethics; comparative social practice in the social professions; professional social work education and practice – especially in respect of practice learning. He has published widely in these fields and his work has been translated into several languages.

Lorie Shekter-Wolfson was Director of the Departments of Social Work and Multicultural Health at the Toronto Hospital, Canada, where she developed the Teaching Centre and collaborated with the Faculty of Social Work on a joint on-site research venture. She was an active member of the Health Research Consortium and co-authored articles with several faculty members on social work practice issues. She has been a lecturer in the Department of Psychiatry, and Social Work Practice Professor, Faculty of Social Work, University of Toronto. She was a former Head, Family and Social Services, Eating

Disorder Centre where she co-authored several articles and two books on family issues related to eating disorders. She has also worked as a consultant for the Government of Ontario.

Alice Tourville is a chemical dependency counselor and instructor of stress management classes at Unity-Hyland Behavioral Health at St. Anthony Medical Center, St. Louis, Missouri, USA. She teaches medical terminology for social work students at the George Warren Brown School of Social Work, Washington University, St. Louis, Missouri, and was the field instructor for community medical social work practicum students at a university–community sponsored neighborhood health clinic.

Dee Underhill is a Practice Learning Co-ordinator. She has responsibility for practice placements within Cambridgeshire Social Services Department, in partnership with Anglia Polytechnic University, England. She is an accredited practice teacher, providing practice teaching and in-house training for practice teachers and supervisors, as well as contributing to other training programmes in the department. Her particular interests include anti-oppressive practice and raising the profile of practice teaching both locally and nationally.

Pauline Woodward is a practitioner with 20 years' experience in mental health social work. She currently works in private practice providing professional supervision, doing part-time teaching in mental health and human development, and provides external supervision for social work students from the University of Canterbury, New Zealand.

Bibliography

Aberdeen Framework Group (AFG) (1998) *The Mental Health Framework in Aberdeen 1998–2004*. Aberdeen: AFG.

Advocacy Services Aberdeen (ASA) (1997) *Memorandum of Association*. Aberdeen: ASA.

Agranoff, R. A. and Pattakos, A. N. (1979) *Dimensions of Services Integration: Service Delivery, Program Linkages, Policy Management, Organisational Structure*. Human Services Monograph Series, 13. Washington, DC: US Department of Health, Education and Welfare, Project SHARE.

Ajdukovic, M., Cevizovic, M. and Kontak, K. (1995) 'Groupwork in Croatia: experiences with older refugees.' *Groupwork 8*, 1, 152–165.

Alcock, P. (1996) *Social Policy in Britain: Themes and Issues*. London: Macmillan.

Allen, J. (1998) National Association of Social Workers President's Lecture at the George Warren Brown School of Social Work, Washington University in St. Louis, 28 March.

Ames, N. (1999) 'Social work recording: a new look at old issues.' *Journal of Social Work Education 35*, 2, 227–237.

Aotearoa New Zealand Association of Social Workers (ANZASW) (1992) *Competent Social Work Practice*. Auckland: ANZASW.

Aotearoa New Zealand Association of Social Workers (1993) *Code of Ethics*. Dunedin: ANZASW.

Atthar, R. (1987) 'A study of policewomen in Greater Bombay.' Unpublished Masters Dissertation, College of Social Work, Bombay.

Balasubrahmanyan, V. (1990) *In Search of Justice, Women, Law, Landmark Judgements and Media*. Shubhada Saraswat Prakashan: Pune.

Bandura, A. and Walters, R. H. (1969) *Social Learning and Personality Theory*. London: Holt Rhinehart and Winston.

Beatty, R. and Ulrich, D. (1991) 'Re-energizing the mature organization.' *Organizational Dynamics 20*, 1, 16–30.

Berengarten, S. (1961) 'Educational issues in field instruction in social work.' Paper presented at a workshop on a Training Center in Social Work Education, co-sponsored by the New York School of Social Work of Columbia University and the Jewish Guild for the Blind.

Bergman, A., Wells, L., Bogo, M., Abbey, S., Chandler, V., Embleton, L., Guirgis, S., Huot, A., McNeill, T., Prentice, L., Stapleton, D., Shekter-Wolfson, L. and Urman, S.

(1993) 'High-risk indicators for family involvement in social work in health care.' *Social Work 38*, 3, 281–288.

Biestek, F.P. (1957) *The Casework Relationship.* Chicago: Loyola University Press.

Bogo, M. and Globerman, J. (1995) 'Creating effective university–field partnerships: an analysis of two inter-organization models.' *Journal of Teaching in Social Work 11*, 1/2, 177–192.

Bogo, M. and Globerman, J. (1999) 'Inter-organizational relationships between schools of social work and field agencies: Testing a framework for analysis.' *Journal of Social Work Education 35*, 2, 265–274.

Bogo, M. and Power, R. (1992) 'New field instructors' perceptions of institutional supports for their roles.' *Journal of Social Work Education 28*, 2, 178–189.

Bogo, M. and Taylor, I. (1990) 'A practicum curriculum in a health specialization: a framework for hospitals.' *Journal of Social Work Education 26*, 1, 76–86.

Bogo, M. and Vayda, E. (1998) *The Practice of Field Instruction in Social Work: Theory and Process*, 2nd edn. New York: Columbia University Press.

Bogo, M., Wells, L., Abbey, S., Bergman, A., Chandler, V., Embleton, L., Guirgis, S., Huot, A., McNeill, T., Prentice, L., Stapleton, D., Shekter-Wolfson, L. and Urman, S. (1992) 'Advancing social work practice in the health field: a collaborative research partnership.' *Health and Social Work 17*, 3, 223–235.

Bradley, J. (1995) 'Totara tree without roots.' *Te Komako. Social Work Review 7*, 1, 6–8.

Braye, S. and Preston Shoot, M. (1998) 'Social work and the law.' In R. Adams, M. Dominelli and M. Payne (eds) *Social Work: Themes, Issues and Critical Debates.* London: Macmillan.

Brearley, J. (1991) 'A psychodynamic approach to social work.' In J. Lishman (ed) *Handbook of Theory for Practice Teachers in Social Work.* London: Jessica Kingsley.

Brenton, M. (1985) *The Voluntary Sector in British Social Services.* London: Longman.

Brown, A. and Bourne, I. (1996) *The Social Work Supervisor.* Buckingham: Open University Press.

Brown, A. L. and Palinscar, A. S. (1989) 'Guided cooperative learning and individual knowledge acquisition.' In L. B. Resnick (ed) *Knowing, Learning and Instruction: Essays in Honor of Robert Glaser.* Hillsdale, NJ: Lawrence Erlbaum.

Browne, C. V., Smith, M., Ewalt, P. L. and Walker, D. D. (1996) 'Advancing social work practice in health settings: a collaborative partnership for continuing education.' *Health and Social Work 21*, 4, 267–276.

Bulmer, M. (1987) *The Social Basis of Community Care.* London: Unwin Hyman.

Butler, B. and Elliott, D. (1985) *Teaching and Learning for Practice.* Aldershot: Gower.

CCETSW (1991) *The Requirements for Post-Qualifying Education and Training in the Social Services* (Paper 30 2nd edn). London: CCETSW.

CCETSW (1995) *Assuring Quality in the Diploma in Social Work – 1 Rules and Requirements for the DipSW (Revised).* London: CCETSW.

CCETSW (1996) *Assuring Quality in the Diploma in Social Work – 1 Rules and Requirements for the DipSW* (2nd revision). London: CCETSW.

Charns, M. P. and Tewksbury, L. S. (1993) *Collaborative Management in Health Care: Implementing the Integrative Organization.* San Francisco: Jossey-Bass.

Cheyne, C., O'Brien, M. and Belgrave, M. (1997) *Social Policy in Aotearoa New Zealand.* Melbourne: Oxford University Press.

Cisneros, H. G. (1995) *The University and the Urban Challenge.* Washington, DC: US Department of Housing and Urban Development.

Clough, R. (1981) *Old Age Homes.* London: Allen and Unwin.

Comas-Diaz, L. and Duncan, J. W. (1985) The cultural context: a factor in assertiveness training with mainland Puerto Rican women. *Psychology of Women Quarterly 9,* 463–476.

Cooper, L. (1992) 'Managing to survive: competence and skills in social work.' *Issues in Social Work Education 12,* 2, 3–23.

Coulshed, V. (1991) *Social Work Practice,* 2nd edn. London: Macmillan.

Cross, T. *et al.* (1989) *Towards a Culturally Competent System of Care.* Washington, DC: National Technical Assistance Center for Children's Mental Health.

Dakshina Murthy, S. (1999) 'Cases of unnatural deaths of women to be part of public interest litigation', *The Hindustan Times* (Delhi), 23 August.

Dalrymple, J. and Burke, B. (1995) *Anti-Oppressive Practice: Social Care and the Law.* Buckingham: Open University Press.

Dattilio, F. M. and Freeman, A. (2001) *Cognitive Behavioural Strategies in Crisis Intervention,* 2nd edn. Hove: Guilford Press.

Davenport, J. and Davenport, J. (1988) 'Individualizing student supervision: the use of androgogical – pedagogical orientation questionnaires.' *Journal of Teaching in Social Work 2,* 2, 83–97.

Department of Health (1989) *Caring for People.* London: HMSO.

Department of Health (1995) *Looking After Children: Assessment and Action Record.* London: HMSO.

Department of Social Work and Social Administration, University of Hong Kong (1997) *Field Instruction Handbook.* Hong Kong: University of Hong Kong.

Deshpande, A. (1990) 'When lawmen take the law into their own hands', *Deccan Herald,* 8 April.

Doel, M. and Marsh, P. (1992) *Task-Centred Social Work.* Aldershot: Ashgate.

Doel, M. and Shardlow, S. M. (eds) (1996) *Social Work in a Changing World: an International Perspective on Practice Learning.* Aldershot: Arena.

Doel, M. and Shardlow, S. M. (1998) *The New Social Work Practice.* Aldershot: Arena.

Doel, M., Shardlow, S. M., Sawdon, C. and Sawdon, D. (1996) *Teaching Social Work Practice.* Aldershot: Arena.

Dominelli, L. (1997) *Sociology for Social Work.* London: Macmillan.

Dominelli, L. (1999) 'Neo-liberalism, Social Exclusion and Welfare Clients in a Global Economy.' *International Journal of Social Welfare 8,* 1, 14–22.

Durie, M. (1995) 'Maori and the State.' *Te Komako. Social Work Review 7,* 1, 2–5.

Falicov, C. (1996) 'Mexican families.' In M. McGoldrick, J. Giordano and J. Pearce (eds) *Ethnicity and Family Therapy,* 2nd edn. New York: Guilford Press.

Falicov, C. (1998) *Latino Families in Therapy: A Guide to Multicultural Practice.* New York: Guilford Press.

Faria, G., Brownstein, C. and Smith, H. (1988) 'A survey of field instructors' perceptions of the liaison role.' *Journal of Social Work Education 2,* 135–144.

Fellin, P. (1982) 'Responsibilities of the school: administrative support of field education.' In B. Sheafor and L. Jenkins (eds) *Quality Field Education in Social Work.* New York: Longman.

Fieldgrass, P. and Fieldgrass, J. (1992) *Snapshots of the Voluntary Sector.* London: National Council for Voluntary Organisations.

Flower, J. (1992) 'New tools, new thinking.' *Healthcare Forum 35,* 2, 62–67.

Fortune, A. and Abramson, J. (1993) 'Predictors of satisfaction with field practicum among social work students.' *Clinical Supervisor 11,* 1, 95–110.

Fortune, A., Feathers, C., Rook, S., Scrimenti, R., Smollen, P., Stemerman, B. and Tucker, E. (1989) 'Student satisfaction with field placement.' In M. Raskin (ed) *Empirical Studies in Field Instruction.* New York: Haworth Press.

Fortune, A., Miller, J., Rosenblum, A., Sanchez, B., Smith, C. and Reid, W. (1995) 'Further explorations of the liaison role: a view from the field.' In G. Rogers (ed) *Social Work Field Education: Views and Visions.* Dubuque, IA: Kendall/Hunt.

Fox, R. and Guild, P. (1987) 'Learning styles: their relevance to clinical supervision.' *Clinical Supervisor 5,* 3, 65–77.

Freire, P. (1972) *Pedagogy of the Oppressed.* Harmondsworth: Penguin.

Froland, C. (1981) *Relating Formal and Informal Sources of Care: Reflections on Initiatives in England and America.* Sheffield: Department of Sociological Studies, University of Sheffield.

Gans, S. P. and Horton, G. T. (1975) *Integration of Human Services: The State and Municipal Levels.* New York: Praeger.

Gardiner, D. (1989) *The Anatomy of Supervision.* Milton Keynes: Society for Research in Higher Education and Open University Press.

Geller, J. L., Fisher, W. H. and McDermeit, M. (1995) 'A national survey of mobile crisis services and their evaluation.' *Psychiatric Services 46,* 1, 893–897.

Gerdman, A. (1989) *Klient, praktikant, handledare: Om att utveckla en egen yrkesteori. Handledning av socionompraktikanter.* Lund: Wahlstrøm and Wildstrand.

Germain, C. (1991) *Human Behaviour in the Social Environment.* New York: Columbia University Press.

Getzel, G. S. and Salmon, R. (1985) 'Group supervision: an organisational approach.' *Clinical Supervisor 3,* 1, 27–43.

Gibson, A. (1991) 'Erikson's life cycle approach to development.' In J. Lishman (ed) *Handbook of Theory for Practice Teachers in Social Work.* London: Jessica Kingsley.

Gilliland, B. E. (1982) *Steps in Crisis Counseling.* Memphis, TN: Department of Counseling and Personnel Services, Memphis State University.

Globerman, J. (1999) 'Hospital restructuring: positioning social work to manage change.' *Social Work in Health Care 28,* 4, 13–30.

Globerman, J. and Bogo, M. (1995) 'Social work and the new integrative hospital.' *Social Work in Health Care 21,* 3, 1–21.

Globerman, J., Davies, J. M. and Walsh, S. (1996) 'Social work in restructuring hospitals: meeting the challenge.' *Health and Social Work 21,* 3, 178–188.

Gould, N. and Taylor, I. (eds) (1996) *Reflective Learning for Social Work.* Aldershot: Arena.

Government of Canada (1984) *Canada Health Act.* Ottawa: Minister of Supply and Services.

Grampian Health Board (GHB) (1998) *Framework for Mental Health Services.* Aberdeen: GHB.

Guetzbow, H. (1966) 'Relations among organisations.' In R. V. Bower (ed) *Studies on Behaviour in Organisations.* Athens, GA: University of Georgia.

Gulbenkian Commission (1996) *Open the Social Sciences: Report of the Gulbenkian Commission on the Reconstruction of the Social Sciences.* Stanford, CA: Stanford University Press.

Hall, N. (1990) *Social Work Training in Africa: A Fieldwork Manual.* Harare, Zimbabwe: Journal of Social Development in Africa.

Haring, K. A. and Lovett, P. L. (eds) (1992) *Integrated Life Cycle Services for Persons with Disabilities: A Theoretical and Empirical Perspective.* New York: Springer-Verlag.

Hayes-Bautista, D. and Chiprut, R. (1998) *Healing Latinos: Realidad y fantasia [Reality and Fantasy]: The Art of Cultural Competence in Medicine.* Los Angeles: Cedars Sinai Health System, Center for the Study of Latino Health, University of California, Los Angeles.

Henderson, R. (1998) 'Devolution of social work in the health sector: a positive development?' *Social Work Review 10,* 3, 18–21.

Hendry, G. D. (1996) 'Constructivism and educational practice.' *Australian Journal of Education 40,* 1, 19–45.

Herbert, M. and Levin, R. (1996) 'The advocacy role in hospital social work.' *Social Work in Health Care 22,* 3, 71–83.

Herrera, R. (1996) 'Crisis intervention: an essential component of culturally competent clinical case management.' In Peter Manoleas (ed) *The Cross-cultural Practice of Clinical Case Management in Mental Health.* New York: Haworth Press.

Hillerbrand, E. (1989) 'Cognitive differences between experts and novices: implications for group supervision.' *Journal of Counselling and Development 67,* 5, 293–296.

Hollis, F. (1964, 1971) *Casework: A Psychosocial Therapy.* New York: Random House.

Homonoff, E. and Maltz, P. (1995) 'Fair exchange: collaboration between social work schools and field agencies in an environment of scarcity.' In G. Rogers (ed) *Social Work Field Education: Views and Visions.* Dubuque, IA: Kendall/Hunt.

Honey, P. and Mumford, A. (1986) *Manual of Learning Styles.* London: P. Honey.

Hong Kong Government (1977) *Integrating the Disabled into the Community: A United Effort.* Hong Kong: Hong Kong Government Printer.

Hong Kong Government (1991) *White Paper: Social Welfare into the 1990s and Beyond.* Hong Kong: Hong Kong Government Printer.

Hong Kong Government (1995) *White Paper on Rehabilitation, Equal Opportunities and Full Participation: A Better Tomorrow for All.* Hong Kong: Hong Kong Government Printer.

Hrafnsdóttir, S. (1995) 'Field instruction in social work education: a study of the views of field instructors in social work education at the University of Iceland.' *Issues in Social Work Education 6,* 1, 48–63.

Hughes, C. (1998) 'Practicum learning: perils of the authentic workplace.' *Higher Education Research and Development 17,* 3, 207–227.

Hughes, L. and Heycox, K.(1996) 'Three perspectives on assessment in practice learning.' In M. Doel and S. M. Shardlow (eds) *Social Work in a Changing World: An International Perspective on Practice Learning.* Aldershot: Arena.

Humphries, B. (1988) 'Adult learning in social work education: towards liberation or domestication?' *Critical Social Policy 23,* 4–21.

Idol, L., Jones, B. F. and Mayer, R. E. (1991) 'Classroom instruction: the teaching of thinking.' In L. Idol and B. F. Jones (eds) *Educational Values and Cognitive Instruction: Implication for Reform.* Hillsdale, NJ: Lawrence Erlbaum.

Jarman-Rohde, L., McFall, J., Kolar, P. and Strom, G. (1997) 'The changing context of social work practice: implications and recommendations for educators.' *Journal of Social Work Education 33*, 3, 573–585.

Johnson, D., Johnson, R. and Holubec, E. (1993) *Circles of Learning: Cooperation in the Classroom.* Edina, MN: Interaction.

Júliusdóttir, S. (1996) 'Utbildning i socialt arbete – identitet och professionellt ansvar.' *Nordiskt Socialt Arbeid 1*, 16, 61–68.

Júliusdóttir, S. (1999) 'Social work competence in the competence society: a professional survival.' *Issues in Social Work Education 19*, 1 (Spring) 75–92.

Júliusdóttir, S. (2000) 'Social work and other social professions in Iceland: educational programmes and professional status.' *European Journal of Social Work 3*, 1, 57–60.

Júliusdóttir, S. and Hrafnsdóttir, S. (1992) *Assessment Scale in Social Work Education.* Reykjavik: University of Iceland.

Kadushin, A. (1992) *Supervision in Social Work.* New York: Columbia University Press.

Kagan, S. L. (1993) *Integrating Services for Children and Families.* New Haven, CT: Yale University Press.

Kagle, J. D. (1984) *Social Work Records.* Homewood, IL: Dorsey Press.

Kamerman, S. B. and Kahn, A. J. (1976) *Social Services in the United States: Policies and Programs.* Philadelphia, PA: Temple University Press.

Kaplan, T. (1991) 'A model for group supervision for social work: implications for the profession.' In D. Schneck, B. Grossman and U. Glassman (eds) *Field Education in Social Work: Contemporary Issues and Trends.* Dubuque, IA: Kendall/Hunt.

Kendall, J. and Knapp, M. (1995) '"A loose and baggy monster": boundaries, definitions and typologies.' In J. Davis, C. Rochester and R. Hedley (eds) *An Introduction to the Voluntary Sector.* London: Routledge.

Kerson, T. S. (1994) 'Field instruction in social work settings.' *Clinical Supervisor 12*, 1, 1–31.

Killén, K. (1992) *Faglig veiledning-et tverrfaglig perspektiv.* Oslo: Universitetsforlaget.

Kimber, D. (1996) 'Collaborative learning in management education: issues, benefits, problems and solutions, a literature review'. Ultibase.rmit.edu.au/Articles/kimbe1.html

Kissman, K. and Van Tran, T. (1990) 'Perceived quality of field placement among graduate social work students.' *Journal of Continuing Social Work Education 5*, 2, 27–31.

Kretzman, J. and McKnight, J. (1993) *Building Communities from the Inside Out: A Path toward Finding and Mobilizing a Community's Assets.* Evanston, IL: Northwestern.

Kristmundsdóttir, K. (1985) 'Handleidsla nema.' *Gedvernd 18*, 1, 66–68.

Kolb, D. A. (1984) *Experiential Learning.* New York: Prentice Hall.

Lathrop, J. P. (1993) *Restructuring Health Care: The Patient Focused Paradigm.* San Francisco: Jossey-Bass.

Lawson, H. (ed) (1998) *Practice Teaching: Changing Social Work.* London: Jessica Kingsley.

Leatt, P., Baker, G. R., Halverson, P. K. and Aird, C. (1997) *Downsizing, Reengineering and Rightsizing: Long-term Implications for Healthcare Organizations.* Hospital Management

Research Unit Technical Report no. 96–04. Toronto: Hospital Management Research Unit, University of Toronto.

Leung, A. Y. L., Hui, H. S. K. and Ip, F. Y. S. (1995a) *People and Services: Neighbourhood Level Integration, an Experiment in Shek Wai Kok.* Hong Kong: University of Hong Kong.

Leung, A. Y. L. Tam, T. S. K. and Chu, C. H. (1995b) *A Study of the Roles and Tasks of a Field Instructor.* Hong Kong: University of Hong Kong.

Leung, A. Y. L. (1996) 'Preparing for change: field work practice in pioneering projects.' In *Participating in Change: Social Work Profession in Social Development.* Proceedings of the Joint World Congress of the International Federation of Social Workers and the International Association of Schools of Social Work.

Li, M. K. Y. (1993) 'Social workers and the issue of discrimination [in Chinese].' *Hong Kong Journal of Social Work 27*, 1, 78–79.

Li, M. K. Y. (1994) 'Reflections on the social networking project.' Paper presented at a seminar on 'Pilot Project on Integrated Service Delivery in Shek Wai Kok Public Housing Estate, Tsuen Wan'. Hong Kong: University of Hong Kong.

Lishman, J. and Wardell, F. (1998) *Changes in the Role of Volunteer Co-ordinators in the Privatisation of Care.* Edinburgh: Scottish Office Central Research Unit.

Lorenz, W. (1994) *Social Work in a Changing Europe.* London: Routledge.

Lum, D. (1996) *Social Work Practice and People of Color: A Process-stage Approach.* Pacific Grove, CA: Brooks/Cole.

Lum, D. (1999) *Culturally Competent Practice: A Framework for Growth and Action.* Pacific Grove, CA: Brooks/Cole.

McClelland, R. W. (1991) 'Innovation in field education.' In D. Schneck, B. Grossman and U. Glassman (eds) *Field Education in Social Work: Contemporary Issues and Trends.* Dubuque, IA: Kendall/Hunt.

Maidment, J. (2000) 'Strategies to promote student learning and integration of theory with practice in the field.' In L. Cooper and L. Briggs (eds) *The Human Services Practicum.* Sydney: Allen and Unwin.

Mallinson, I. (1995) *Key Working in Social Care.* London: Routledge and Kegan Paul.

Manoleas, P. G. (1994) 'An outcome approach to assessing the cultural competency of M.S.W. students.' *Journal of Multicultural Social Work 3*, 1, 43–57.

Manoleas, P. G., Organista, K. C., Negron-Velasquez, G. and McCormick, K. (2000) 'Characteristics of Latino mental health clinicians: a preliminary examination.' *Community Mental Health Journal 36*, 4, 383–394.

Marris, P. (1974) *Loss and Change.* London: Routledge and Kegan Paul.

Marsh, P. and Triseliotis, J. (1996) *Social Workers and Probation Officers: Their Training and First Year in Work.* Aldershot: Avebury.

Maslow, A. (1970) *Motivation and Personality*, 2nd edn. New York: Harper and Row.

Maxwell, J. (1990) 'Cultural values as determinants of service integration: some examples in international perspective.' *International Social Work 33*, 2, 175–184.

Midgley, J. (2001) 'Issues in International Social Work: Resolving Critical Debates in the Profession.' *Journal of Social Work 1*, 1, 21–36.

Miranda, J., Azocar, F., Organista, K. C., Dwyer, E. and Arean, P. (2000) 'Treatment of depression in disadvantaged medical patients.' Unpublished manuscript. Washington, DC: Georgetown Medical Center.

Moore, L. S. and Urwin, C. A. (1990) 'Quality control in social work: the gate-keeping role in social work education.' *Journal of Teaching in Social Work 4*, 1, 113–128.

Moore, S. T. and Kelly, M. J. (1996) 'Quality now: moving human service organizations toward a consumer orientation to service quality.' *Social Work 41*, 1, 33–40.

Morell, E. (1980) 'Student assessment: where are we now?' *British Journal of Social Work, 2*, 4, 431–442.

Morrison, J. D., Alcorn, S. and Nelums, M. (1997) 'Empowering community-based programs for youth development.' *Journal of Social Work Education 33*, 2, 329.

Munson, C. E. (1987) 'Field instruction in social work education.' *Journal of Teaching in Social Work 1*, 1, 91–109.

Nai-Ming Tsang (1993) 'Shifts of students: learning styles on a social work course.' *Issues in Social Work Education 12*, 1, 62–76.

National Council for Voluntary Organisations (NCVO) (1996) *Report of the Commission on the Future of the Voluntary Sector.* London: NCVO.

Nisivoccia, D. (1990) 'Teaching and learning tasks in the beginning phase of field instruction.' *Clinical Supervisor 8*, 1, 7–22.

Nixon, S., Shardlow, S.M., Doel, M., McGrath, S. and Gordon, R. (1995) 'An empirical approach to defining quality components of field education.' In G. Rogers (ed) *Social Work Field Education: Views and Visions.* Dubuque, IA: Kendall/Hunt.

Office of Policy Development and Research (1995) *Empowerment: A New Covenant with America's Communities. President Clinton's National Urban Policy Report.* Washington, DC: US Department of Housing and Urban Development.

O'Hagan, K. (1994) 'Crisis intervention: changing perspectives.' In C. Hanvey and T. Philpot (eds) *Practising Social Work.* London: Routledge.

O'Neill, J. (1999) 'Profession dominates in mental health.' *NASW News, 44*, 6, 1.

Organista, K. C. and Valdes Dwyer, E. (1996) 'Clinical case management and cognitive-behavioral therapy: integrated psychosocial services for depressed Latino primary care patients.' In P. G. Manoleas (ed) *The Cross-cultural Practice of Clinical Case Management in Mental Health.* New York: Haworth Press.

Orme, J. and Glastonbury, B. (1993) *Care Management.* Houndmills, Basingstoke: Macmillan

Parlamentul Romaniei (1991) *Constitucia Romaniei.* Bucharest: Monitorul Oficial.

Parlamentul Romaniei (1998a) Legea 108 pentru aprobarea Ordonancei de urgenc a Guvernului nr.25/1997 cu privire la adopcie. Bucharest: Monitorul Oficial al Romaniei, Partea I, nr.205/1998.

Parlamentul Romaniei (1998b) Legea 87 pentru aprobarea Ordonancei de urgenc a Guvernului nr.26/1997 cu privind protectia copilului aflat in dificultate. Bucharest: Monitorul Oficial al Romaniei, Partea I, nr.168/1998.

Payne, M. (1997) *Modern Social Work Theory*, 2nd edn. London: Macmillan.

Peters, T. (1992) *Liberation Management.* New York: Alfred A. Knopf.

Piaget, J. (1972) 'Intellectual evolution from adolescence to adulthood.' *Human Development 15*, 1, 1–12.

Pincus, A. and Minahan, A. (1973) *Social Work Practice: Model and Method*, Itasca, IL: Peacock.

Pressman, J. and Wildavsky, A. (1979) *Implementation*, 2nd edn. Berkeley, CA: University of California Press.

Ranade, S. N. (1994) 'New directions in social work.' In K. K. Jacob (ed) *Social Work Education in India, Retrospect and Prospect*. Delhi: Himanshu.

Randal, H. (1994) 'Student supervision.' *Social Work Review 6*, 5 and 6, 34–36.

Raphael, F. B. and Rosenblum, A. (1987) 'An Operation Guide to the Faculty Liason Rule.' *Social Casework 68*, 3, 156–163.

Rapp, C. A., Chamberlain, R. and Freeman, E. (1989) 'Practicum: new opportunities for training, research and service delivery.' *Journal of Teaching in Social Work 3*, 1, 3–16.

Raskin, M., Skolnik, L. and Wayne, J. (1991) 'An international perspective of field education.' *Journal of Social Work Education 27*, 3, 258–270.

Redburn, F. S. (1977) On 'Human Services Integration'. *Public Administration Review 37*, 3, 264–269.

Rennie, G. (1998) 'Graduate diploma in not for profit management as a counter to new managerialism.' *Social Work Review 10*, 3, 15–17.

Reynolds, B. (1942) *Learning and Teaching in the Practice of Social Work*. New York: Rhinehart.

Rogoff, B. (1990) *Apprenticeship in Thinking: Cognitive Development in Social Context*. New York: Oxford University Press.

Rosenfeld, D. J. (1989) 'Field instructor turnover.' In M. Raskin (ed) *Empirical Studies in Field Instruction*. New York: Haworth Press.

Sabel, C. (1994) 'Learning by monitoring.' In N. Smelser and R. Swedberg (eds) *The Handbook of Economic Sociology*. Princeton, NJ: Princeton University Press.

Sabogal, F., Marin, G., Otero-Sabogal, R., VanOss Marin, B. and Perez-Stable, E. J. (1987) 'Hispanic familism and acculturation: what changes and what doesn't?' *Hispanic Journal of Behavioral Sciences 9*, 4, 397–412.

Sanger, V. (2000) 'Eve-teasing: will it ever end?' *The Times of India* (Bombay), 8 March.

Schön, D. A. (1987) *Educating the Reflective Practitioner*. New York: Basic Books.

Schön, D. A. (1995) *The Reflective Practitioner*. Aldershot: Arena.

School of Social Work, University of Leicester (1990) *Practice Guide: Information on the Administration, Teaching and Assessment of Students in their Practice Placements*. Leicester: University of Leicester.

Schuftan, C. (1996) 'The community development dilemma: what is really empowering?' *Community Development Journal 31*, 3, 260–264.

Scottish Office (1997) *A Framework for Mental Health Services in Scotland*. Edinburgh: HMSO.

Secker, J. (1993) *From Theory to Practice in Social Work*. Aldershot: Avebury.

Seed, P. and Lloyd, G. (1997) *Quality of Life*. London: Jessica Kingsley.

Selby, R. (1995) 'Watch out for the quicksand.' *Te Komako. Social Work Review 7*, 1, 19–20.

Shardlow, S. M. and Doel, M. (1996) *Practice Learning and Teaching*. London: Macmillan.

Sharma, P. (1999) 'A hazardous road for single women: eve-teasing continues to be the source of major trauma for women commuters.' *The Pioneer* (Delhi), 1 March.

Sheafor, B., Horejsi, C. and Horejsi, G. (1988) *Techniques and Guidelines for Social Work Practice.* Boston, MA: Allyn and Bacon.

Shearer, A. (1986) *Building Community with People with Mental Handicaps, their Families and Friends.* London: Campaign for People with Mental Handicaps.

Shennon, G. (1998) 'Are we asking the experts? Practice teachers' use of client views in assessing student competence.' *Social Work Education 17,* 4, 407–418.

Sim, A. J. and Mackay, R. (1997) 'Advocacy in the UK.' *Practice 9,* 2, 5–12.

Skovholt, M. and Rönnestad, M. H. (1992, 1995) *The Evolving Professional Self: Stages and Themes in Therapist and Counselor Development.* New York: John Wiley.

Sue, S., Fujino, D. C., Hu, L., Takeuchi, D. T. and Zane, N. W. S. (1991) 'Community mental health services for ethnic minority groups: a test of the cultural responsiveness hypothesis.' *Journal of Consulting and Clinical Psychology 59,* 4, 533–540.

Tanner, K. and Le Riche, P (1995) 'You see but do not observe: the art of observation and its application to practice teaching.' *Issues in Social Work Education 15,* 2, 66–80.

Te Kaiawhina Ahumahi (1997) *Guidelines for Providers of Education and Training in the Social Services.* Wellington, NZ: Industry Training Organisation for Social Services.

Thorsteinsdóttir, G. and Júliusdóttir, S. (2000) 'Breytt námsskipan í félagsráogjöf.' *Rannsóknir í félagsvísindum III.* Reykjavik: Háskólaútgáfan Félagsvísindastofnun 453–463.

Tidikis, F. and Strasen, L. (1994) 'Patient-focused care units improve service and financial outcomes.' *Healthcare Financial Management 48,* 9, 38–44.

Tong, H. S. K., Ip, F. Y. S., Leung, A. Y. L. and Lai, O. K. (1994) 'The promotion of integrating service delivery via students' placements: a reflection on students' learning.' In *Social Work Education in Chinese Societies: Existing Patterns and Future Development.* Proceedings of the Conference of the Asian and Pacific Association for Social Work Education in Hong Kong.

Trevillion, S. (1997) 'The globalisation of European social work.' *Social Work in Europe 4,* 1, 1–9.

Tribe, R. and Shackman, J. (1989) 'A way forward: a group for refugee women.' *Groupwork 2,* 2, 159–166.

Tsang, N. M. (1983) 'Students' perspectives of field instruction in undergraduate social work education in Hong Kong.' M.Phil thesis. Hong Kong: University of Hong Kong.

Ulas, M. and Connor, A. (1999) *Mental Health and Scoial Work: Research Highlights 28.* London: Jessica Kingsley.

Ulas, M., Myers, F. and Whyte, B. (1994) *The Role of the Mental Health Officer.* Edinburgh: Scottish Office Central Research Unit.

UNAIDS/WHO (1998) *Epidemiological Fact Sheet.* Geneva: UNAIDS and WHO.

UNAIDS/WHO (1999) *Epidemic Update: December.* Geneva: UNAIDS and WHO.

Urbanowski, M. and Dwyer, M. (1988) *Learning through Field Instruction.* Milwaukee, WI: Family Service America.

US Bureau of the Census (1994) *The Hispanic Population in the United States: March 1993. Current Population Reports.* Series P20–475. Washington, DC: US Government Printing Office.

Vayda, E. and Bogo, M. (1991) 'A teaching model to unite classroom and field.' *Journal of Social Work Education 27*, 3, 271–278.

Vega, W. A., Kolody, B., Aguilar-Gaxiola, S., Alderete, E., Catalano, R. and Caraveo-Anduaga, J. (1998) 'Lifetime prevalence of DSM-III-R psychiatric disorders among urban and rural Mexican Americans in California.' *Archives of General Psychiatry 55*, September, 771–782.

Vygotsky, L. S. (1978) *Mind in Society: The Development of Higher Psychological Processes.* Cambridge, MA: Harvard University Press.

Walker, D. and Boud, D. (1994) 'Learning from the pastoral placement.' *Ministry, Society and Theology 8*, 1, 7–21.

Wan-lau, S. O. (1994) 'Integrated service delivery from the perspective of services for the elderly [in Chinese].' Paper presented at a seminar on 'Pilot Project on Integrated Service Delivery in Shek Wai Kok Public Housing Estate, Tsuen Wan.' Hong Kong: University of Hong Kong.

Washington University Medical Center Redevelopment Corporation (1995) *US Department of Housing and Urban Development Joint Community Development Program Application Executive Summary.*

Wintersteen, R. T., Mupedziswa, R. and Wintersteen, L. B. (1995) 'Zimbabwean families of the mentally ill: experiences and support needs.' *Journal of Social Development in Africa 10*, 1, 89–106.

Wong, D. (1994) 'Field instruction in unstructured community settings: contributions and constraints to student learning.' In *Social Work Education in Chinese Societies: Existing Patterns and Future Development.* Proceedings of the Conference of the Asian and Pacific Association for Social Work Education in Hong Kong.

Yau, Y. C. (1994) 'Integrated service delivery from the perspective of services for young people [in Chinese].' Paper presented at a seminar on 'Pilot Project on Integrated Service Delivery in Shek Wai Kok Public Housing Estate, Tsuen Wan'. Hong Kong: University of Hong Kong.

Yng, H. (1998) 'Recruitment, continuity and the problem of turnover of practice teachers in social work education.' Unpublished lecture at a Conference on Social Work Education, Stavanger, 16–19 April.

Zakutansky, T. (1993) 'Ethical and legal issues in field education: shared responsibility and risk.' *Journal of Social Work Education 29*, 3, 338–346.

Zastrow, C. (1995) *The Practice of Social Work.* Pacific Grove, CA: Books/Cole.

Subject Index

academic settings, pros and cons
110–11
acculturation 201, 203
adoption work 134, 143–4
advocacy 138
  levels of 189–90
Advocacy Services Aberdeen (ASA)
185–93
Africa 167, 173
Age Concern 181
agencies
  culture 95, 102–3
  evaluation and continuity 116
  inter-agency linkages 65, 66, 67,
216
  orientation through case records
149
  placement incomes 77, 182
  recruitment 115–16
agency-school relations see
  university/school-field relations
AIDS see HIV/AIDS
Alameda County community crisis
  response team (CCRT) 215–18
anti-discriminatory practice 82, 83,
  87, 88, 187, 193–4
Aotearoa New Zealand Association
  of Social Workers
  Code of Ethics 98, 102
  Competency Standards 98, 102
apprenticeship model 153
assertiveness training 205–6
assessment, client
  assessment algorithm 212–13
  child and family services 135, 137,
  143
  mental health services 169–70, 204
assessment, organizational 139–41
assessment, student
  concrete tools used 119–21

dynamic process and concrete tool
  117–18
external supervision 96–7, 99
'job description' model 145
marginal performance 126–8
outcome forms 63–4
over time 118–19
two-stage placement model
  112–14, 121–5
assessment scales 119–21
asylum seekers project, England 13,
  77–90
  background 78–9
  emergent themes 88–9
  involvement of practice learning
  coordinator 80–1
  media vitriol 19, 85
  practice teachers' perspectives 86–7
  project leader's perspective 86
  social work response 79
  students' accounts 81–5
  team manager's perspective 88
Asylum Support (interim)
  Regulations (1999) 79

Barnado's 181
bereavement theory 195
biculturalism 102, 203
'biculturation' 205
Building Communities from the
  Inside Out (Kretzman and
  McKnight) 28

Cambridgeshire 78–9
Canada, university teaching hospitals
  16, 20, 222–36
Canada Health Act (1984) 228
care in the community 62, 66, 181,
  184, 189, 190
case records, practice teaching using
  18, 147–63
  changing practice environment 148
  group discussion 158–62
  new initiative 149
  selecting case records 153–4
  stimulating effective learning
  149–53

strategies in action 156–7
strategies used by practice teachers 154–6
childcare and family services
   Iceland 122–3
   Romania 130–46
children
   abuse and neglect 125, 138–9, 210
   busing 27
   community work 30, 39
   and police 44
   rehabilitation work 170–3
   unaccompanied asylum seekers 79
Children Act (1989) 79
Church of Scotland 181
class setting, keywords 237
clients
   empathic understanding 122–3
   integration 61–3
   inter-clientele linkages 65, 66
   respecting points of view 35–6, 39
   responsiveness to needs 38, 67
   rights and empowerment 190–2
clinical algorithms 208–14
clinical case management (CCM) 204, 207–8
Cluj Child Protection department 131–44
cognitive apprenticeship 153
Cognitive Behavioural Depression Clinic, San Francisco General Hospital 203–8
cognitive behavioural therapy (CBT) 205–7
cognitive conflict 151
cognitive development 151–2
cognitive restructuring 206, 214
cognitive skills 188
cognitive strategies 154–5
   clarifying 155, 159–60
   predicting 155, 160
   questioning 155, 159
   summarizing 155, 158–9
College of Social Work, Nirmala Niketan (NN) 43, 45, 46, 50, 55, 57, 58
committee meetings 186–7
communal riots, Mumbai 19, 54–5
communication
   across different worlds 34
   external supervision 95
   maintaining clear patterns 36–7
   shared cultural metaphors 212
communication skills 82, 83, 188–9
   police, India 51
community care see care in the community
community revitalization partnerships 25–42
community work, police station placements 54–5
competence-based approach 18, 89, 182
competencies, keywords 237–8
   see also core competencies; professional competence
conscious competence/incompetence 83
Constitution of Romania 144
constructivist views of learning 151–2
consultant, keywords 238
Convention of the Rights of the Child (1989) 144
core competencies 77, 78, 199n
   Assessment and Care Planning 80, 81, 82, 84, 86, 87, 190
   Communication Skills 82
   Social Work Intervention 80, 190
   Working in Organizations 185–6
crisis intervention models 84, 86
   six-step 216–17
crisis theory 195
Critical Incident Review 191–2
culturally competent practice 20, 31
   with asylum seekers 83
   with Latinos 200–21
   in New Zealand 101–2
   in Zimbabwe 169, 170, 174

depression, outpatient treatment
   with Latinos 203–8
   in Zimbabwe 168–70
Diploma in Social Work (DipSW) 77, 78, 80, 179, 182, 197
disabled people
   integration 62, 63, 65–6, 67

rehabilitation work with children
170–3
Discrimination Disability Ordinance
(1995), Hong Kong 62
distal/proximal causes 213
diversity and difference 20–1
see also culturally competent
practice
domestic violence 44, 50
using case records 156–60

ecological model 19, 98–108
limitations 108
transactional outcomes 98–9
use by educators 106–7
use by students 106–7
economic rationalist ideology 95
educational coordinators, university
teaching hospitals 224, 225,
226, 227, 232
elopement 53–4
employment referral center 30, 31,
39
empowerment 32, 198
community 29, 32–3
user rights and 190–2
engagement algorithm 209–12
England, asylum seekers project 13,
77–90
European Convention in respect of
Children's Adoption (1967) 144
'eve-teasing' 44
experimentation 13, 18, 60, 67
effects of prescriptive curricula 89
external ('long-arm', off-site)
supervision 87, 93–109
attention to process 95–7
contextual influences 95
ecological perspective 98–108
linking literature with experience
94
stakeholder interest 97–8
voluntary sector 183–4, 185

faculty-based field instruction unit
model 63
families

caring for mentally ill relatives,
Zimbabwe 169
centrality in Latino lives 203, 205
of HIV/AIDS patients, Zimbabwe
175
see also childcare and family
services
family work, police station
placements 52–4
field liaison staff 77, 145–6, 226,
232
keywords 238
foster care 124–5, 143–4
fundraising 138

Ganesh festival 54
gatekeeping function of placements,
Iceland 13, 110–29
assessment in practice placements
121–8
concrete tools used in assessment
119–21
high quality placements 115–19
infrastructure of education 112–15
institutional context and
professional competence 110–12
gay/bisexual issues 211
gender issues 211
group closeness 82, 88
group learning 18, 73, 147–8, 149,
150–1, 158–62, 163
group meetings 29–31, 47
group rehabilitation work 172–3
group therapy 205–7
groupwork, in the community 54–5
Gypsy communities, Romania 135

Hague Convention on Protection of
Children and Cooperation in
respect of Intercountry Adoption
(1993) 144
healthcare
interprofessional partnerships 16,
36, 175–8
Saturday Free Clinic 34–6
see also hospital-based settings;
university teaching hospitals

HIV/AIDS patients 48, 173–5
home visits 53, 135, 171, 191
Hong Kong, Shek Wai Kok
   integration project 13, 16,
   59–76
Hong Kong government 61, 62
hospital-based settings, Zimbabwe
   167–78
   children in the Rehabilitation
   Department 170–3
   HIV/AIDS patients 173–5
   psychiatric outpatients 168–70
   social work in general hospitals
   167–8
   teamwork 175–8
   see also university teaching
   hospitals
Hungarian minorities, Romania 131

Iceland, gatekeeping function of
   placements 13, 110–29
Immigration and Asylum Act (1999)
   79, 89
incompetent practice 191–2
India
   police station placements, Mumbai
   18, 43–58
   use of term 'social worker' 13,
   43–4
Indian Penal Code 48, 50
information technology 138
integration see university-community
   integration placements
interdisciplinary approaches 16
   community settings 31, 36
   hospital settings 175–8, 225–6,
   230
International Classification of
   Non-Profit Organizations
   (ICNPO) 180
International Federation of Social
   Workers (IFSW) 11
interpersonal skills 28–9, 39, 71, 73
   police, India 51
Interpreting Service 82

'job description' approach, Romania
   130–46
   first year: observation 132–3
   second year: direct practice
   placement 133–5
   third year: more advanced direct
   practice 136–7
   fourth year: networking skills
   137–41
   fifth year: masters level 142–4
   general issues 141–2
   outline of model 145–6
Juvenile Justice Act (1986) India 44

keywords 237–41
Kosovan culture 82

Latinos 13, 16, 20, 200–21
   culturally competent practice with
   202–3
   hospital-based outpatient clinic
   203–8
   mental health profile 201
   outpatient private practice 208–14
   socio-demographic profile 200–1
   urban mobile crisis team 214–20
learning
   constructivist views 151–2
   graduated levels 97
   group 18, 73, 147–8, 149, 150–1,
   158–62, 163
   phases 118–19
'learning by doing' 63, 72
learning (practicum) contracts 28, 97,
   103
'learning outcomes' 80
legal context 20
   Romania 144
   UK 188–9
life cycle theory 195
life history 193
link supervisor role, 'long-arm'
   model 183–4
'long-arm' supervision see external
   supervision

Mahila Dakshata Samitis (women's vigilance groups) 58
managerialist paradigm 95
Maori culture 100, 102, 109n
'marketization' 12
mental health services
  culturally competent, for Latinos 200–21
  policy and practice 184–5
  voluntary sector 179–99
meta-learning 97
Mexican American Prevalence and Services Survey (MAPS) 201
modelling behaviour 153
modelling thinking 153, 156

National Assistance Act (1948) 79
National Asylum Support Service (NASS) 89
NCH (National Children's Homes) 181
networking approach 62
New Zealand
  culturally competent practice 101–2
  external supervision 93–109
NGOs 52, 54, 63, 167
NHS and Community Care Act (1990) 182, 188

object relations theory 196
off-site supervision see external supervision
older people, integration project 63, 65–6
organizations, learning about 185–7
outreach 29, 30–1, 40, 202, 204

Pakeha culture 100, 102, 109n
partnership 15–16
  school-agency 67–8
  university-community 26–7
  university-hospital 224–5
pedagogue, keywords 239
peer group learning 151, 152
  practice teachers' comments 160

students' comments 162
personal safety 19, 134
placements
  developing high quality 115–17
  educational paradigm 14–15
  functions 59–60
  keywords 239
  as vehicles for social change 15–17, 43
police station placements, Mumbai 18, 43–58
  brief analysis 58
  initiation 45–6
  methodology of working 50–2
  objectives 46–7
  procedure 47
  rationale for 44–5
  reactions of police 49–50
  research study 56–7
  summary of students' work 52–5
  student tasks 48–9
  timings and duration 47
political action vs. 'care management' 13
power relations
  inter-professional 17
  practice learning 17
  work with asylum seekers 78, 83
practice, keywords 240
practice curriculum 187, 189
practice learning coordinator role 77–8, 80–1, 89
practice settings
  diversity 19
  keywords 240
  matching with students 76
practice teachers/field instructors
  assessment and gatekeeping 113, 114, 117, 118, 120–1, 121–8
  attitude to case recording 147, 149
  in changing models, university teaching hospitals 224–8, 230–2, 233–5
  cognitive strategies 154–6
  collaboration with academic staff 147–8
  comments on using case records 160

community revitalization program 29
desired attributes, external supervisors 94, 101, 109
equal partnership 17
facilitator role 73
importance of recognition 17–18
keywords 241
manager role 72
payment 141–2
perspectives on asylum seekers project 86–7
promoting continuity 116–17
responses to two-stage placement model 114–15
role in England 77
role in 'job description' model 133, 135, 145
role in 'long-arm' model 183
Shek Wai Kok project 71–5
teacher role 72–3
Teaching Centre model 225, 226–7
'practice teaching', diverse meanings 20–1
practicum contracts see learning contracts
practicums see placements
private outpatient psychotherapy practice 208–14
professional competence, institutional contexts and 110–12
professional development 36
programme, keywords 241
programme management model 230–2
proximal/distal causes 213
psychiatric outpatients 168–70, 203–8
psychoanalytical theory 150
psychosocial medicine 203–4

reciprocal teaching 152–3
rehabilitation services 62, 170–3
research 223
  integration into placement 113
  neglect in social work 111
  policewomen study, Mumbai 55–7
residential settings 193–7

rights-based approach 190–2
Romania
  'job description' approach 130–46
  law 144
  social worker's role 131, 145, 146

San Francisco General Hospital 203
Save the Children in Scotland 182
school-field relations see university/school-field relations
Scotland 13
  'mental health framework' 189, 190
  voluntary sector placements 19, 179–99
service integration 60–3
Shek Wai Kok integration project, Hong Kong 13, 16, 59–76
  attainment of objectives 66–8
  background information 63–4
  conceptual basis 60–3
  development and results 64–6
  practice-teaching-learning experience 69–75
social learning theory 153
social policy context 189–90
social work
  in Canadian hospitals 223–4, 228–9, 232–3
  contribution to social sciences 111
  familiarity with controversy 85
  in general hospitals, Zimbabwe 167–8
  globalization and localization 11–14
  IFSW definition 11
  response to asylum seekers 79
  role in community partnerships 32–3
  role in rehabilitation 171
Social Work (Scotland) Act (1968) 188
social workers
  numbers in USA 200
  role in Romania 131, 145, 146
  use of term in India 43–4
socio-political context 95
St. Louis, Missouri 27

stakeholder interest 97–8
student logs 40, 69–70, 72–3, 187
student perspectives
  accounts of work with asylum
    seekers 81–5
  comments on using case records
    161–2
  reflections on community-focused
    practice learning 38
  responses to two-stage placement
    model 114
substance abuse 36, 45, 52–3, 204

Tata Institute of Social Sciences
    (TISS) 44
Te Kaiawhina Ahumahi 102
Teaching Centre model 20, 224–8
team meetings 73, 86, 186
teamwork 175–8, 193
theory and practice 14, 64, 114,
    121, 193–7
Times of India 57
transculturation 210
treatment algorithm 213–14

UK
  development of mental health
    services 184
  national training curriculum 18, 77,
    80
  voluntary sector service provision
    180–2
  see also England; Scotland
unethical practice 106
University of Canterbury, New
    Zealand 93
University of Hong Kong
    Department of Social Work and
    Social Administration 60,
    61, 63
University of Iceland School of
    Social Work 110, 114, 120
University of Toronto 235
university-community revitalization
    partnerships 25–42
  community-focused practice
    learning activities 29–32

community setting 27–9
diverse skill development 37
maintaining goal-directed focus and
  clear communication 36–7
obstacles 33–4
review of practice learning 38–42
Saturday Free Clinic 34–6
social work's role 32–3
student professional development
  36
student reflections 38
university-community partnerships
  26–7
university/school-field relations
  collaboration on projects 67–8,
    147–8, 149
  developing a model of cooperation
    115–19
  inter-organizational factors 222–36
  need for improved links 142
  obstacles 16, 33–4
  tensions 59–60
  university-community partnerships
    26–7
university teaching hospitals, Canada
    16, 20, 222–36
  changing context for social work
    228–9
  emerging context for social work
    232–3
  evolving model 233–5
  history of social work 223–4
  programme management model
    230–32
  Teaching Centre model 224–8
urban mobile crisis team 214–20
US Department of Housing and
    Urban Development (HUD)
    26–7, 32
  Office of University Partnerships
    27
USA
  community revitalization programs
    25–6
  mental health practices with Latinos
    200–21
  number of social workers 200
  university-community partnerships
    25–42

voluntary sector placements, Scotland
19, 179–99
connecting theory to practice
193–7
practice learning 184–93
role of assessed practice learning
and teaching 182–4
UK service provision 180–2

Washington University Medical
Center Redevelopment
Corporation 26
Washington University School of
Social Work 26, 28, 29, 32
women
assertiveness training, Latino
women 205
in Kosovan culture 82
research into policewomen, India
55–7
treatment by police in India 44–5,
50

young people, integration project 63,
65–6

Zimbabwe
cost of burial 176
hospital-based settings 167–78
prevalence of AIDS 173
Zimbabwe School of Social Work
167, 168
zone of proximal development 152

Author Index

Aberdeen Framework Group 190
Advocacy Services Aberdeen (ASA)
    185
Agranoff, R. A. and Pattakos, A. N.
    61
Ajdukovic, M., Cevizovic, M. and
    Kontak, K. 84
Alcock, P. 181
Allen, J. 25
Ames, N. 147
Aotearoa New Zealand Association
    of Social Workers (ANZASW)
    98, 102, 106
Atthar, R. 55

Balasubrahmanyan, V. 44
Bandura, A. and Walters, R. H. 153
Beatty, R. and Ulrich, D. 229
Berengarten, S. 59
Bergman, A., Wells, L., Bogo, M.,
    Abbey, S., Chandler, V.,
    Embleton, L., Guigis, S., Huot,
    A., McNeill, T., Prentice, L.,
    Stapleton, D., Shekter-Wolfson,
    L. and Urman, S. 227
Biestek, F. P. 134
Bogo, M. and Globerman, J. 98, 222,
    224, 226, 233, 234
Bogo, M. and Power, R. 233
Bogo, M. and Taylor, I. 225
Bogo, M. and Vayda, E. 59, 93, 95,
    225
Bogo, M., Wells, L., Abbey, S.,
    Bergman, A., Chandler, V.,
    Embleton, L., Guirgis, S., Huot,
    A., McNeill, T., Prentice, L.,
    Stapleton, D., Shekter-Wolfson,
    L. and Urman, S. 227
Bradley, J. 100

Braye, S. and Preston Shoot, M. 191
Brearley, J. 196
Brenton, M. 180
Brown, A. and Bourne, I. 89
Brown, A. L. and Palinscar, A. S.
    152, 153
Browne, C. V., Smith, M., Ewalt, P. L.
    and Walker, D. D. 229
Bulmer, M. 62
Butler, B. and Elliott, D. 59, 191

CCETSW 77, 96, 179, 182, 185,
    188, 193, 199
Charns, M. P. and Tewksbury, L. S.
    228
Cheyne, C., O'Brien, M. and
    Belgrave, M. 95
Cisneros, H. G. 26
Clough, R. 195, 196
Comas-Diaz, L. and Duncan, J. W.
    205, 206
Cooper, L. 94
Coulshed, V. 84, 87
Cross, T. et al 83

Dakshina Murthy, S. 44
Dalrymple, J. and Burke, B. 192
Dattilio, F. M. and Freeman, A. 84
Davenport, J. and Davenport, J. 97
Department of Health 137, 189
Department of Social Work and
    Social Administration,
    University of Hong Kong 59
Deshpande, A. 54
Doel, M. and Marsh, P. 85, 196
Doel, M. and Shardlow, S. M. 12, 83,
    113
Doel, M., Shardlow, S. M., Sawdon,
    C. and Sawdon, D. 187, 189
Dominelli, L. 12, 108
Durie, M. 102

Falicov, C. 203, 210
Faria, G., Brownstein, C. and Smith,
    H. 96
Fellin, P. 97

Fieldgrass, P. and Fieldgrass, J. 180
Flower, J. 229
Fortune, A. and Abramson, J. 94
Fortune, A., Feathers, C., Rook, S.,
    Scrimenti, R., Smollen, P.,
    Stemerman, B. and Tucker, E. 94
Fortune, A., Miller, J., Rosenblum, A.,
    Sanchez, B., Smith, C. and Reid,
    W. 96, 97
Fox, R. and Guild, P. 97
Freire, P. 186
Froland, C. 62

Gans, S. P. and Horton, G. T. 61
Gardiner, D. 97, 149
Geller, J. L., Fisher, W. H. and
    McDermeit, M. 219
Gerdman, A. 118
Germain, C. 98, 99–100
Getzel, G. S. and Salmon, R. 150
Gibson, A. 195
Gilliland, B. E. 216
Globerman, J. 231, 233
Globerman, J. and Bogo, M. 229
Globerman, J., Davies, J. M. and
    Walsh, S. 229, 231, 235
Gould, N. and Taylor, I. 94
Government of Canada 228
Grampian Health Board 190
Guetzbow, H. 61
Gulbenkian Commission 111

Hall, N. 171
Haring, K. A. and Lovett, P. L. 62
Hayes-Bautista, D. and Chiprut, R.
    209
Henderson, R. 95
Hendry, G. D. 151
Herbert, M. and Levin, R. 229
Herrera, R. 219
Hillerbrand, E. 151
Hollis, F. 111
Homonoff, E. and Maltz, P. 96
Honey, P. and Mumford, A. 81
Hong Kong Government 61, 62
Hrafnsdóttir, S. 121
Hughes, C. 95

Hughes and Heycox 117
Humphries, B. 108

Idol, L., Jones, B. F. and Mayer, R. E.
    153

Johnson, D., Johnson, R. and
    Holobec, E. 150
Júliusdóttir, S. 110, 111, 112, 117
Juliusdóttir, S. and Hrafnsdóttir, S.
    119

Kadushin, A. 72
Kagan, S. L. 61
Kagle, J. D. 149–50, 153, 154
Kamerman, S. B. and Kahn, A. J. 61
Kaplan, T. 150
Kendall, J. and Knapp, M. 180, 181
Kerson, T. S. 59
Killén, K. 118, 124
Kimber, D. 151
Kissman, K. and Van Tran, T. 93, 94
Kolb, D. A. 187
Kretzman, J. and McKnight, J. 26
Kristmundsdóttir, K. 118

Lathrop, J. P. 229
Lawson, H. 183, 184
Leatt, P., Baker, G R., Halverson, P.
    K. and Aird, C. 229
Leung, A. Y. L. 69
Leung, A. Y. L., Hui, H. S. K. and Ip,
    F. Y. S. 64
Leung, A. Y. L., Tam, T. S. K. and
    Chu, C. H. 72, 73
Li, M. K. Y. 62, 67
Lishman, J. and Wardell, F. 181, 182
Lorenz, W. 11
Lum, D. 202, 203, 204

McClelland, R. W. 60
Maidment, J. 97
Mallinson, I. 196
Manoleas, P. G. 202

Manoleas, P. G., Organista, K. C.,
    Negron-Velasquez, G. and
    McCormick, K. 209
Marris, P. 195
Marsh, P. and Triseliotis, J. 94
Maslow, A. 82, 195
Maxwell, J. 61, 68
May 44
Midgley, J. 11–12
Miranda, J., Azocar, F., Organista, K.
    C., Dwyer, E. and Arean, P. 207,
    208
Moore, L. S. and Urwin, C. A. 129
Moore, S. T. and Kelly, M. J. 229
Morell, E. 117, 128
Morrison, J. D., Alcorn, S. and
    Nelums, M. 25
Munson, C. E. 60

Nai-Ming Tsang 117
National Council for Voluntary
    Services 180
Nisivoccia, D. 118
Nixon, S., Shadlow, S., Doel, M.,
    McGrath, S. and Gordon, R. 95

Office of Policy Development and
    Research 26, 27
O'Hagan, K. 84, 87
O'Neill, J. 200
Organista, K. C. and Valdes Dwyer,
    E. 203
Orme, J. and Glastonbury, B. 181

Parlamentul Ronamei 144
Payne, M. 98, 99, 111
Peters, T. 229
Piaget, J. 151
Pincus, A. and Minahan, A. 111, 113
Pressman, J. and Wildavsky, A. 26

Redburn, F. S. 61
Ranade, S. N. 44
Randal, H. 95
Raphael, F. B. and Rosenblum, A. 96

Rapp, C. A., Chamberlain, R. and
    Freeman, E. 12, 60
Raskin, M., Skolnik, I. and Wayne, J.
    12, 60
Rennie, G. 95
Reynolds, B. 83, 118
Rogoff, B. 151
Rosenfeld, D. J. 116

Sabel, C. 63
Sabogal, F., Marin, G.,
    Otero-Sabogal, R., VanOss
    Marin, B. and Perez-Stable, E. J.
    203
Sanger, V. 44
Schön, D. A. 12
School of Social work, University of
    Leicester 119–20
Schuftan, C. 32
Scottish Office 190
Secker, J. 95
Seed, P. and Lloyd, G. 179
Selby, R. 100
Shannon, G. 78
Shardlow, S. M. and Doel, M. 63, 94,
    117
Sharma, P. 44
Sheafor, B., Horejsi, C. and Horejsi,
    G. 32
Shearer, A. 67
Sim, A. J. and Mackay, R. 192
Skovholt, M. and Rönnestad, M. H.
    110
Sue, S., Fujino, D. C., Hu, L.,
    Takeuchi, D. T. and Zane, N. W.
    S. 208

Tanner, K. and Le Riche, P. 96
Te Kaiawhina Ahumahi 102
Thorsteindóttir, G. and Juliusdóttir, S.
    113
Tidikis, F. and Strasen, L. 228
Tong, H. S. K., Ip, F. Y. S., Leung, A.
    Y. L. and Lai, O. K. 69, 72
Trevillion, S. 111
Tribe, R. and Shackman, J. 84
Tsang, N. M. 59

Ulas, M. and Connor, A. 184
Ulas, M., Myers, F. and Whyte, B. 185
UNAIDS/WHO 173
Urbanowski, M. and Dwyer, M. 59, 63
US Bureau of the Census 200, 201

Vayda, E. and Bogo, M. 60
Vega, W. A., Kolody, B., Aguilar-Gaxiola, S., Alderete, E., Catalano, R. and Caraveo-Anduaga, J. 201
Vygotsky, L. S. 152

Walker, D. and Boud, D. 95
Wan-lau, S. O. 67
Washington University Medical Center Redevelopment Corporation 26
Wintersteen, R. T., Mupedziswa, R. and Wintersteen, L. B. 169
Wong, D. 69

Yau, Y. C. 67
Yng, H. 116

Zakutansky, T. 97
Zastrow, C. 133